08- BAX - 678

DATE DUE

Demco, Inc. 38-293

Professional Development Schools

Schools for Developing a Profession

Edited by
Linda Darling-Hammond

Reissued with a New Introduction

Teachers College, Columbia University
New York and London

Published by Teachers College Press, 1234 Amsterdam Avenue, New York, N.Y. 10027

Library of Congress Cataloguing-in-Publication Data

Professional development schools : schools for developing a profession /
    edited by Linda Darling-Hammond.
        p.   cm.
    Originally published: New York : Teachers College, c1994. With new introd.
    Includes bibliographical references and index.
    ISBN 0-8077-4592-8 (pbk.)
    1. Laboratory schools — United States.   2. Teachers — Training of—
    United States.   3. Teachers — In-service training — United States.
    I. Darling-Hammond, Linda, 1951–
    LB2154.A3P75 2005

                                                    2005043068

ISBN 0-8077-4592-8 (pbk.)

Printed on acid-free paper

Manufactured in the United States of America

12 11 10 09 08 07 06 05   8 7 6 5 4 3 2

Contents

Introduction

Our world is changing rapidly. Whereas a century ago, more than 95% of all people in the world worked as unskilled laborers in factories, mills, mines, and farms, today more than 70% must acquire specialized skills to engage in the knowledge-based economy that has arrived. There is no doubt that, in the 21st century, the demands of societies for more widespread education will continue to grow. Consequently, the demands made of schools for more powerful and effective teaching will continue to increase. This kind of teaching will necessarily require that teachers do much more than just "covering the curriculum" or "getting through the book." Teachers must be able to enable all students to actually learn effectively—given their different backgrounds, starting points, and approaches to learning—which is a much more challenging undertaking that requires much greater knowledge and skill.

There are several dilemmas in creating a profession full of such teachers. One is that teacher education must become an ever more powerful intervention to overcome the long "apprenticeship of observation" prospective teachers have experienced in their own prior schooling—an apprenticeship that often prevents them from learning more effective approaches than what they, themselves, experienced as students. This means that new teachers must see and experience state-of-the-art practice in their training so that they can understand the broader possibilities for their work. A second dilemma is that schools must become ever more supportive organizations for the lifelong learning of teachers and the productive learning of all students if every child is to achieve higher levels of learning. A third dilemma—born of the intersection of these two—is that schools and universities must change in tandem, so that universities can prepare teachers not for schools as they have been, but for schools as they should become. In this way, knowledge and practice can advance together to the ultimate benefit of children and their learning.

This is where the professional development school (PDS) comes in. Advanced by such reformers as the Holmes Group and the National Network on Education Renewal during the late 1980s, the PDS is an undertaking of schools and schools of education to create places in which entering teachers can combine theory and practice in a setting organized to support their learning; veteran teachers can renew their own professional development and assume new roles as mentors, university adjuncts, and teacher leaders; and school and university educators together can engage in research and rethinking of practice. In these sites, new teachers learn to teach alongside experienced veterans who plan and work together, and university and school-based faculty work collaboratively to design and implement learning experiences for new and experienced teachers, as well as for students. Ideally, the university program and the school develop a shared conception of good teaching that informs their joint work.

The power of this idea made real is one I have personally experienced in my work as the faculty sponsor of the Stanford Teacher Education Program (STEP). When I took that role in 1998, the program was typical of many: The program had 60–80 secondary education students who student taught in nearly as many different schools, often in classrooms with teachers who took student teachers because they needed an extra pair of hands or wanted a break from teaching. Candidates only occasionally saw practice that reflected the research they read about in their classes, and they often worked in schools where there was little evidence or guidance for how to teach all students equitably and powerfully. This model of clinical training required prospective teachers to imagine rather than directly experience most of what they hoped to accomplish and that provided little opportunity for schools to benefit from the efforts of the novice teachers or from the resources of the university.

Over the last 6 years, my colleagues have developed PDS relationships with a number of schools serving very diverse student populations—several large, comprehensive high schools that are in the process of restructuring to allow more personalization, more in-depth teaching, and greater equity, and several new small high schools recently founded (three of them with support from the university) to develop new models of education that involve teams of teachers working with shared groups of heterogeneously grouped students around performance-based instruction and assessment. Student teachers are concentrated in these schools, where their year-long placement allows them to learn about all of the aspects of the school and to function like members of the faculty; the teachers of the schools are committed to a shared venture of mutual improvement of both the university and school programs; and the schools also work with each other on problems of practice. For example, a mathematics initiative involves teachers from several of the schools visiting a departmental team where a reform-oriented approach to practice has been successful in allowing de-tracked classes of diverse students to learn college preparatory mathematics. The teachers in the consortium have engaged in joint professional development and curriculum development to strengthen practice across all the sites. School faculty members provide feedback and advice to the Stanford program and sometimes co-teach classes. University faculty and supervisors support mentoring, curriculum development, and reform initiatives in the schools. The resulting community of practice is powerful for all of the members, an engine for continual learning for students, student teachers, veteran teachers, and teacher educators, and a source of renewal. As student teachers in the PDSs have observed:

> This is just an amazing place to be while in the STEP classes. . . . I can take the things we learn and see it in action here rather than . . . understand it only as theory. . . .

> The environment is wonderful for giving us a chance to try new things. If I came to my cooperating teacher and I said, "Hey we learned this in class, can we try it?" she'd say "Sure! Let's go for it." Everyone here seems to be open to try new things that come out of Stanford. It wasn't like in big schools where all the teachers say "That sounds great, but we really can't do that in our class." We have a lot of freedom here to try to figure it out.

> Right off the bat we were treated as colleagues by all of the staff, not just the teachers we were working with. We were able to get really involved with the school at all levels and participate in a lot of different things. From the beginning we really had the opportunity to sit down at the cooperative planning meetings and be a part of the team as much as anyone else.

> I have learned more than I ever could have imagined. . . . I was really able to come and try to implement things that I learned in my Curriculum & Instruction class [and] to use some of theory and practice ideas from Adolescent Development [and] the Special Education class—I really applied it to our classroom.

We have found that teachers who graduate from this kind of PDS training not only become strong teachers from their first days in the classroom, they also become change agents in the schools they enter, and, frequently, founders of new schools that are designed to help all students engage in ambitious learning successfully.

Developing sites where state-of-the-art practice is possible has been one of the difficulties in constructing clinical experiences for prospective teachers: Quite often if novices are to see and emulate high-quality practice, especially in schools serving the neediest students, it is necessary not only to seek out individual cooperating teachers but to develop the quality of the schools, so that prospective teachers can learn productively, and to create settings where advances in knowledge and practice can continue to occur. Thus PDSs aim to develop *school practice* as well as the *individual practice* of new teacher candidates. In this sense, professional development schools are a special case of school restructuring: As they simultaneously

restructure school programs and teacher education programs, they redefine teaching and learning for all members of the profession and the
school community

Sometimes thought of as the analogue to a teaching hospital, professional development schools are intended not only to support the learning
of teachers who happen to be placed in such buildings, but also to support
and strengthen the entire profession of teaching. Such schools support
advances in knowledge by becoming places in which new practices can be
instantiated, and where practice-based and practice-sensitive research can
be carried out collaboratively by teachers, teacher educators, and
researchers.

Barely more than a dream a decade ago, professional development
schools are now becoming a reality, and this vision guides many of them.
As of 1998, the American Association of Colleges for Teacher Education
estimated that there were more than 1000 such schools in 47 states in operation across the country. Recent research has suggested that PDSs typically include more extensive school experience for prospective teachers,
more frequent and sustained supervision and feedback, more collective
planning and decision making among teachers at the school as well as
among school- and university-based faculty, and participation in research
and inquiry about teaching and teacher education by novices, veteran
teachers, and university faculty. In addition, novices in these schools are
not limited to an individual classroom but gain school-wide experience ny
working with school teams on such tasks as curriculum development,
school reform, and action research. In most of these sites, university faculty teach courses and organize professional development at the school-
site and are also involved in teaching children.

The case studies in this book describe what these kinds of practices
look like and how they were constructed in professional development
schools as varied and far-flung as Wells, Maine; New York City; Los
Angeles; Columbia, South Carolina; Seattle, Washington; and Jefferson
County, Kentucky. The university partners involved are public and private universities, both large and small, with strong missions to improve
teacher education and ambitious goals for contributing to public schools.
These early efforts planted the seeds for successes that have borne fruit
elsewhere.

Accomplishing the difficult work of creating these practices has positive consequences for teacher preparation, veteran teacher learning, teaching practice, and student learning. Studies of highly developed PDSs have
suggested that teachers who graduate from such programs feel better
equipped to teach.[1] For instance, a study of one middle-level teacher education program found that graduates trained in a PDS felt more knowledgeable about early adolescents, more prepared to teach middle school,

and better able to make connections between ideas in coursework and their clinical experiences; by contrast, graduates of the traditional program felt significantly less sure of their ability to support student learning by using different teaching strategies.[2] A longitudinal study of four cohorts of graduates from a PDS-based program at the University of California-Riverside found that PDS program graduates rated their preparation for teaching and their sense of self-efficacy higher than graduates of traditional teacher preparation programs in the area.[3]

Some studies have evaluated outcomes of PDS participation for teaching practice and student achievement. In studies polling employers and supervisors, PDS graduates were viewed as much better prepared than other new teachers. Veteran teachers working in highly-developed PDSs have reported changes in their own practice and improvements at the classroom and school levels as a result of the professional development, action research, and mentoring that are part of the PDS. Comparison group studies have found that PDS-prepared teachers are rated stronger in areas of teaching ranging from classroom management and uses of technology to content area skills.[4]

Studies have also documented gains in student achievement tied directly to curriculum and teaching interventions resulting from the professional development and curriculum work professional development schools have undertaken with their university partners.[5] In a study of a group of PDS sites associated with a Midwestern university, student achievement gains were significantly related to faculty ratings regarding the professional development efforts at the site.[6]

Although research has also demonstrated how difficult these partnerships are to enact, many schools of education and some districts are moving toward preparing all of their prospective teachers in such settings, both because they allow prospective teachers to learn to teach in professional learning communities—and this concern can be addressed more consistently and systematically through PDS partnerships—and because such work is a key to changing school cultures so that they become more productive environments for the learning of all students and teachers.

However, like all reform ideas, the ideals of professional development schools have been unevenly implemented, and many sites that have adopted the label have not created the strong relationships or adopted the set of practices anticipated for such schools. The work is hard and models are much needed. This volume offers those who are struggling to develop such schools a variety of examples in different kinds of communities, ranging from New York City to Seattle, Washington, from to rural Maine to Louisville, Kentucky. These case studies illustrate how the concept has evolved in various settings, what it looks like in operation, how partnerships have been forged, what models are being developed, and what barriers and obstacles have been encountered and overcome. The volume also evaluates the ways in which these evolving institutions support teacher development and teaching practice and considers the kinds of policy initiatives that will be required to support their continued development and institutionalization.

Linda Darling-Hammond
Stanford, California
January 2005

[1] For a review of research on the outcomes of professional development schools noted in this preface, see chapter 11 in L. Darling-Hammond & J. Bransford (eds.), *Preparing teachers for a changing world: What teachers should learn and be able to do* (San Francisco: Jossey-Bass, 2005).

[2] S. Yerian & P. L. Grossman (1997), "Preservice teachers' perceptions of their middle level teacher education experience: A comparison of a traditional and a PDS model," *Teacher Education Quarterly*, 24(4), 85–101.

[3] J. H. Sandholtz & S. H. Dadlez (2000), "Professional development school trade-offs in teacher preparation and renewal," *Teacher Education Quarterly*, 27(1), 7–27.

[4] See, for example, Darling-Hammond & Bransford, 2005; I. Guadarrama, J. Ramsey, & J. Nath (Eds.), *Forging alliances in community and thought: Research in professional development schools* (pp. 3–30; Greenwich, CT: Information Age Publishing, 2002); R. Trachtman, *The NCATE professional development school study: A survey of 28 PDS sites.* (Professional Development School Standards Project, National Council for Accreditation of Teacher Education, Washington, DC, 1996); G. A. Neubert & J. B. Binko, "Professional development schools: The proof is in the performance," *Educational Leadership, 55* (5), 44–46 (1998).

[5] N. Frey, Literacy achievement in an urban middle-level professional development school: A learning community at work. *Reading Improvement, 39* (1), 3–13 (2002); Guadarrama et al., 2002 (*see* J. Fischetti & A. Larson, "How an integrated unit increased student achievement in a high school PDS, and B. C. Glaeser, B. D. Karge, J. Smith, & C. Weatherill, Paradigm pioneers: A professional development school collaborative for special education teacher education candidates); D. L. Wiseman & D. Cooner, Discovering the power of collaboration: The impact of a school-university partnership on teaching, *Teacher Education and Practice 12*(1), 18–28 (1996).

[6] G. J. Marchant, Professional development schools and indicators of student achievement, *The Teacher Educator 38*(2), 112–125 (2002).

Chapter 1

DEVELOPING PROFESSIONAL DEVELOPMENT SCHOOLS: EARLY LESSONS, CHALLENGE, AND PROMISE

Linda Darling-Hammond

A major aspect of the restructuring movement in education is the current effort to invent and establish professional development schools (PDSs). PDSs aim to provide new models of teacher education and development by serving as exemplars of practice, builders of knowledge, and vehicles for communicating professional understandings among teacher educators, novices, and veteran teachers. They support the learning of prospective and beginning teachers by creating settings in which novices enter professional practice by working with expert practitioners, enabling veteran teachers to renew their own professional development and assume new roles as mentors, university adjuncts, and teacher leaders. They allow school and university educators to engage jointly in research and rethinking of practice, thus creating an opportunity for the profession to expand its knowledge base by putting research into practice—and practice into research.

PDSs are a special case of school restructuring: as they simultaneously restructure schools and teacher education programs, they redefine teaching and learning for all members of the profession and the school community. Extending beyond the analogue of the teaching hospital that supports medical internships and clinical research, the PDS intends not only to support the learning of individual faculty members, it also aims to redesign university programs for the preparation of educators and to transform the teaching profession.

In many reform models, such as those offered by the Holmes Group (1986, 1990), the Carnegie Forum on Education and the Economy (1986), the RAND Corporation (Wise & Darling-Hammond, 1987), and the National Board for Professional Teaching Standards, all prospective teachers would undertake an intensive internship in PDSs. There they would encounter state-of-the-art practice and a range of diverse experiences under intensive supervision so that they learn to teach effectively, rather than merely to cope or, as many do, to leave the profession entirely. Ideally, PDSs will also provide serious venues for developing the knowledge base for teaching by becoming places in which practice-based and practice-sensitive research can be carried out collaboratively by teachers, teacher educators, and researchers.

Although the concepts underlying PDSs have a long history (described in Brainard, 1989; Stallings and Kowalski, 1990), the most recent rebirth of these ideas occurred in 1986, with the "second wave" school reform reports that called for dramatic improvements in the preparation of teachers as a foundation for other school reforms. The Holmes Group's (1986) proposal for PDSs recognized that efforts to reform teacher education must also be accompanied by efforts "to make schools better places for teachers to work and to learn" (p. 4).

Since then, a remarkable flurry of effort has produced hundreds of school-university collaborations across the country that call themselves PDSs. Though the exact number is unknown, well over 100 PDS initiatives have been identified (Darling-Hammond, Adams, Berry, & Snyder, in press). Some of these fledgling initiatives were aided originally by small grants from the Ford Foundation and local community funds. Most, however, have had little funding. The movement has been encouraged by the Holmes Group, the National Network for Educational Renewal, the American Association of Colleges for Teacher Education, the National Education Association, and the American Federation of Teachers. Local consortia have also emerged to support the wider establishment of PDSs in certain regions: The Michigan Partnership at Michigan State University, the Gheens Professional Development Academy in Louisville, and the Puget Sound Educational Consortium at the University of Washington in Seattle, all provide support for clusters of PDSs. A few state licensing systems, including Minnesota's and Michigan's, are envisioning that all entering teachers will have been prepared in PDSs. In Michigan, proposals to include PDS preparation as a prerequisite for licensing are under active consideration. In Minnesota, such a plan has already been adopted by the Board of Teaching, and pilot sites are being developed and studied. These encouragements have emboldened teachers and teacher educators to imagine and invent new institutions and images for teaching and teacher development.

This volume offers an in-depth look at a number of the newly emerging PDSs. It examines how the PDS concept has evolved, how partnerships have been forged, what models are being developed, and what barriers and obstacles have been encountered and overcome. Chapters 2 through 8 present case studies of seven different PDS models in very different communities, ranging from urban centers such as New York City,

Los Angeles, and Louisville, to rural Maine to suburban schools near Seattle and Columbia, South Carolina. Chapters 6 through 8 are collaboratively authored by university and school participants, giving first-hand accounts of both points of view about the PDS and its birthing process. The final chapter examines how partners must collaborate in order to create these changes and how they must, at the same time, change old practices in order to effectively collaborate.

The invention of such new institutions creates many challenges, struggles, and pitfalls. Turfism, tradition, scarce resources for change, inexperience with collaborative decision making, and uncertain environmental constraints and supports in and outside of each institution, all contribute to a need for creative problem solving each step of the way. "Systematic ad hocism" is the term coined by PDS inventors in southern Maine to describe the approach they have used to work through and adapt to the many challenges and changing realities they have faced. "Who owns the knowledge?" "Whose knowledge counts?" and "What is our knowledge?" are the more fundamental questions of school–university collaboration that emerge and must be grappled with as PDSs—and the profession of teaching—strive to grow up.

For all the barriers and obstacles, it is clear that many of these joint ventures between local schools and teacher education institutions are restructuring teaching knowledge, the form and content of teacher education, and the nature and governance of teaching. In short, they are redesigning both teacher preparation and the practice of teaching, building the foundations that will support a profession of teaching.

This introductory chapter examines the promise PDSs offer and the challenges they face. It does so from a perspective that views PDSs as central to teaching's transition from a bureaucratized occupation to a profession. It evaluates the ways in which these evolving institutions support teacher learning and the kinds of policy initiatives that will be required to support their continued development and institutionalization.

PROFESSIONAL DEVELOPMENT SCHOOLS IN CONTEXT: DEVELOPING THE FOUNDATION FOR A PROFESSION

Teaching has long been numbered among the professional occupations. . . . [Yet,] teaching has developed the characteristic features of a profession very slowly and is still in the process of achieving equal status with other professions. (Anderson, 1962, p. 140)

The quasiprofessional status of teaching has long been noted by scholars of the professions. Three decades after Anderson's tenuous prognosis was published in *Education for the Professions,* questions of the extent to which teaching is or should be treated as a profession still abound. These questions focus on the role of knowledge and expertise, ethical commitment to clients, and responsibility for setting standards (Darling-Hammond, 1990a). These professional cornerstones are only haphazardly developed in teaching, where preparation is not always required for practice and where bureaucratic rules and employer-employee contracts are often developed and implemented without regard to professional knowledge or the needs of clients. At the same time, teachers as a group exercise little control or responsibility for defining, transmitting, and enforcing standards of professional practice in teacher education and certification policies, school personnel decisions, or on the job review of practice.

Among the promises PDSs offer are new structures and approaches for deepening and sharing knowledge for teaching and developing shared norms for learner-centered practice, and enabling teachers to assume responsibility for professional standard setting and for inducting new entrants into the profession. To actualize these ideals, PDSs must confront longstanding obstacles to the creation of a knowledge-based and client-oriented profession of teaching (Darling-Hammond, 1990a).

Professionalism starts from the proposition that thoughtful and ethical use of knowledge must inform practice. Yet school reform has rarely focused on the support and improvement of teacher education programs or the development of teacher knowledge. In most universities, colleges of education receive the fewest resources, and teacher training is the least well-funded activity within the school of education (Ebmeier, Twombly, & Teeter, 1991). School districts spend less than one half of 1% of their budgets on professional development for teachers, as compared with nearly 10% of revenues spent on employee education by corporations. Even during those periods of intense interest in improving education that seem to occur about once a generation, neither federal or state governments nor colleges or school systems seem inclined to spend much money on the education of teachers.

This may be because policymakers are unsure whether a teaching knowledge base exists or whether its acquisition would improve teaching. Or it may be because insisting on serious preparation for all entrants would require raises in teacher salaries, which few governmental bodies have been willing to support. To avoid having to hike salaries, most states have routinely managed recurrent teacher shortages by waiving preparation requirements, allowing entry via emergency certificates, or, more recently, "alternate routes" to teaching (Darling-Hammond, 1992). On the assumption that what teachers know (or do not know) matters little to their teaching or to their students' learning, teachers are often treated as conduits for policies rather than as important actors in determining what goes on in classrooms.

In the bureaucratic view of teaching that has evolved since the late 19th century, the key to educational improvement is the correct definition of procedures for teachers to follow rather than the development of teachers' capacities to make complex judgments based on deep understandings of students and subjects. As bureaucrats, teachers need not be particularly expert, since most major teaching decisions are handed down through policy and encapsulated in curriculum and teaching materials. It is better that they not be especially "empowered," as correct implementation depends on a certain degree of uniformity controlled from above. In this commonly held conception of teaching there is no rationale for substantial teacher preparation, induction, or professional development, aside from "inservicing" designed to ensure more exact implementation of prescribed teaching procedures. There is no need and little use for professional knowledge and judgment, or for collegial consultation and planning. Problems of practice do not exist; the only problems are failures of implementation.

This view of teaching as an occupation has prevailed for over a century in the United States, with brief efforts to create a vision of teaching as complex, thoughtful work alternating with renewed attempts to teacher-proof education (Darling-Hammond, 1990b). In different eras, Horace Mann, John Dewey, Jean Piaget, and others sought to create a reflective and knowledgeable profession of teaching as the foundation for child-centered education. Their efforts were stymied, according to Cremin (1965), by the fact that such education requires "infinitely skilled teachers." Because of the conditions of teaching work, such teachers could not be recruited in sufficient numbers to sustain this more demanding kind of teaching and learning.

The Demands of Current School Reforms

The desires of today's reformers for schools that educate all students to higher levels of performance, accommodate and celebrate student diversity, and ensure that all students learn to create, analyze, produce, adapt, and invent their own ideas and products, require such "infinitely skilled" teachers: teachers who understand learning as well as teaching, who can address students needs as well as the demands of their disciplines, and who can create bridges between students' experiences and curriculum goals. Furthermore, the goals of school restructuring can only be served if such teachers are available in sufficient numbers to serve students in all schools in all communities, not just the affluent, where the relative few have traditionally been hired. Gary Fenstermacher (1992) observes that the outcomes we want and need from teacher preparation, particularly at this moment in history, require substantial new investments in teacher learning:

In a time when so many advocate for restructured schools, for greater decision autonomy for teachers, and for connecting the schools more intimately with homes and communities, it is more important than ever that teachers have the capacity to appraise their actions, evaluate their work, anticipate and control consequences, incorporate new theory and research into practice, and possess the skills and understanding needed to explain their work to other teachers, and to students and their parents.

These reflective capacities are not innate to human beings, nor are they acquired quickly. They are not acquired during a planning period sandwiched somewhere in between classes, or during evening "mini-courses" after a full day's work. They are, rather, the outcome of sustained and rigorous study, and of dialogue and exchange with master teacher educators. (p. 182)

These understandings are precisely the kind that must be developed at the nexus of theory and practice, combining the knowledge base built in the academy with the knowledge derived in close interactions with children, parents, and colleagues. The PDS—developed at the intersection of preservice education and inservice teaching—is a critical linchpin in developing teachers who can create learner- and learning-centered schools.

The PDS can provide the kind of thoughtful introduction to practice needed to enable teachers to make informed judgments in complex situations with the support of colleagues in a reflective, knowledge-rich environment. In contrast to most other professions, which require structured, intensively supervised internships prior to licensing, teaching has offered prospective teachers little assistance in learning to teach. Beyond a relatively short and idiosyncratic student teaching experience, beginning teachers are generally left to "sink or swim" during their first years of teaching (Wise, Darling-Hammond, & Berry, 1987).

Because the development of learner-centered practice is difficult, the early attempts of untutored novices often fail. Applying knowledge about learning, teaching, curriculum-building, development, motivation, and behavior to the diverse needs of students is a daunting task requiring skillful observation, diagnosis, and integration of many different concepts and abilities. Unless this occurs with the support of an able mentor, the effort can become overwhelming. This is one reason why the knowledge acquired in preservice courses is often not put to use—and why beginning teachers' practices often become less sensitive to students' needs rather than more so during their initial year in teaching.

Beginning teachers must develop the ability to apply knowledge appropriately in different contexts while handling the dozens of cognitive, psychological, moral, and interpersonal demands that simultaneously require attention in a classroom. Learning to manage the different personalities and needs of 25 or 30 children while prioritizing and juggling often conflicting goals doesn't happen quickly or easily. These skills have to be developed. Clinical experiences must enable teachers to learn first hand about the variability in students' development and approaches to learning while they are supported by guided instruction and opportunities to reflect on their teaching and its effects on learners. These educative complements to classroom work should assist novices to acquire wider repertoires of teaching strategies and help them relate problems of teaching practice to research on teaching and human development. These kinds of opportunities should encourage beginners to teach reflectively; to evaluate what they are doing; to assess what's working and why; to understand how to make better decisions; and to juggle the many concerns of teaching.

CURRENT INDUCTION INTO TEACHING

Research on the experiences of beginning teachers confirms that the likelihood of long-term success for many is impaired by the absence of expert guidance, support, and opportunities to reflect on their efforts (McDonald, 1980; Ryan, 1979; Tisher, 1978; Veenman, 1984). Initial teaching experiences have far-reaching effects, for they influence the attitudes and competences a teacher develops and maintains over a career, as well as decisions about whether to continue in teaching (National Institute of Education, 1979).

Alternate routes to teaching that minimize or eliminate traditional preservice courses frequently make the argument that on-the-job supervision of early teaching will be more effective than coursework at preparing teachers. However, research on these programs demonstrates that this is not true: such programs leave recruits underprepared in a number of areas (Darling-Hammond, 1992). But, where it actually materializes, the importance of supervision in learning to teach is confirmed. In Los Angeles, a state evaluation of the alternate certification program compared several different kinds of teaching recruits, including one group of entrants who decided to enroll in regular university teacher education programs rather than the alternate route program's short summer program, while still receiving state-funded mentor support providing them assistance in their 1st year of teaching. This group far outscored any of the other recruits (those with university teacher education but no mentors and those with mentors but no university preparation) on every criterion of classroom effectiveness, suggesting the cumulative power of adding adequate preservice preparation to intensive on-the-job supervision (Wright, McKibbon, & Walton, 1987, p. 124).

Because they join professional education with intensively supervised opportunities for practice, PDSs promise to develop more effective teachers and to reverse three aspects of socialization to teaching that have defined schools' approaches to teacher learning in the past: "Figure it out yourself"; "do it all yourself"; and "keep it to yourself."

Even the best preparation in a school of education can go only part way toward developing clinical skill, that very important and difficult process of applying knowledge to the many problems of practice that teaching presents. Furthermore, beginning teachers are usually placed in the least advantageous situations, with the most challenging students to teach, in the schools where turnover has been highest (because many teachers with seniority have transferred out), and where, consequently, potential mentors are fewest (Wise, Darling-Hammond, & Berry, 1987). Often the only help occurs when the principal hands the beginner a key to a practically empty bookroom at the beginning of school saying. The message is "Figure it out yourself. We'll see you in June . . . if you make it that long!"

In addition, beginning teachers receive the message that they should "do it all themselves." Teaching does not yet have highly developed structures for consultation and collegiality, so novices and veterans are on their own in dealing with problems of practice. While physicians consult with one another about patients, and lawyers conduct case reviews, asking for advice in teaching is viewed as stigmatizing. "Do it all yourself" is one of the more damaging expectations conveyed to beginners and veterans alike. The reinforcement of teacher isolation greatly reduces teacher learning and opportunities for sharing knowledge.

Similarly, incentives in teaching create the companion dictum "keep it to yourself." Because of the closed-door ethic, it is unconventional to offer advice to another colleague in many schools. And competitive incentive systems currently being urged upon schools in an effort to apply "business principles" to education further discourage cooperation and sharing among teachers. Colleagueship and the development of shared standards of practice are essential to professions. These are among the most fundamental objectives of PDSs, which encourage knowledge sharing, team planning and teaching, and collective reflection.

POSSIBILITIES OF PROFESSIONAL DEVELOPMENT SCHOOLS

PDSs struggle against traditional school norms as they offer the possibility for socializing new teachers to a different set of expectations about practice within and outside the bounds of their classrooms. Because they are schoolwide innovations, they go beyond the particularistic relationship a student teacher may have with a cooperating teacher by creating an overall environment for professional practice, professional colleagueship, and for ongoing collective work and inquiry. If PDSs become the doorways that all new teachers pass through as they launch their careers, they can transform the culture of teaching and the expectations for collaboration along with the nature of teaching and learning in individual classrooms. One of the most striking features of current PDSs is their emphasis on collaboration—via shared decision making in teams within schools and between schools and universities, team teaching within both the schools and universities, and collaborative research among teachers, student teachers, and teacher educators (Darling-Hammond et al., in press; see also chapter 9, this volume).

In the view of many proponents, internships in PDSs would provide for both modeling and mentoring, enabling novices to observe what experts do, even when it is not articulated, while also profiting from the tutelage of those who analyze teaching. PDS internships, like those of other professions, would offer opportunities to observe, practice, debrief, and be counseled, as well as to consult, attend seminars, and reflect with colleagues. This combination would help interns acquire a broad set of understandings and abilities rather than a formulaic set of behaviors that ultimately prove inadequate.

PDS internships could also strengthen the profession by reducing the revolving door phenomenon in the early years of teaching. Rates of early attrition from teaching are very high: most studies find that 30–50% of new teachers leave within 3–5 years of entry (Grissmer & Kirby, 1987). Settings that provide assistance and support to beginning teachers can make a large difference in retention in teaching. One of the strongest predictors of commitment to the profession is a sense of efficacy—the teacher's sense that he or she is making a positive difference in the lives of students (Bredeson, Fruth, & Kasten, 1983; Chapman & Hutcheson, 1982; Rosenholtz & Smylie, 1983). People enter teaching for the satisfaction of making that contribution. Many leave if they feel unsuccessful in reaching students. Thus, helping beginners to become more successful could enhance commitment as well as expertise throughout the profession.

Professional development schools are linchpins in the movement to restructure education, as the form of learner-centered education demanded by the restructuring movement depends first and foremost on the knowledge and capacities of teachers. More complex forms of teaching are required to support the growth and development of diverse learners with a wide range of learning styles, multiple intelligences, family and cultural backgrounds, and life experiences. More sophisticated understandings of students and subjects are required to help these diverse learners acquire "higher order" skills and performance abilities beyond those expected in the past. These capacities can only be developed if teacher preparation enables entering teachers to put theory into practice in settings that model and encourage both state-of-the-art practice and an inquiry ethic that sustains continued professional growth.

Given that nearly 4 million teachers will be hired into U.S. schools over the next two decades (Darling-Hammond, 1990c), PDSs could provide a critical opportunity to transform the ways that teachers come into the profession—in fact, to create the means to prepare teachers for learner-centered schools. By supporting the development of individual and collective knowledge about teaching, strong commitments to students and school improvement, and a sense of professional responsibility for defining and supporting good practice, PDSs hold promise for building the foundation of a profession as well.

ENACTING THE PROMISE OF PROFESSIONAL
DEVELOPMENT SCHOOLS

The case studies in this volume detail how many of these possibilities for PDSs are being enacted. Individually and collectively, the cases explain how PDSs are transforming teaching, schooling, and professional development as their efforts extend beyond those of other school reform projects or of bells and whistles added to traditional teacher education programs. First, PDSs are creating entirely new frames for teacher learning—frames that provide opportunities for *learning by teaching, learning by doing, and learning by collaborating*. These enhance the learning of teacher educators and veteran teachers as well as beginning teachers.

Second, as they integrate the work of teachers and teacher educators, of schools and universities, of teachers as researchers and researchers as teachers, PDSs are creating possibilities for building entirely new ways of knowing and kinds of knowledge for the profession as a whole.

Finally, as they begin to restructure schools and universities, PDSs are eliciting unanticipated potentials and challenges for rethinking teaching and schooling. The implications for education in both kinds of institutions reach to the fundamental relationships between and among students and teachers, the conceptualizations of what it means to know and to learn, and the obligations that organizations have to those who work and learn in them. The implications for teaching extend to its character as an occupation and a profession as well as its development as a reflective activity deeply connected to students and their welfare.

NEW FRAMES FOR TEACHER LEARNING

Traditional frames for teacher education, like those for elementary and secondary students, have envisioned teaching primarily as information transmittal, and learning as individual knowledge acquisition. Whether in courses or student teaching, clear distinctions between teacher and learner, expert and novice, have been maintained, along with tidy compartments separately housing theory and practice, knowledge and application.

In PDSs, these distinctions begin to disappear. Veteran teachers find themselves learning more about both the theory and practice of teaching as they teach novices. The old saw that you really learn something when you teach it to someone else has proven true for PDS participants across all of the sites. As one teacher at Wells Junior High (see chapter 2) put it, "Watching somebody else teach and thinking how I might change it . . . forced me to really think about teaching . . . in a different way." Another echoed, "it helps you reflect on what you're doing as well as reflect on what the interns do." As classroom teachers become teacher educators, they find their own knowledge base deepening and their teaching becoming more thoughtful.

At Norwood Elementary in Los Angeles (see chapter 7), university and school faculty created another avenue for student teacher learning by developing a series of problem-solving clinics for interns, based on common concerns and problems. This, along with other responsibilities of the project teachers, stimulated a great deal of learning and development for them as well as for their interns:

> Our involvement with teacher education and the study of how student teachers learn to teach has made a significant impact on our own professional practice at Norwood. We have reviewed models of teaching and have seen how to implement them. We have become aware of the value of peer coaching and the need to foster collegial relationships. . . . The [problem-solving] clinics have had a definite impact on the project teachers, as some of us have helped write cases and lead seminars. This puts a fair amount of pressure on in-service professionals to keep current on educational issues and help identify causes of (and remedies for) poor student achievement and other classroom concerns.

In these restructuring PDSs, teachers also find that they are learning by actually engaging in the work of thinking through, researching, debating, and implementing innovations. Whitford, in chapter 4, describes how teachers at Fairdale High in Louisville were propelled into professional readings and conversations to answer the questions that emerged as they planned and experimented with their own reforms. In this case as others, "much professional development occurred in a learning-by-doing approach."

Grossman, in chapter 3, comments about the excitement of student teachers at Lark Creek Middle School at "being a participant in school reform efforts." As one put it: "It's important that we know it can happen. It's not just theory." At Fairdale, Lark Creek, and other PDS sites, experts and novices learn together about teaching—in newly forged intersections between research, theory, and application—as they do the work of school restructuring together.

Finally, all PDS participants learn through collaboration. Perhaps one of the most promising aspects of the schools described in this volume is that they emphasize collaborative planning, teaching, and decision making within and across institutions in such a variety of ways that they begin to redefine both the act of teaching and the nature of their home institutions. Virtually all of these PDSs have introduced or strengthened existing arrangements for team teaching at the school sites and, frequently, for teacher education courses as well. Teacher educators learn more about teaching as they teach collaboratively with veteran teachers. Beginners and veterans both learn in new ways as they engage in cooperative team planning and teaching. Interns, particularly when they are organized in intern pairs or teams, have many opportunities to collaborate with each other as well as with the teaching teams they work in at school. Shared decision making creates still other "teachable moments" within and across the several role groups of PDS inventors and participants.

Grossman describes how the new integrated core seminar offered for interns at the PDS has created a team-teaching structure that contributes to the professional development of university faculty. "As the content of the course goes well beyond the expertise of any individual, all instructors acquire new knowledge and perspectives from interactions in planning and teaching the class." In addition, a collaborative approach has begun to permeate the school, snowballing in ways that develop a cooperative culture: an instructional council was formed for site-based decision making, the staff was organized into interdisciplinary teams, more integrated team teaching developed among both veteran and student teachers.

The ongoing opportunities for collaboration in all these PDSs create an environment for continuous learning among all parties. Teachers comment at the extent to which they find themselves learning from the interns or student teachers as well as from each other and from their experiences as mentors. Inspired by new opportunities to collaborate with colleagues, one veteran teacher at P.S. 87 (see chapter 5) said:

> The support I received through this ongoing informal and formal sharing was what gave me the courage to try something new. I never would have done it alone. Schools need to change so that we all have more contact with each other because teachers are out there alone. Ideas need to be passed amongst teachers just like they need to be passed amongst children.

At I.S. 44, where the "January Experience" described by Lythcott and Schwartz (see chapter 6) is a giant exercise in interdisciplinary cross-role collaboration, the benefits of collegial learning extend from school and university faculty to student teachers and students. Just as faculty enjoyed the collaboration, so did the students, who worked in groups on their interdisiplinary projects. They enjoyed the teamwork, the opportunities for friendship, and the chance to teach and learn from each other.

Other research has found that teachers are most likely to engage students in these kinds of cooperative learning experiences when they themselves have been involved in such opportunities. In this hands-on experience of curriculum invention and interdisciplinary team teaching at I.S. 44, teaching and learning roles become fluid and inseparable. Learning by teaching, learning by doing, and learning by collaborating occur simultaneously within both the teaching teams and the student groups:

> This was not a program in which "experts" mentored "apprentices"; rather everyone was learning together. . . . Released from a self-conscious mentor role, cooperating teachers began to focus on what they themselves had been able to achieve in doing things differently, and to build on those. Rather than explicitly focusing on what student teachers were learning about teaching, they assumed that that was going on and they simply talked, analyzed, invented, modified, and shared in conversation with them as one set of colleagues to another—a new model for student teaching.

As a consequence of this model, student teachers acquired entirely new frames for thinking about their teaching—frames that include professional collaboration and collegial problem-solving, interdisciplinarity, and "whole child" perspectives as foundations upon which to build their future learning and experience. They described themselves as "collaborating constantly," and able to understand more about their students by seeing them in other classrooms and subjects. A transformation of thinking about both students and subjects occurred as a result:

> Originally [each of us four student teachers] thought of ourselves as "experts" only in one insular discipline. Now at the conclusion of this program it would seem awkward for me to address a student as just a reader of English Literature and not as the rounded individual he/she is. . . . The student and the discipline would suffer from this artificial narrowness.

In chapter 8 the differences between learning in a collegial PDS setting and the "fragmented and lonely" experiences of traditional student teachers are summarized by one MAT intern in the University of South Carolina program at Pontiac elementary school:

> We were a close group, and we had teacher support teams. We knew the school and the staff. . . . We were more confident. . . . We supported each other. We had no competition among ourselves. . . . We helped each other and shared materials and ideas with each other.

In the University of Southern California's Collegial Teacher Preparation Program where student teachers work in pairs (chapter 7), teacher educators have documented how novice teachers gain insight into teaching processes by observing each other, reflecting not only on what is happening in the classroom, but why it is happening. As they focus on the "other" instead of just the "self," their discussions become substantive and reflective rather than visceral.

Snyder (chapter 5) also documents fundamental shifts in perspective that deeply influenced the learning of interns in the collaborative settings at both P.S. 87 and I.S. 44. Interns noted that they were able to shift their concerns from survival skills to student learning, to learn the value of and means for cooperation with colleagues, and to understand that teaching is a process of continual learning.

These kinds of experiences for new teachers create a different frame from which they will learn throughout their professional lives. Because they see learning as continuous, collegial, integrated, and child-centered—and because they see collaboration and reflection as opportunities for learning—they will build new kinds of knowledge for practice, and they will also use knowledge differently.

New Ways of Knowing and New Ways of Building Knowledge

All of the PDSs described in this volume have had to affirm, negotiate, and redefine two different kinds of knowledge: the formal, research-based knowledge that is the basis for much university teacher education and the less formal, context-based knowledge that is the basis for much practice in schools. Nearly all of these PDSs have had to confront the issues of "privileged" knowledge, struggling to define what ways of knowing are considered most valid as the basis for teaching and for teacher education. As Whitford explains in chapter 4:

> The university's claims to expertise are based largely on norms of disciplined ways of knowing, such as knowledge of theory and research gained through scholarship. A good part of the expertise of those in schools is based on custom, tradition, and daily practice inside particular school cultures. Unlike university scholarship, much experience-based knowledge is tacit and not easily articulated. Because of the isolation of teachers from one another, much of that knowledge also remains privately held rather than publicly debated. The status and prestige of those in uni-

versities relative to those in schools reinforce the view that publicly-held "university" knowledge is superior to school-based knowledge. . . . These conditions work against the best intentions of those who see collaboration within a professional development school as a means of improving the education of teachers and public school students.

In chapter 2, Miller and Silvernail describe how this traditional status distinction is disrupted and reshaped in the PDS as the perspectives and insights of practicing teachers are acknowledged and incorporated into the preservice program. This occurs as experienced teachers talk about the tacit understandings and informal rules of practice that underpin their knowledge of teaching. "Through continuous conversation in the context of real schools and classrooms, teacher voice assumes a privileged authority and often challenges the more formal knowledge base that university professors represent."

As they create this "rub between theory and practice," PDSs have found themselves creating new, hybrid ways of knowing and forms of knowledge that have a special power and energy of their own. As one Teachers College, Columbia University professor put it:

> I think what we get in interacting with experienced practitioners are new ways to look at what we're looking at through a research perspective. This is not only useful in terms of our work with prospective teachers, but useful in terms of the way we do our research: the way we interpret our findings; the way we conceive our research questions; what we think are the important agendas to pursue.

Miller and Silvernail similarly suggest that "what is happening at Wells are a series of private epiphanies about conceptions of knowledge and the appropriate role of schools and university faculty for sharing that knowledge."

There are many features of these new ways of knowing and new forms of knowledge:

- knowing through direct action and reflection, as well as by understanding and appreciating the findings of others
- knowing through sharing different experiences with colleagues
- knowing through research conducted by teachers along with researchers that is informed by the diverse experiences of individual children as well the aggregated outcomes codified in empirical studies

Growing up where theory rubs practice, these kinds of knowledge-building activities resemble those that Cronbach (1975) called for when he realized the limits of a positivist research paradigm for establishing causality in teaching and learning. Having discovered the difficulties of deriving generalizable rules for teaching practice from research methods unable to accommodate the nearly infinite number of variables and interactions, he concluded that the search for empirical generalizations should give way to "response sensitive" research. By this he meant research that takes exceptions seriously and makes continual adjustments on the basis of individual, context-specific responses (p. 119).

This is precisely what good teachers must do. They must adapt and respond on the basis of individual needs and interactions to a complex, everchanging set of circumstances, taking into account the real knowledge and experiences of learners: their cultures, their communities, and the conditions in which they live. The implication, then, is that research on teaching must reflect and build upon teaching as it exists in classrooms.

Some of the most central features of these new ways of knowing that are being enacted in PDSs are extensions of the constructivist understandings of knowledge that teachers and teacher educators have appreciated on behalf of children, and are just now beginning to extend to themselves and the knowledge base for their own work. Knowledge that is coconstructed by experienced teachers, novices, and teacher educators in conjuction with the children they serve, informs both research and practice in ways that create new possibilities for each.

NEW POSSIBILITIES FOR MUTUAL RESTRUCTURING

The dual goals of exemplary practice and exemplary induction in PDSs create other creative tensions that press for the mutual restructuring of schools and universities. Answering the questions that underlie PDS planning opens a Pandora's box of potentially radical rethinking: How do we envision the school as a community of learners? What do we want children to know? What do we want prospective teachers to know? How do we want teachers to be, to act? What opportunities do we want for teachers as lifelong learners? What do all of these things mean for the ways in which we structure teaching and learning opportunities for all of the actors in the PDS?

Acting on the ideals that are articulated in the planning process brings to light the disjunctures that exist between the real and the ideal, ultimately stimulating change. As pointed out in chapter 6, the experience of one student teacher at I.S. 44 made clear to him how the efforts of the PDS to create an integrated, crossdisciplinary community of learners would ultimately demand more fundamental school restructuring:

> For an interdisciplinary course to work, teachers need to work together, to not feel ownership of children, time periods, classes and materials, to

accommodate and to eliminate feelings of competition and insecurities among cohorts. But this is not easy to change. School is structured in a way that does not allow teachers to see and talk to each other, and often teachers are not even allowed to talk about kids and classrooms in the faculty lounge. Rooms are too small to allow for two classes to meet together with two teachers; separate schedules and different grade levels all make collaborating difficult . . . to ask what comes first, interdisciplinary teaching or collaboration is like asking what came first, the chicken or the egg.

Similarly at Norwood Elementary School, teachers keenly feel the need to restructure the school schedule and create time for collaboration as they proceed with fundamental reforms. As they explore new models of teaching, develop units for thematic, interdisciplinary learning and link these with authentic assessment, initiate peer coaching and collegial planning, and launch problem-based clinics for student teachers, the need to use school time differently has become apparent. Though part of a school-based management initiative, their requests to "bank" time for joint work have not been approved by the Los Angeles School District. Like other schools engaged in restructuring, the work of a PDS bumps up against the "regularities of schooling" (Sarason, 1982).

These kinds of recognitions have occurred in virtually all PDSs—that to accomplish the goals of the new enterprise, more fundamental changes in the school and the teacher education program will be required. These frequently also require changes in the larger institutions—districts and universities—within which the PDS participants must operate. The model for pursuing such changes is also a new one. Rather than the traditional model of school reform in which external change-agents develop a plan that is then carried out by the inside implementors, a model for mutual problem-solving about joint matters of concern has begun to emerge. Frequently, these internally generated solutions press outward (and hierarchically upward) for more systemic change rather than the reverse scenario anticipated by top-down change models.

Snyder, in chapter 5, describes the "SIP," the school improvement program model in which universities go out to improve schools, and the "flip-SIP," the inverse SIP in which school practitioners see the university as the defective partner, as the precursors to a third model—the PDS. Unlike a SIP or flip-SIP where the goal is for one party to change the other, the PDS is based on a realization that all of the participating experts must together invent a new system that is built upon the knowledge of all parties. Whitford, in chapter 4, describes a similar shift from an *interventionist* stance previously associated with university attempts to "help" schools— one often viewed from the inside of schools as interference—to an *interactive* approach in which the parties collectively identify problems and create solutions.

These kinds of shifts are evident in all of the PDS initiatives described in this volume, with a range of important results for the ways in which schools and universities function as learning communities. The emphasis on cooperative learning for students and teachers intersects with many of the school restructuring activities that are concurrently underway with PDS projects. This cooperative emphasis has spilled over to university terrain as well. Team teaching and joint planning among university faculty as well as school faculty have begun to create more integrated approaches to the curriculum for prospective teachers, while team teaching and intern structures in the PDS are doing the same for students. Snyder reports that, at P.S. 87 and I.S. 44, "*all* collaborating educators, no matter their depth of experience or whether school or university based, reported creating totally new curriculum units—some for the first time in years."

Curriculum changes on both sides of the school-university divide are provoking discussions of broader changes in the core programs to which PDS projects are generally attached (though, as discussed below, these attachments are generally quite loose). At the University of Southern California, for example, experience with the Norwood professional practice school has given university teacher educators insights about what their student teachers "know and understand about teaching" as well as "what they do not know or misunderstand." These insights have translated into adjustments in curriculum and methods classes, new initiatives to strengthen recruitment and teacher education for bilingual and second language teaching, and the development of problem-solving clinics. At the same time, participation in the professional practice school has stimulated restructuring of curriculum and student assessment at Norwood in ways that support the goals of the teacher education program to reflect professional standards of student-centered practice.

Structural changes in other programs are helping them better serve the needs and interest of learners rather than the demands of school and university schedules, calendars, and compartments. Interns at Southern Maine are selected into the PDS by both school and university faculty, and their program follows the school year rather than the college calendar. This enables them to learn the real job of teaching in a more holistic, integral way while also being more respectful of the influence of the interns' comings and goings on the lives and learning of the children and teachers in the school. Interns, and the PDS program, become part of the school rather than an extra add-on.

The University of Washington's PDC has created possibilities for more comprehensive, less compartmentalized services within schools by connecting others of the university's social service schools with the PDS schools, placing social work interns alongside teaching interns, and creating an interdisciplinary effort to prepare professionals who work with children. In Louisville, similar initiatives are underway to link in-school health and social services agencies to the preparation of future professionals. Meanwhile, the parallel efforts to restructure secondary schooling, through linkages to the Coalition of Essential Schools, and to create a PDS, through linkages to the Holmes Group and the Gheens Professional Development Academy, are leading the way for a broader restructuring of teacher education at the University of Louisville. There the possibility exists for the development of a new model of teacher preparation aimed at preparing teachers explicitly for the redesigned schools of the future.

In all of these efforts, broader networks for school and university reform have played critical roles in initiating and legitimizing these innovations. The Coalition of Essential Schools, the NEA's Mastery in Learning Project, the 21st Century Schools Project, and others are providing impetus for rethinking the education of elementary and secondary school students. At the same time, initiatives like those of the Holmes Group, Goodlad's Network for Educational Renewal, the AFT's Professional Practice Schools project, and the Gheens Academy have been providing a stimulus for rethinking the education of teachers. These stimuli for change help provide the external "blessing" many local reformers need to leverage the status quo; they open up opportunities for new ideas and learning through their networking activities; and they help support the new social dynamics that emerge in times of change.

Nonetheless, the work of restructuring—and the ideas that finally count—are entirely local. In chapter 2, Wells Junior High staff describe the philosophy they have developed through much experience with self-initiated, though externally supported, change as a commitment to continual inquiry. While using knowledge from research and theory to examine their teaching and school structures, "they understand that the answers to educational questions must ultimately come from within their educational community." A Wells teacher explains their development as empowered decision makers through their experience with the Mastery in Learning project, connecting their practical knowledge of children and classrooms with research knowledge, and choosing to use those strategies that seem appropriate: "We began to see ourselves as problem solvers."

In chapter 4, Whitford explains that "while externally developed frames are affecting the content of the changes, what both Fairdale and the Department of Secondary Education are inventing will be unique. This approach to reform can take local context into account and build ownership and commitment." Similarly, Snyder in chapter 5 describes how shared problem-solving around the particular concerns of the individuals and groups in the local context was what enabled the emergence of "one common, new voice—that of the PDS."

Involvement in decision making and empowerment to make positive changes are connected and contagious, as one Norwood teacher explains:

> On a personal level, I would venture to say that no project member feels exactly the same about teaching as before. Ever since Norwood came into partnership with USC, there has come to exist a renewed sense of professionalism, of true pride in one's work, that makes our campus an exciting place to be. Teachers have begun to view students as problem solvers who are more likely to learn if they are allowed to have input into their units of study. We see ourselves as colleagues with the administration in formulating and assessing educational opportunities and with the university in determining the student teacher's course of study.

In each PDS, success has rested upon the development of participants as joint, self-empowered problem-solvers, framing their own unique PDS questions and wrestling with their own unique circumstances to develop locally appropriate strategies for change.

POSSIBILITIES AND PITFALLS:
POLICIES AND STRUCTURAL SUPPORTS

For all of the possibilities painted in these cases, the challenges to the growth and survival of PDSs are very real. In the long-run, institutional, financial, and policy supports will all be needed if PDSs are to fulfill their promise.

INSTITUTIONAL CHALLENGES

The many institutional challenges to PDS development derive from the collaborative demands PDSs place on individual and institutional participants, the threats PDSs pose to core institutional traditions and practices in each institution, the low status that teacher education holds in universities and that professional development activities hold in schools, and the related lack of institutional incentives for this kind of work. In all of these areas, the case studies point up not only the potential of PDSs but also their fragility.

A common theme is the difficulty of establishing and maintaining the collaborative relationships that are at the heart of the PDS mission and that are prerequisites for its success. Collaboration takes time, the resource in shortest supply in most schools and among overstretched teacher education faculty. As Berry and Catoe note in chapter 8, there are few incentives or resources for cross-institutional collaboration from either of the parent institutions, which in a time of scarce resources must first maintain those activities they see as their own independent missions and functions. Nor are there yet many incentives from outside sources, such as state agencies, whose funding methods and programs will often support certain projects and activities in schools and others in schools of education, but little in the interstices between the two.

In addition, the capacity to collaborate is part of a developmental process that cannot be short-circuited by the arrival of a grant or the pronouncement of a new initiative. It is no accident that among the PDSs described in this volume, those that got off to the most propitious starts are the ones that grew out of preexisting personal and organizational relationships. These relationships had engaged people in collaborative work around a variety of shared goals over a period of time. This common history enabled a shared vision to emerge in the new context built on a sturdy foundation of shared understandings from the previous ones.

As other cases painfully detail, where such relationships do not exist, there are many obstacles to be negotiated: development of trust, identification of individual interests and objectives that can become the basis for common goals and mutual interests, creation of ways of talking and ways of working together that bridge cultural and communication differences. Even where preexisting relationships smooth the way, the development of the more intimate, even intrusive, form of collaboration required by a PDS is not straightforward.

In contrast to many other kinds of school-university collaboration that result in projects that do not tamper much with the core of either institution, the work of jointly restructuring schools and schools of education is doubly difficult. The two different cultures are not easy to harmonize in any event, but in this case, where a new organization is being invented that requires fundamental changes in both of the parent organizations, the work is both daunting and devoid of guidelines. At the same time, the traditional lack of respect for and attention to professional development in teaching must be overcome. PDSs are especially challenging collaborations because they seek to reshape fundamental values, beliefs, and paradigms for schools and school change while they are negotiating two worlds and inventing new programs.

For related reasons, PDSs have often grown up on the peripheries of school and university organizations, creating a small intersection set between the different missions and activities of the two, but not infiltrating the core of either. In chapter 3, Grossman talks about the history of reform initiatives as "detachable projects" that both result from and contribute to the complexities of organizations that function in multiple contexts with multiple agendas. She notes that these studies of PDSs make apparent the organizational complexity of collaborative arrangements between schools and universities. As a "small ad-hocracy wedged in the cracks of the formal organizational structure of the college" the PDS avoids bureaucratic imperatives that might kill it. This same ad-hocracy, however, "may relegate it to the permanent periphery of university life." Institutionalizing a PDS will require new organizational arrangements that address issues of funding, governance, and university and school culture.

The usual dilemma of school reforms is magnified here. Because new ideas and projects threaten the "behavioral and programmatic regularities" of schools (Sarason, 1982), they frequently need to be created at the margins of the institution where they can be ignored long enough to take root. The dilemma, of course, is that if such initiatives continue to live at the periphery, they fail at their overall mission. In the case of the PDS, the difficulties double, since it is the core of two previously separate institutions that must be infiltrated, connected, and simultaneously transformed. These case studies demonstrate that all of these innovations have grown up on the margins, and only a few are making progress at working their way toward the center of either the school or the university. As Grossman notes, changes in organizational culture, funding, and governance must all be tackled for reform at the center to occur.

Among the most tenacious issues of organizational culture are the low values placed upon teacher education in the university and upon professional development activities in the school—and the concomitant lack of rewards for teacher learning in both places. Since teacher learning is the primary mission of the PDS, its disdain by these organizations (which both reflects and reinforces the fundamental problems of the profession), threatens the long-term viability of the PDS concept—and the prospects of teaching becoming a profession.

A number of the case studies point out how the low status of teacher education and teacher development result in low levels of resources for PDS work from either universities or schools. They also detail the ways in which PDS work goes unrewarded by the incentive structures of both organizations. While professors are rewarded for research, and to a lesser extent, teaching university courses, school faculty are rewarded for working with students, not with other teachers. For the most part, incentive structures that would provide additional time, recognition, or remuneration for the work of PDS development are absent. In chapter 2, Miller and Silvernail aptly capture the questions that result:

> Will involvement in preservice education help redefine the teacher role within the school and enhance teacher leadership? Or will teacher involvement come to be viewed as one more burden in an already overburdened profession? . . . Will teacher education become central to the worklife of faculty in the College of Education or will it maintain its contradictory status as both highly visible and ultimately marginal?

Many of the answers to these questions depend on how the financial and policy parameters for PDSs evolve.

FINANCIAL CHALLENGES

Despite substantial moral support, the PDS movement has been launched with remarkably little funding. Ford's support lasted only a few years; no major foundation has made a long-term commitment to these new initiatives, and federal or state support has been largely absent. With the exception of the Michigan Partnership, where a business-education partnership has raised a sizeable sum of corporate, foundation, and state money to support PDS development and Minnesota's seed money for pilot projects, few PDSs have been launched with substantial external support.

The prospects for institutional support are also limited. As already noted, teacher education is generally less well supported by universities than are most other programs. There is usually no cushion on which to build substantial labor-intensive innovations. Individual schools or districts have few resources as well as few incentives to invest in the preparation of novice teachers, many of whom will leave to develop their careers in other schools and districts. Since most beginning teachers are hired by less affluent schools where teacher turnover is highest, the prospects for funding model induction programs with the existing resources of schools where most induction occurs are not good.

As one of Berry and Catoe's respondents notes in chapter 8, for funding issues to be successfully resolved, a persuasive case for PDSs will have to be made to a number of key constituencies not yet well informed or substantially involved:

> It's difficult to get money for collaboration. Who's going to give it up? . . .
> You would have to have support from the college presidents and either the
> local superintendents, the teachers' association, or the school board associ-
> ation. . . . Some key people in those groups are going to have to under-
> stand what a PDS is.

The hope for institutionalizing PDSs is that states will begin to acknowledge them as part of the infrastructure for building a strong education system and will fund them through basic aid allocations as they do other integral parts of the educational system. Massachusetts had taken a step in the direction of establishing a statewide network of PDSs before its economy collapsed several years ago, and Michigan is in the process of taking similar initial steps. Minnesota has enacted a provision that will make an internship in a PDS-like "clinical site" a prerequisite for initial licensing, and the state is funding a set of pilot programs. Ultimately, the intention is to provide state support for these sites. Since states assume the responsibility of licensing teachers for the schools they approve, it is appropriate for them to assume some significant role in ensuring that teachers are adequately prepared to be responsible practitioners.

In addition, the federal goverment has many reasons to invest in PDS development, just as it has invested in the development and support of teaching hospitals as part of its efforts to improve medical education and ensure an adequate supply of qualified health professionals. Investing in the capacity of the teaching profession to develop and transmit knowledge, to prepare new entrants effectively, and to stem unnecessary attrition are all appropriate and much needed federal interventions that would offer significant support for the pursuit of other federal education goals.

POLICY CHALLENGES

As PDSs begin to take root, a number of policy supports will be needed to sustain their further growth and sustenance. In addition to financial support, PDSs will need to become part of the licensing and certification parameters for entry into teaching. They will need to be taken into account in procedures for approving and accrediting teacher education institutions. These changes are beginning to be discussed as states increasingly envision internships as part of the teacher preparation process, and as the National Council on Accreditation of Teacher Education (NCATE) adjusts its standards to allow for innovations in strategies for preparing teachers.

In addition, as PDSs strengthen and act upon a growing knowledge base for teaching, they will confront the after effects of a policy era in which teaching practice became increasingly defined by state legislatures rather than by a professional knowledge base. In chapter 8, Berry and Catoe provide poignant illustrations of how prescriptive state policies enacted during the 1980s governing school curriculum and testing practices, along with teacher evaluation standards, are at odds with emerging standards of practice for teaching and for PDSs. While creating programs that teach prospective teachers to use and conduct research, to reflect, and to adapt their practice to the needs of students, South Carolina teacher educators must simultaneously train them to pass a beginning teacher evaluation regimen that undermines these qualities, hoping that the mandated routines do not unduly affect their later practices. While preparing their charges to use state-of-the-art teaching methods in line with the standards of national professional associations, these same teacher educators know that schools under pressure to score high on "decontextualized, multiple choice basic skills tests" are unlikely "to encourage a curriculum that prepares educators to teach for understanding."

As policy rethinking occurs, it is important that efforts to restructure elementary and secondary schools become more closely joined to these efforts to restructure teacher education. This connection is extremely important for the future of all of the reforms thus far undertaken. There has always been a chicken and egg problem with efforts to improve schools and schools of education. Schools, especially those in the vanguard of practice, frequently complain that education programs don't send them candidates prepared to teach in the ways they require. Schools of education traditionally complain that they must prepare teachers to cope in a preponderance of schools that require retrogressive practices as well as a very few that entertain progressive ones—and that they cannot get too far ahead of traditional practice in the field without disadvantaging their students when they encounter "real" schools, particularly those in less advantaged communities that tend to hire most new teachers. And, schools of education must prepare teachers to pass licensing requirements that themselves do not encourage state-of-the-art conceptions of teaching and learning. Coherent, connected progress in all of these arenas must occur simultaneously if school restructuring is to take hold.

A related challenge for PDSs is the intensity and fragmented character of the very reform movement that has spawned them. Due in part to inherent conservatism and in part to lack of capacity for more integrative action, both governments and private funders have a tendency to seek change at the margins rather than at the core of established practice, relying on a plethora of small projects and demonstrations rather than on more coherent and substantial redesign. As a consequence of this project mentality, the most innovation-minded schools and schools of education are overwhelmed with innumerable (often temporarily funded) reform initiatives. Their efforts to manage these separate projects alongside the sequential waves of reform policy that have swept over schools in the last decade result in the "overstuffed agendas and curricular discontinuities" described in chapter 8 and evident in many of the other case studies as well.

The frantic pace of life in schools is exacerbated further by efforts to keep all of these projects spinning like so many plates on their separate sticks—some of them colliding due to conceptual dissonance—and expending extraordinary amounts of time, energy, and invention without benefit of the synergistic, coordinated efforts a more coherent set of change strategies would allow. Well-intentioned reformers—at the policy and funding levels as well as among school and university practitioners—would do well to consider how fragmented and disjointed initiatives may ultimately reduce the likelihood that any of their efforts will become institutionalized. Establishing some coherence and integration of direction and effort is a critical part of the challenge for policy makers and organizational leaders as well as for classroom practitioners.

Unless policy and practice are jointly reconstructed across institutional and state bureaucracy boundaries, the possibilities for creating a foundation for learner-centered teaching and teacher education will, once again, go unrealized. On the other hand, if policymakers and practitioners together seek to create PDSs that push the edges of teaching knowledge forward while restructuring teacher education and schooling, they will have made a profound contribution to real and lasting educational reform.

REFERENCES

Anderson, A. W. (1962). The teaching profession: An example of diversity in training and function. In N. B. Henry (Ed.), *Education for the professions*, The Sixty-First Yearbook of the National Society for the Study of Education (pp. 140–167). Chicago: University of Chicago Press.

Brainard, F. (1989). *Professional development schools: Status as of 1989*. Seattle: Institute for the Study of Educational Policy, University of Washington.

Bredeson, P. V., Fruth, M. J., & Kasten, K. L. (1983). Organizational incentives and secondary school teaching, *Journal of Research and Development in Education, 16*, 52–56.

Carnegie Forum on Education and the Economy. (1986). *A nation prepared: Teachers for the 21st century*. New York: Author.

Chapman, D. W., & Hutcheson, S. M. (1982). Attrition from teaching careers: A discriminant analysis. *American Educational Research Journal, 19*, 93–105.

Cremin, L. (1965). *The genius of American education*. NY: Vintage Books.

Cronbach, L. J. (1975). Beyond the two disciplines of scientific psychology. *American Psychologist, 30*(2), 116–127.

Darling-Hammond, L. (1990a). Teacher professionalism: Why and how? In A. Lieberman (Ed.), *Schools as collaborative cultures: Creating the future now* (pp. 25–50). New York: The Falmer Press.

Darling-Hammond, L. (1990b). Teachers and teaching: Signs of a changing profession. In W.R. Houston (Ed.), *Handbook of research on teacher education*. NY: Macmillan.

Darling-Hammond, L. (1990c). *Teacher supply, demand, and quality: A mandate for the National Board*. Paper prepared for the National Board for Professional Teaching Standards.

Darling-Hammond, L. (1992). Teaching and knowledge: Policy issues posed by alternate certification for teachers," *Peabody Journal of Education, Vol. 67*(3), 123–154.

Darling-Hammond, L., Adams, C., Berry, B., & Snyder, J. (in press). *The evolution of professional development schools*. NY: National Center for Restructuring Education, Schools, and Teaching, Teachers College, Columbia University.

Ebmeier, H., Twombly, S., & Teeter, D. J. (1991). The comparability and adequacy of financial support for schools of education, *Journal of Teacher Education, 42*(3), 226–235.

Fenstermacher, G. (1992). The place of alternate certification in the education of teachers," *Peabody Journal of Education, 67*(3), 155–185.

Grissmer, D., & Kirby, S. N. (1987). *Teacher attrition: The uphill climb to staff the nation's schools.* Santa Monica, CA: The RAND Corporation, R-3512-CSTP.

Holmes Group. (1986). *Tomorrow's teachers: A report of the Holmes Group.* East Lansing, MI: Author.

Holmes Group. (1990). *Tomorrow's schools.* East Lansing, MI: Author.

McDonald, F. (1980). *The problems of beginning teachers: A crisis in training (Vol. 1).* Study of Induction Programs for Beginning Teachers. Princeton, NJ: Educational Testing Service.

National Institute of Education (1979). *Beginning teachers and internship programs.* Report Number 78-0014. Washington, D.C.: U.S. Department of Education.

Rosenholtz, S. J., & Smylie, M. A. (1983). *Teacher compensation and career ladders: Policy implications from research.* Paper commissioned by the Tennessee General Assembly's Select Committee on Education.

Ryan, K. (1979). Toward understanding the problem: At the threshold of the profession. In K. Howey and R. Bents (Eds.), *Toward meeting the needs of beginning teachers.* Minneapolis, MN: U.S. Department of Education/Teacher Corps.

Sarason, S. (1982). *The culture of the school and the problem of change.* Boston: Allyn and Bacon.

Stallings, J., & Kowalski, T. (1990). Research on professional development schools. In W. R. Houston (Ed.), *Handbook of research on teacher education,* (pp. 251–263). NY: Macmillan.

Tisher, R. (1978) (ed.) *The induction of beginning teachers in Australia.* Melbourne: Monash University.

Veenman, S. (1984). Perceived problems of beginning teachers. *Review of Educational Research, 54,* 143–178.

Wise, A. E., & Darling-Hammond, L. (1987). *Licensing teachers: Design for a teaching profession.* Santa Monica, CA: The RAND Corporation.

Wise, A. E., Darling-Hammond, L., & Berry, B. (1987). *Effective teacher selection: From recruitment to retention.* Santa Monica, CA: The RAND Corporation, R-3462-NIE/CSTP.

Wright, D. P., McKibbon, M., & Walton, P. (1987). *The effectiveness of the teacher trainee program: An alternate route into teaching in California.* California Commission on Teacher Credentialing.

Chapter 2

WELLS JUNIOR HIGH SCHOOL: EVOLUTION OF A PROFESSIONAL DEVELOPMENT SCHOOL

Lynne Miller and David L. Silvernail

Wells Junior High School, in its 2nd year as a professional development school (PDS), is pursuing the three goals associated with such an enterprise: (1) to provide for continuing development and professional growth of experienced teachers; (2) to provide a context for thinking and reinventing schools for the purpose of building and sustaining the best educational practice, and (3) to contribute to the preservice education of teachers and induct them into the teaching profession (Lieberman & Miller, 1990).

We believe that the school presents a working example of the dual agenda that Goodlad (1986) terms "simultaneously improving schools and the education of educators." This chapter takes the form of a retrospective case study that describes the evolution of Wells Junior High School as a PDS, its history and context, the model's various components and characteristics, and the challenges it presents to school and university faculty about their most fundamental notions of teacher education and school renewal.

HISTORY AND CONTEXT

The PDS at Wells Junior High School represents a high stakes partnership between the University of Southern Maine (USM) and the Wells School District, and with roots in the Southern Maine Partnership, a school/university collaboration committed to Goodlad's simultaneous agenda, it is deeply embedded in the history of the two collaborating institutions. It is best understood as an evolution of relationships among institutions, policies, practices, individuals, and groups of people. Both the university and the school district came to the project with what Sarason (1982) calls rich individual "prehistories," as well as with dispositions toward and experiences in partnerships.

THE WELLS SCHOOL DISTRICT AND ITS JUNIOR HIGH

The Wells School District with a total student population of approximately 1,550 divided among two elementary schools, a junior high school, and a high school is in a coastal community in southern Maine with a year-round population of 9,000. The population base is a mixture of long-term residents and urban professionals, who have moved north to Maine for the "quality of life." Though overwhelmingly white, the population is by no means homogeneous. A range of socioeconomic and regional ethnic groups is represented in the schools. About 35% of high school graduates go on to 4-year colleges and universities; the rest seek local employment and reside in or near the community.

The school system, through its superintendent and school board, encourages systemic improvement, based on collaboration, inquiry, and school-based governance. It takes seriously the notion that classroom teachers should lead school change. The district describes itself this way:

> The staffs in Wells . . . are committed to the practice of continual inquiry. They use the knowledge from research and theory to examine both their instruction and practice and the structure within which they work in order to continually improve the educational program for their students, but they understand that the answers to educational questions must ultimately come from within their educational community. (Wells Junior High School, 1989, p. 3)

Despite the economic hardships, the Wells district has continued to commit itself to K–12 restructuring and has aggressively sought outside resources to sustain its efforts. The district has received foundation grants for faculty development and school change, has maintained a relationship with the National Education Association's Center for Innovation, and has just received major grant support for its work in curriculum and assessment.

The Wells district was not always so forward looking and inventive. Until recently, the district was viewed as the poor relation of its better known and better financed neighboring school district to the north. The transformation of the Wells district is due, in large part, to its superintendent. Since becoming the superintendent, he has promoted a culture characterized by optimism, high expectations, experimentation, and risk-taking. How he led the district in its transformation is a lesson in large-scale vision and small-scale change. The emergence of Wells Junior High School as a center for teacher education is grounded in the district's initiatives and support for teacher learning that the superintendent encouraged.

Teachers at Wells Junior High School had been involved in a process of rethinking and redirecting their own professional development long before they agreed to become a PDS. Beginning in 1979, with assistance from the National Diffusion Network, the school participated in a district-wide experiment with building-based staff development. Procedures were developed that helped the school staff make decisions about its own developmental activities and build an appropriate staff development budget. This early initiative led to a centralized and teacher-driven process but it did not challenge assumptions about the content of staff development and how professional growth activities should be delivered. There was a continuous reliance on outside consultants and on disconnected workshops throughout the life of the project.

It was not until 1986, 1 year into the Mastery of Learning Project, that the staff confronted the substantive and adult learning issues related to staff development. The school, with project funding, hired a change facilitator—a person who had wide experiences as an alternative school teacher and director and university instructor. Together, the school faculty and this change facilitator began to put in place many of the tenets of the Mastery in Learning Project.

> Three rules governed a faculty's participation in the project; 75% staff approval, full faculty particpation in the Faculty Inventory, and commitment that no decision about a reform initiative would be made without the consideration of options available

The last tenet, "consideration of options available," came to be called "using the knowledge base" at Wells Junior High. "Using the knowledge base" meant that teachers became consumers of research as well as doers of research.

"Using the knowledge" became the starting point for developing a new view of staff development at Wells. The school staff redefined its use of the district's allocated workshop days. Rather than providing time for formal presentations by outside consultants, the days were used for teachers' review of research and for critical discussion and reflection. For example, on one such day teachers spent 2 hours individually reading research about grouping. During another day, they worked in cooperative learning groups to share their perceptions on the research they had read. On yet another day, the staff met to engage in the process of concensus building with the goal of reaching a decision about grouping practises in the school.

In the course of these meetings and activities, the whole notion of staff development was turned on its head. The emphasis shifted from outside consultants to in-house experts. Collaborative learning groups replaced the traditional lecture/demonstration format. Problem posing and problem solving supplanted the recipes and prescriptions for effective schools that teachers had heard for years and never managed to implement. It was in this environment for professional development that the PDS model took hold.

The junior high school itself serves approximately 310 students in grades 6, 7, and 8. It was an original member of NEA's Mastery in Learning Project, "a site-based, faculty-led school empowerment project. It attempts to learn what happens to educational quality when a school faculty, organized knowledge, and the authority to act are brought together in a school" (McClure, 1991, p. 221). Wells Junior High School's experience in Mastery in Learning was very successful. During the time of its involvement, the faculty developed a consensus-based decision-making process and began to move away from a traditional junior high school toward a school that is "appropriate to the developmental needs of 10–14 year olds within a learning atmosphere that is productive for students and adults" (Wells Junior High School, 1990, p. 2). For the junior high school staff, the Mastery in Learning notion of "reflecting on practice" and "using the knowledge base" were particularly powerful. As Susan Walters, a Wells teacher who later became a pivotal figure in the PDS, indicates:

> The staff embraced the emphasis on teacher decision making and its connection to instruction. They resonated with the possibilities and connected their practical knowledge of children and classrooms with the professional research. There was a sense there was not a right answer. We began to see ourselves as problem solvers and we got a sense that if it doesn't work, we can always retool and change.

In 1988, after Mastery in Learning had been in place for 3 years, a new principal arrived at the school. With a recently earned doctorate in hand, she encountered a school staff that was ambivalent at best about having a strong administrative leader. Some initial friction arose between the principal and her staff around issues of teacher and administrative roles in decision making. Today, the relationship is still evolving and this evolution is now an accepted ingredient in the life of the school.

THE UNIVERSITY OF SOUTHERN MAINE AND ITS TEACHER EDUCATION PROGRAMS

The University of Southern Maine (USM) traces its roots to teacher education. Initially chartered as the Western Maine Normal School in 1878, USM now has over 10,000 students and serves a diverse student population in a wide metropolitan area.

Like many universities with a history in the normal school movement, USM has devoted a large portion of its time and resources to broadening its base beyond the preparation of teachers, and in deemphasizing, if not denying, its normal school origins. As its programs in arts and sciences, business, and the health professions grew, the university's ability to commit to quality teacher education was stretched.

In the late 1980s, the College of Education enrolled approximately 350 undergraduates who had the option of selecting between the two elementary teacher education programs. One program, a traditional university course sequence, was complemented by a 14-week supervised student teaching experience in local schools. The other, a site-based internship program, involved students in a full year's internship in a school setting; all method courses were taught on site; and students were placed in cohort groups and encouraged to develop collegial bonds with their peers and their cooperating teachers. The internship program was originally designed to replace the traditional student teaching option. In fact, it failed to establish a firm hold in the college as more and more students opted for the less rigorous program. Efforts to maintain the internship program were undermined by a lack of resources and ambivalent college-wide commitment. Undergraduate teacher education became less of a priority as more resources and attention were shifted to graduate programs and the college relied increasingly on part-time faculty to deliver its teacher education courses and to supervise its students in the field.

Faculty members were divided into two distinct groups: the undergraduate and graduate faculties. The undergraduate faculty worked exclusively in teacher education and were assigned 12 credit hours of course work and supervision each semester. Graduate faculty taught at the masters level and carried a 9 credit load. It was assumed they would devote the equivalent of 3 credit hours toward scholarship. As Goodlad (1990) described, those responsible for teacher education were awarded less status and more work than other professors of education. Quite simply, undergraduate teacher education was not accorded a privileged place in the College.

At the same time, the college supported two small, postgraduate teacher preparation programs. These were designed to attract mid-career professionals with liberal arts degrees into teaching. One program focused on elementary teacher preparation, the other on the secondary level. The programs admitted a cohort of students who took their required courses in the fall semester and did an intensive supervised student teaching semester in the spring. These programs were staffed primarily by graduate faculty, who developed and offered the programs with little or no consultation with their undergraduate colleagues. Professors engaged in postgraduate teacher education carried the graduate level teaching load and often divided their time between teacher education and existing masters degree programs. Thus, the division that already existed between undergraduate and graduate faculty was exacerbated by the fledgling postgraduate programs, which never came under formal faculty scrutiny and approval.

All this began to change in May, 1989. In response to the national debate about the inadequacy of the preparation of teachers, the dean of the college—with the encouragement and support of the president of the university—urged the faculty to replace its undergraduate program with a postgraduate year of professional preparation. In a vote of the entire college faculty, a resounding majority supported the elimination of the bachelors degree in education. The only nine dissenting voices were from the undergraduate teacher education faculty. In large measure, these nine faculty members thought the existing programs were well-designed, but lacked the necessary resources to prove their effectiveness. But, the majority rule prevailed and undergraduate teacher education, long the mainstay of the college, and the normal school that preceded it, ceased to exist.

The next few months at the College of Education were filled with tumult and promise. A planning committee, comprised of four faculty and the Dean, was formed. Only one member of the committee had been involved in preservice teacher education. The others held appointments in graduate programs in adult education, counselor education, and leadership and administration. The committee was charged with developing a process for planning a new "fifth year" teacher education program. It formed four investigative task forces charged with examining four topics: (1) baccalaureate offerings and the development of a minor in educational studies; (2) development of a postbaccalaureate professional preparation program; (3) degrees and certification; and (4) admission criteria and procedures. At the end of the summer, members of the task forces and the planning committee met in a retreat to share their findings and consider the next steps in planning a new program. A panel of three school administrators was invited to the retreat to react to the initial plans and to offer suggestions. This was the first instance of school-based involvement in the planning process and it was short-lived. The College of Education faculty continued to assume exclusive responsibility for teacher education planning for months to come.

The planning committee, enlarged to include two additional faculty who had been involved in preservice teacher education, met again in the Fall of 1989. Its first task was to consider the recommendations presented by the task force during the summer retreat. One of the earliest committee decisions was to discontinue using phrases like "5th year" and "postgraduate" to describe the emerging program and to begin calling it by its new name, Extended Teacher Education Program or ETEP. The decision on a name signalled a major departure from the previous notions about program assumptions and design. The committee consciously discarded the idea that quality teacher education could occur during one postgraduate or "5th year." Instead it embraced the idea of continued teacher development, beginning with one's entry into a liberal arts curriculum as an undergraduate and extending through preparation, induction, and continuation in the teaching profession. In keeping with this new definition and nomenclature, the committee viewed ETEP as having three distinct, but interrelated, components: an undergraduate major in arts and sciences with an accompanying minor in educational studies, an intensive postgraduate year of professional preparation, and finally a clinical masters degree available to interns once they became practicing teachers. The planning group assigned development of the minor to a small subgroup comprised of undergraduate faculty who had expressed a particular interest in this component of the program. The committee as a whole turned its attention toward the design of the postgraduate year of professional preparation.

The planning committee made two additional important decisions early in the fall. One was to admit students who sought elementary, middle, or secondary certification. This was a departure from the earlier undergraduate programs, that only prepared elementary teachers, and from the postgraduate programs and admitted only small groups of elementary and secondary candidates. The second decision was more immediate and more dramatic: to pilot a middle-level program for the following academic year.

There is no agreement as to who first suggested a middle-level pilot program. Some believe the idea originated with the dean, some think it came from the superintendent of Wells, and some say it grew out of initial discussions of the planning group. Whatever its origins, by early November the group had decided to ask Cherie Major, an undergraduate faculty member with extensive experience and training in middle level education and an advocate of the former site-based undergraduate internship program, to organize the new pilot program. In the words of Major, "I was itching to do it. I wanted to create a program that retained the good components of the internship program and included some of my own experiences from teaching in a lab school."

So began the process for planning and implementing ETEP's first PDS. It was a process authorized by an ad hoc faculty group with the blessings of the dean and stewarded by an undergraduate faculty member, who had directed one of the site-based internship programs. It is no small irony that she had also cast one of the nine dissenting votes in the May 1989 decision to create a new approach to teacher education.

FORGING COLLABORATIONS

After exploring four possible school sites for the pilot program, Major settled on Wells. Many qualities recommended it. It was an active member of the Southern Maine Partnership whose forums for the exchange of ideas among school and university faculty members laid the foundation for reciprocal dialogue and planning. Additionally, Wells had put in place major changes in school structure and design, such as site-based management, a middle level and developmental philosophy, teaching teams and block scheduling, and a fledgling advisor/advisee program. Its involvement in NEA's Mastery in Learning Project was further evidence that Wells took school restructuring seriously and that it was committed to systemic change, and support from the district and the superintendent seemed assured. Equally important were personal factors. The principal saw the pilot program as an opportunity not only for teacher development but also for forging her own connection to the university. Having just completed her doctorate, she was eager to continue an academic affiliation. "I personally wanted to be involved in teacher education as an equal partner." There also was a personal friendship between the principal and Major who had known each other for several years through professional association and middle school connections. They were confident that "our mutual respect and trust for each other would help in developing a 'true' partnership between the school and College."

By early 1990, the idea of the middle-level pilot program had been discussed extensively by the Wells district central administration and endorsed in concept by the superintendent. However, in keeping with the philosophy of site-based governance, the superintendent left the final decision about participation in the hands of the Wells faculty. When presented with the idea, the faculty were intrigued but cautious. Many had memories of less than satisfying experiences with traditional student teaching programs. To alleviate these fears, three teachers who had experience working with Major in the earlier site-based undergraduate internship program, met with the Wells faculty and shared their experiences of working with interns in general, and with Major in particular. By the end of these discussions, the Wells faculty reached a consensus to participate as the pilot program. There were no dissenting votes.

Planning for the program began in earnest in mid-March. The dean of the college authorized Major to convene a planning team for this new approach to teacher education. The planning team was markedly different from the earlier groups convened to design ETEP. It had seven members: two college faculty, the school principal and guidance counselor, two teachers, and the school district certification officer. Meeting biweekly, this committee designed the curriculum, identified instructors, planned practicum experience, and developed a recruitment, application, and selection process of students. Almost all of the team's work took place in Wells, not on the university campus. The program that emerged focused on an intensive internship at Wells Junior High School where on-site course work and real-life experiences were to be woven together over an entire academic year. This new program borrowed from both the former undergraduate intern and the postbaccalaureate programs at the university. What was different about the new Wells site was the nature of interaction between the school site and the university that the PDS model promised to promote. While actual program design is discussed later in this case, it is important to note that many of the characteristics that have been identified as essential to PDSs emerged almost de novo from the joint planning that took place at the school level in Wells. A core group of school and university faculty made a public commitment to working together as teacher educators and school improvers. While the college faculty's voice was important, it was not dominant. Their knowledge of teacher education practice and familiarity with new directions in the field informed, but did not dictate, program design. The idea for teacher education that developed was, in many ways, like reinventing the wheel. While many of the spokes were not original, the way they were joined was unique to the setting. The result was a new wheel.

Two parts of this planning process are particularly worthy of mention. For the first time in the college's history, public school faculty had a major voice in designing a teacher education program. As a result, the principal reports, "teachers developed a real sense of responsibility for the preparation of future teachers." The planning process was also unique in that it took place outside the traditional departmental and college-wide committee structure. Although attempts were made to keep faculty informed about the planning, and the original six-member college planning committee endorsed the program design, the pilot program was not formally reviewed and approved by the college faculty. That came later. In a real sense, the school faculty were first among equals in creating the new middle-level teacher preparation program. Once the program was underway, it became a model for future development of PDSs in other locations throughout the Southern Maine Partnership.

By late spring, after only 6 months of planning, the program was ready to accept applications for admission. Coincidental to this process, Major and a university colleague wrote and submitted a federal grant proposal designed to enhance the project, a proposal subsequently funded for 2 years beginning October 1990. Although not critical to implementing the program, the federal grant provided opportunities to expand its scope. It provided support for the training and development activities that would assist school and university-based teacher educators to put the program in place. In particular, it provided support for course development by university/school teams and for the later training of cooperating teachers. The grant also provided resources for assessing the development of the interns and the impact of the program on Wells Junior High and the College.

THE PDS MODEL

PRESERVICE EDUCATION PROGRAM

The ETEP preservice education program that was developed for Wells consists of a 30-credit hour graduate program embedded in a 1-year internship at Wells Junior High School. In the 1st year, 15 teacher candidates interned at Wells Junior High School. In the 2nd year, 26 candidates were placed in four PDSs that now exist in the district. About half of the interns were at Wells Junior High.

The PDS program is structured around a core of common principles and practices that distinguish it from previous preservice efforts at the university. The most important of these principles are:

• *Joint Coordination.* The program is codirected by Major and a teacher leader, Susan Walters, who serves as the teacher certification officer in the district. The teacher leader is released from half the time of her regular district responsibilities to coordinate the preservice program and to link preservice education to ongoing teacher development and school renewal efforts. The university pays the Wells school district the equivalent of one half of Walters' teaching salary to support her time as site coordinator. Working together, Walters and Major model the collaboration and teambuilding the program promotes.

• *Innovative and Collaborative Admissions Procedure.* The interns' program officially begins in August, but actually the learning and development of the future teachers starts with the application process. This includes traditional criteria (e.g., standardized test scores, transcripts, letters of recommendation, etc.) as well as formal and informal interviews. The planning team felt an important ingredient in the program would be the match of the teacher interns with their cooperating teachers, and the ability of the interns to interact with middle level students. Each candidate is interviewed by a team of school and college faculty and a middle school student; is given a tour and orientation to the school by a team of middle school students; and interacts informally with teachers and students throughout the daylong selection process. Final selection of the interns is made by the school and college faculty team that relies heavily on teacher and student impressions of the candidates.

One of the innovations built into the new program is the manner in which it determines the size of its class. Traditionally, the number of participants in a teacher preparation program is driven by the size of the applicant pool. If 30 qualified applicants are identified, then the College faculty seeks 30 field placements. In contrast, in the new program, the size of the intern group is determined by the capacity of the school to provide quality placements. As a result, qualified candidates may be turned away because the site can only support a given number of interns.

• *Cohort Placement of Interns.* Interns work as a cohort group throughout the year. They work alongside each other as junior colleagues in the school and as students in graduate courses. Weekly seminars and other site-based activities reinforce the cohort nature of the program.

• *Adherence to School Calendar.* Interns follow the school, not the university, calendar. They begin the internship when school begins; they take school vacations, honor school semesters, attend school staff development programs, and follow school protocol.

• *Team Building.* The program actively promotes team building for the cohort group and within the district. In August, interns participate in an Outward Bound semi-wilderness experience designed to develop a supportive cohort group. They then join with the entire Wells faculty and staff in a retreat that focuses on team building. "These experiences proved to be very important," reported one intern graduate. "It helped us learn we could rely on each other for help and support, and it helped the teachers see that we had many unique contributions we could make in their classrooms." Team building continues throughout the year through ongoing Outward Bound and other cohort activities.

• *Integration of Theory and Practice.* Beginning with the first day of school, interns divide their time between observing and teaching in classrooms, and taking graduate level teacher preparation courses. Successful completion of the year-long program results in initial teacher certification for the interns, and the earning of 30 graduate credits that may be applied toward the clinical masters degree in teaching. During the fall semester the interns earn 15 graduate credits for coursework. They also take a semester long practicum that includes a two week observation of the opening of the school year, followed by twelve weeks of half-time work in classrooms. Interns work with mentor teachers as well as with subject matter specialists. In addition, each intern is assigned to an advisor/advisee group and participates in grade level team activities. In the spring semester, interns continue taking university courses and spend full days in classrooms at both the elementary and secondary level.

• *Valuing of Teacher Voice.* Integration of theory and practice goes beyond combining academic course work and field experiences. In general, teacher's voices have been uninvited, unheard, and devalued in professional discourse about teacher education. The Wells PDS makes teacher voice central to its preservice program and acknowledges the unique perspectives, insights, and wisdom that practicing teachers have accumulated and incorporates these into the preservice program. Through ongoing, daily discussion, story telling, and reflective interaction, experienced teachers talk about the tacit understandings and informal rules of practice that underpin their knowledge of the teaching craft. Through continuous conversation in the context of real schools and classrooms, teacher voice assumes a privileged authority and often challenges the more formal knowledge base that university professors represent.

• *Site-based Cooperative Course Delivery.* All graduate level courses are delivered on site and taught by combinations of university and school faculty during the afternoons. In some cases, school faculty are released from their normal duties during the school day. In others, the faculty co-teach courses beginning in midafternoon, after the students' school day. The school faculty are reviewed and approved as adjunct faculty by the college department faculty and are paid the normal university rate for teaching courses part-time. Some courses are conducted exclusively by university faculty while others are delivered by school faculty alone. Academic work includes: an interdisciplinary course in learning theory, work in models of teaching and content methods, adolescent development, technology, curriculum development and organization, education for exceptional children, and weekly seminars focusing on middle level education, team teaching and school restructuring, and reflective teaching. All courses require observation and demonstration within the school.

• *Intensive Supervision of Practice.* Supervision of interns is shared by the university and school-based site coordinators; this results in a supervisor-intern ratio of 1 to 7 or less. All interns are observed weekly or even biweekly by a supervisor and interns receive regular systematic coaching from their cooperating teachers. Supervision and coaching involve pre and postconferences around a teaching episode. Twice during the semester the interns, their cooperating teachers, and the supervisors participate in "the videotaped observation conference." Developed specifically for Wells Junior High School interns, the process has the following components:

1. The intern teaches a lesson which is videotaped.
2. The intern, the cooperating teacher, and the supervisor view the videotape of the lesson; only the intern comments and is encouraged to analyze his/her teaching.
3. The cooperating teacher and the intern have a conference, which is videotaped by the supervisor.
4. The intern leaves and the cooperating teacher and the supervisor view the tape of the conference; only the cooperating teacher comments and is encouraged to analyze his/her coaching.
5. The cooperating teacher and the supervisor discuss the conference.

This process is viewed as particularly helpful in guiding interns through the complexity of teaching and drawing on the knowledge of both school and university-based teacher educators.

•*Reflective Practice.* Throughout the program, interns are provided opportunities for reflecting on their own practice and on the schoolroom practices they observe. Journaling, is done through "intern notebooks" and weekly seminars are forums for group reflection and analysis. The program assumes that theory and practice will "rub against each other" in the school. Interns are expected to observe and process contradictions between the knowledge base the university promotes and the knowledge base that practicing teachers use in their daily life in classrooms. Interns are encouraged to embrace these contradictions and to struggle through them. They are expected to reach a personal, if tentative, stance on teaching and learning as they complete the year's internship.

PROFESSIONAL DEVELOPMENT OF EXPERIENCED TEACHERS

While the decision to become a clinical site for teacher education introduced a new agenda for staff development into Wells—preservice teacher education—it also served to enhance the existing agenda for school renewal based on reflective practices. At least three professional development activities resulted from the infusion of teacher education into the life of the school.

Training for Cooperative Teachers.   Systematic preparation for cooperating teachers was not a component of any of the earlier teacher education programs. In fact it was not even a component of the initial Wells Junior High School program. It was not until the 2nd year of Wells' involvement as a PDS that university and school faculty acknowledged the need for such training. As Susan Walters, the school's teacher leader, reports, "By the end of the 1st year, teachers felt the need for a common language, for a way to understand what they were doing and needed to be doing with interns." Thus, during the summer preceding the program's 2nd year, 35 teachers from the district, 12 of them from the middle school, participated in a voluntary 2 day institute that focused on developing coaching skills and on discussing intern-related issues. At the end of the summer institute, teachers requested follow-up activities. A monthly seminar is now in place as is a regular cooperating teacher newsletter. Teachers who participate in cooperative teacher training may earn credit toward renewal of their certification. Credits are also awarded for working with interns during the school year. In order to earn these, teachers are asked to submit written reflections. The intention of the reflections is to promote professional earning, not to burden teachers with extra work or unnecessary red tape.

Videotaped Observation Process.   Originally designed to assist interns' growth, the videotaped observation process has proved to be a powerful tool in professional development of the participating Wells faculty. As noted above, during the final phase of the process the cooperating teacher and the preservice supervisor view and discuss the videotape of the coaching conference held between the intern and the cooperating teacher. Cooperating teachers have an opportunity to assess themselves as coaches and to observe how much of what they learned in the summer institute has actually been assimilated and used. In addition, teachers have commented that the opportunity to meet with the supervisor provided for reflection on their own teaching and on the teaching-learning process. As one teacher noted:

> I think it's very positive. One of the things I was very impressed with was the evaluation system that we're using with the interns because it helped me as well. That's when they videotape the intern's lesson. Then, I talk with the intern and it's videotaped, and then we critique my observational and conferencing skills with a college professor. So it's an observation and it's a growing process for me. That's something I found very valuable for me personally.

The Presence of Interns.   Perhaps the most powerful professional development experience at work in Wells was relatively unplanned; the professional development and refinement of educational practices that flows from the mere presence of interns in the schools. Although it has often been assumed that supervising a student teacher would promote professional development, this has functioned more as an anecdotal myth than as documented reality. In Wells, teachers view interns as junior colleagues and they gain insight into their own teaching by close interaction with and observation of these novices. As one teacher says,

> I think the biggest benefit for me was watching somebody else teach and thinking how I might change it. It forced me to really think about teaching, which I think I do but it made me think about it in a different way.

Interns also provide access to new ideas and strategies. The knowledge they bring from formal coursework into daily classroom practice influences their cooperating teachers. One teacher reports "The interns come with great ideas. The fact that they were learning the latest things that education is about and were able to bring it back into the classroom was very helpful." Another teacher describes her experience this way, "I got to see a variety of new teaching techniques. It was a real eye-opener and opportunity to teach in a different light—interdisciplinary unit, teaching reading in a different way, more hands on." Because interns ask naive questions about teaching and learning, they challenge practicing teachers to give reason for what they do. A teacher states,

One of the things I like is that it forces me to verbalize my thinking and planning patterns and think twice or three times about what I do. I think it's a great method of staff development because it helps you reflect on what you're doing as well as reflect on what the interns do.

Finally, because interns break the pattern of isolation that most teachers experience, they provide motivation for teachers to do their best work and to improve their own practices. A teacher reports,

I think it was good for me to be observed by the interns. It made my teaching better because I knew there was another adult in the classroom who was watching me and talking about me later, so it made me really want to get prepared even more, and it develops good habits. When someone is there watching you everyday, then you're a lot more critical.

Teacher development at Wells has been enhanced and extended by the presence of interns and by the introduction of the teacher education agenda into the life of the school. Furthermore, as these teacher comments reveal, the interns and preservice program has provided a context for teachers to reflect on their teaching, to refine it, and to improve practice.

RESHAPING TEACHER EDUCATION: THORNY ISSUES

The principal at Wells often says, "We're all teacher educators." She means that university and school faculty are authentic partners in teacher education. This seems to be the case. The collaborative nature of the teacher education project and the connections it makes between the preparation of novice teachers, the professional development of experienced teachers, and the sustaining of best practices all lend credence to the belief that the school and the university have succeeded in their efforts to engage in common work for a common good. In many ways, the effort has been successful. However, unresolved core issues and professional tensions exist alongside the sense of harmony and shared vision that seems to permeate Wells as a PDS. In most cases, these concerns originate with the university faculty, but they impact on the program as a whole. They speak to the very nature of the teaching profession, how professional knowledge is constructed, and how university and school faculties do business together.

RESPONSIBILITY FOR TEACHER EDUCATION

As indicated earlier, the development of Wells as a PDS took place largely outside formal university channels. This, by and large, was not a problem for professors in the College of Education. While faculty expressed some concern about course and instructor approval, these were easily assuaged by attention to departmental protocol and time lines. Concerns about procedure seemed to be more important than concerns about substance.

For all practical purposes, the teacher education program is planned and implemented by the site steering committee. Governance and day-to-day management of teacher education has become localized in Wells. Most important, program decisions are made on site. Such a situation seems ripe for school/university conflict about issues concerning control and responsibility. But little such conflict has emerged. Although university faculty may raise concerns about inclusion in the formal approval process, they do not seem to mind that the more important program decisions are located in the school under the auspices of a group that they have no control over and little influence on. One way of reading this response is to say that the collective faculty has vested its authority in the university coordinator and is confident that she represents their interests without requiring their involvement. Another reading says that faculty members are not so interested in the teacher education program as they are in those particular components of the program that affect them individually. This interpretation makes sense when one considers that general faculty concern has been limited to course and instructor approval, areas where they have traditionally had control. Professors are used to working in teacher education programs which are collections of courses. It may be that they bring this predisposition and experience to the new PDS model. The effect is that for most college faculty, the commitment to teacher education is marginal and motivated by particular interests and not by a concern for a coherent integrated program.

If the College of Education faculty does not have a collective self-interest in teacher education, then who does? In this instance, it seems fair to conclude that the site steering committee has assumed stewardship for teacher education for the Wells interns. This steering committee represents a new formation in teacher education, one that combines people who share an interest in and a commitment to common values in an environment that is removed from the university. Major, the university coordinator, as the representative of the college, works with a sympathetic and supportive group of public school educators to reshape teacher education. The far reaching implications of such an arrangement have yet to be addressed by the university or the school.

What is also clear is that the steering committee provides a primary affiliation group for the university coordinator that replaces the university faculty as her major source of colleagueship and professional identity. The public school faculty, with its collective engagement in teacher education and the education of young adolescents, presents an attractive alternative to university culture with its emphasis on individual accomplishment and its continued marginalization of teacher education. If the site coordinator feels so strong an allegiance to and affiliation with the PDS, this raises issues about the university's ability to support the work of committed teacher educators within its traditional boundaries.

DEFINING KNOWLEDGE AND ROLES

The PDS at Wells raises issues about the roles that school and university faculty should and do play in the development and teaching of professional knowledge for the interns. Below, we profile three key university faculty, their varying perspectives on these issues, and how the issues are being enacted and challenged.

The university site coordinator occupies a unique position among university faculty. She strongly identifies with the culture of the junior high school—a culture, as noted, that strongly values teacher knowledge and leadership. During the program's 1st year, the coordinator stated publicly that she wanted to see all the teacher preparation courses at Wells eventually taught by Wells teachers, with teachers assuming full responsibility for the supervision of student teaching. She envisioned the site becoming an exemplar of teacher-directed, teacher-managed teacher education. Given this position, she often became impatient with the instructor review and approval process in place at the university and challenged professors on their reluctance to assign course responsibility to Wells teachers. Now in her 2nd year at Wells, the coordinator has changed her perspective.

> I've come to realize that the partnership is the really important piece. In many ways, the professors gain as much as everyone else. I see the need now for a range of possibilities, some solo teaching by university professors, some team teaching, and some solo teaching by public school teachers. The players will change and so must our approach. What's important is having the rub between theory and practice.

The coordinator recognizes the value of both the practical craft knowledge that classroom teachers bring to teacher education and the more theoretical, research-driven knowledge of the university professors.

Other professors align themselves with the coordinator, but they voice more concern for the integrity of content being taught. While these professors have adapted courses to accommodate the needs of the setting and have worked to incorporate practical work into their academic course requirements, they still want to serve as gatekeepers for the teaching of specific methods and content. The professor of mathematics education is a case in point. She believes that teachers can assume leadership in mathematics and in teacher education, but she takes measures to insure quality control. She has organized a cadre of what she calls, "leaders in mathematics." This group has been in existence for 2 years and its goal is the exchange of effective teaching practices in mathematics and the development of the capacity to teach mathematics-teaching to others. Teachers who have been involved in this work are now ready to assume responsibility for teaching the mathematics methods course in teacher education sites. One of these teachers will be assigned to Wells during the next academic year.

This mathematics educator takes the notion of combining practical and theoretical knowledge a step further than most university professors. She sees herself as both a classroom teacher and as a teacher educator and feels that she should be able to demonstrate what she is teaching to novice teachers by teaching children. She regularly schedules classroom teaching for herself and invites both interns and experienced teachers to observe her and offer feedback. Her approach blurs the boundaries between practical and theoretical knowledge even as she maintains a clear role for herself as a champion of mathematics education within the PDS. Her role is to broker between university and school knowledge about the teaching and learning of mathematics.

Other professors involved in the program articulate and act on more traditional assumptions about professional knowledge and role differentiation. The professor of literacy education at Wells represents this perspective quite eloquently.

> I see my role as working to certify or establish that the basic theoretical constructs of literacy learning are being acknowledged. I am a resource who represents the construction of knowledge of the field. I provide the framework and organization for understanding literacy learning.

Like the mathematics educator, the literacy professor serves as champion of the teaching of content and method in his discipline. In many ways, his role is more gatekeeper than bridge. Like the mathematics educator, he certifies and approves instructors who assume a teaching function in the program. He does this by identifying outstanding students in the university's graduate literacy program and teachers in the field and by offering them opportunities for apprenticeships and coteaching before authorizing them to teach full courses on their own.

In the Wells site, the issue of literacy education has become the focal point of much discussion and debate. While the math and literacy educators take positions that are quite similar, there are noticeable differences in nuance and meaning. And these differences are noted by the school staff. More than the mathematics professor, the literacy specialist makes obvious the distinction between university and public school work—a distinction that teachers in the PDS, with its ideology of teacher leadership and in-house expertise, have not been quick to acknowledge or embrace. While the literacy professor has come to see the need for more teacher involvement in his courses, his notion of involvement still holds to the distinction between teacher and professorial roles. He states, "I feel an emptiness in the course by not having a teacher in there with me. I think it is essential to have a teacher who is a liaison with the process and helps to interpret and implement. I feel the absence of verification."

In many ways, this last statement is an adaptation of the professor to the demands and expectations of the Wells site, just as the site coordinator's affirmation of the importance of partnership and the rub between theory and practice represents a rethinking of her earlier notion of an exclusively teacher-driven program. While these shifts and adaptations speak well of the potential of the PDS to promote faculty reflection and growth, they represent private and individual changes. There is no public acknowledgement of where people stand and where they are moving. What is happening at Wells are a series of private epiphanies about conceptions of knowledge and the appropriate role of school and university faculty for sharing and building that knowledge. As positions sharpen and blur, there is no public discourse about what is happening. There is real potential in the school site for the development of new understandings, but it is a potential that is not being realized. It is indeed ironic that a teacher preparation program, premised on the value of reflective practice, provides little opportunity for the university faculty to engage in public and collaborative reflection on their own work. Such reflection would contribute to the development of internal critiques of practice that the PDS promises but does not yet deliver.

THE WELLS EXPERIENCE: CONCLUSIONS AND CONJECTURES

We began this case study by noting that the PDS in Wells could best be understood as the evolution of relationships. In this final section, we would like to revisit this early understanding and unpack the notions of relationship and evolution that underpin the development of the model.

Throughout the case study, we have been struck by the centrality of relationships, personal and professional as well as individual and institutional, at the Wells site. The principal and the university site coordinator represent a relationship that has both personal and professional dimensions. Having known each other previously, they were eager to work together in this new venture. In the course of the 2 years that Wells has been a PDS, they have cotaught courses, presented jointly at regional and national conferences, and worked closely together in supporting intern development within the school culture. For both, their prior relationship laid the foundation for their present collaboration. They were able to draw from their own history to create new patterns of interaction around site specific issues as well as around general educational concerns. The site coordinator also developed close professional relationship with many teachers at the school, especially with the school-based coordinator. These new relationships were built on frequent interaction, shared work, common interests, and continual dialogue. They established a context for making decisions and resolving conflicts that was effective and acceptable to all interested parties. Some of this ease in interaction may be due to the fact that the university coordinator is, herself, a middle school specialist and shares with her public school colleagues common beliefs about the importance of teamwork and collaboration.

It should not go unacknowledged that the PDS at Wells is managed exclusively by women. The university coordinator, her school-based counterpart, and the principal are all women. It may be that they bring to their work what Gilligan (1982) describes as an ethic based on "caring and relationship" and that this sets the tone for the site. This is clearly conjecture, but it seems well worth exploring as researchers accumulate multiple case studies of PDSs. It is clear that an ethos of care and relationship pervades the Wells site and characterizes much of the work of the PDS. Also, the "match" between people is very important. In many ways, Cherie Major was ideal for the Wells site. Her interest in middle schooling, her respect for teacher knowledge, and her ability to build personal and professional relationships with colleagues especially recommended her for the site. This issue of personal and professional matching also seems worthy of further study and analysis.

Relationships at Wells are also institutional. They involve the school, the school district, and the university. The university and the district share a history. The Wells school district and the University of Southern Maine had been involved together in the Southern Maine Partnership for 3 years before the teacher education agenda changed at the university and before the idea of a PDS was posed to the district. This is a matter of considerable importance. The two institutions had established patterns of interaction and had taken advantage of opportunities to establish ways of working together. They had come to know each other in a context outside of teacher education and to understand what each could offer to the other. They had, in effect, established a readiness to engage in a high stakes partnership because they had had time to practice partnership in less charged environments. These conditions of history and time to practice partnership may be key elements in developing a successful PDS.

That the importance of relationships goes hand in hand with the evolutionary character of the PDS at Wells is obvious, not only in its developing relationships, but also in its emergent design. The model is clearly not a product of rational linear planning. Rather it epitomizes what we have come to call "systematic ad hocism" (Miller & Wolf, 1974). Systematic ad hocism is characterized by having a map rather than an itinerary, being long-range, being adaptive, and being value-based. This approach to planning has been advantageous to the development of the Wells model. It has produced a program that, by and large, runs smoothly and supports innovative practice. It has enabled experimentation and risk-taking and encouraged authentic partnership. Most important, it has encouraged constant assessment and invention—which may well be essential ingredients in the transformation of teacher education.

However, systematic ad hocism is a double-edged sword. Because roles and expectations are not fixed, there is room for confusion and ambiguity. Witness the conflicting notions about professional knowledge and the roles of university and school faculty. Because procedures and policies are not firmly established, areas of responsibility and accountability are fragile and unclear. There is also the tenuous legitimacy of site-based decision making and program management. All of this can make life hard for everyone involved. Over time, there may be a longing for a more settled, more predictable program—for a finished production rather than for an improvisation. Yet, it is this very ambiguity, unpredictability, and sense of being engaged in a work-in-progress that continues to engage and engross the participants in the Wells PDS and to make the experience and the program unique. The ad hoc nature at Wells does not preclude our making conjectures about the problems and concerns that the project will face in the future. The thorny issues identified earlier provide a foundation for raising questions that the university and the Wells schools will have to confront as the program develops and matures. Among them are:

Will the university faculty assume—or want to assume—more direct responsibility for the daily operation of the intern program?

How will school and university faculty modify their roles and develop their interactions?

Will parity be sustained and enhanced, or will hierarchy and status issues undermine collaboration and partnership?

Will teacher and school development become more interdependent or will they become two separate projects within the school?

Will involvement in preservice education help redefine the teacher role within the school and enhance teacher leadership?

Or will teacher involvement come to be viewed as one more burden in an already overburdened profession?

And finally, will teacher education become central to the worklife of faculty in the College of Education or will it maintain its contradictory status as both highly visible and ultimately marginal?

The case study we have presented here is, by necessity, a snapshot of the PDS at Wells. Given the evolution of relationships on which the school is based, it is very difficult—if not impossible—to capture a more definitive view of the school. As researchers, we have been frustrated and challenged by the task of describing Wells. We have struggled to get a "fix" on the school and its developing agendas for school renewal and teacher education. We have had an equally difficult time coming to an understanding of our home institution, the university, and the changing role it is playing in teacher education. We have found the process of putting together the pieces of the puzzle demanding and useful work. We have shared the case with the participants of the PDS and have been pleased to see its utility as a tool for reflection and analysis. It is our intention that the case provide insights about the emergence of one PDS and that, as part of a volume of diverse cases, it make a contribution to our profession's developing knowledge about connecting teacher education and school renewal.

NOTE

The authors are faculty members at the University of Southern Maine and have some familiarity with the program described but they also depended on interviews with people involved in program development and implementation as well as documents, artifacts, and reported proceedings developed at both the school and university sites. Their primary responsibilities are removed from the day-to day-operations of the Wells PDS. In order to reconstruct a unified history, the authors triangulated the interviews and other available data sources.

REFERENCES

Gilligan, C. (1982). *In a different voice: Psychological theory and women's development.* Cambridge, MA: Harvard University Press.

Goodlad, J. (1986). Linking schools and universities: symbiotic partnerships. *Occasional Paper #1.* Seattle, WA: National Network for Educational Renewal.

Goodlad, J. (1990). *Teachers for our nation's schools.* San Francisco: Jossey-Bass.

Lieberman, A., & Miller, L. (1990). Teacher development in professional practice schools. *Teachers College Record,* 92(1), 105–122.

McClure, R. (1991). Individual growth and institutional renewal. In A. Lieberman & L. Miller (Eds.) *Staff development for education in the 90s.* New York: Teachers College Press.

Miller, L., & Wolf, T. (1974). Staff development for school change: Theory and Practice. In A. Lieberman & L. Miller (Eds.) *Staff development for education in the 90s.* New York: Teachers College Press.

Sarason, S. (1982). *The culture of the school and the problem of change.* (2nd edition) Boston: Allyn and Bacon.

Wells Junior High School. (1990) Mission Statement.

Chapter 3

IN PURSUIT OF A DUAL AGENDA:
CREATING A MIDDLE LEVEL
PROFESSIONAL DEVELOPMENT SCHOOL

Pamela L. Grossman

"Kids Count Here" proclaims a sign over the front office of the Lark Creek Middle School, one of the professional development schools (PDSs) participating in the Puget Sound Professional Development Center (PSPDC) located in Washington state. Perhaps a more accurate sign would read "People Count Here," as the principal, Melissa Gray, concerns herself as much with helping teachers grow as she does with encouraging all students to become successful learners. This dual emphasis on teacher and student development captures the mission of Lark Creek Middle School.[1]

To spend time at Lark Creek Middle School is to witness the phenomenon of on-going school renewal at work, with all its expected and unexpected turbulence and attainments. A clear vision of an effective middle school oriented around the goals of Outcome-Based Education guides the on-going work of school renewal, while a process for dialogue and decision-making helps teachers and administrators negotiate the rough waters of school change. As a school consumed with the business of restructuring itself, Lark Creek provides a unique context for the professional preparation of preservice teachers, as well as myriad opportunities for the professional development of experienced teachers.

COLLABORATION IN CONTEXT

Lark Creek Middle School's future as a PDS had its beginnings in a flurry of grant writing that took place at both the school and the University of Washington during 1987–88. Influenced by recent reports on teacher preparation reform that advocated the creation of PDSs as contexts for career-long teacher education (e.g., Carnegie Forum on Education and the

Economy, 1986; Holmes Group, 1986), the Ford Foundation requested proposals for the creation of what they termed "clinical training schools." Ann Lieberman, then Executive Director of the Puget Sound Educational Consortium (PSEC), a collaborative venture between the University of Washington and 13 local school districts, and Nathalie Gehrke, an associate professor of curriculum and instruction at the University of Washington, wrote a proposal to fund a planning year. Because they believed that middle-level education had been largely ignored by the educational community, the grant proposal concentrated on middle schools, despite the fact that the state of Washington did not offer a separate credential for middle grade teachers nor did the University of Washington currently have a program of teacher education aimed at the middle level.

At the same time, a core of faculty at Lark Creek Middle School was writing a grant proposal to the state of Washington to become a School for the 21st Century. This program, begun by Governor Booth Gardner to stimulate school reform, provided selected schools with additional funds and releases from bureaucratic restrictions to help schools reform themselves. Schools proposing a specific plan of action for restructuring could qualify for 6-year grants to fund 10 additional days of staff time and up to $50,000 for staff development activities per year. Lark Creek Middle School had decided to apply for a Schools for the 21st Century grant to implement Outcome-Based Education at their school. This grant proposal grew out of several years of school-wide planning and had the support of most of the faculty members of the school.

While waiting to hear about the grant, Principal Gray became aware of the Ford-sponsored project on clinical training schools. She and two teachers leaders decided to apply for this as well. In retrospect, Gray reflected, "The first decision to go with the [professional development center] was really [ours]. Consensus was not gotten. . . . We saw the PDC as helping us in all our missions" (Sagmiller, 1992, pp. 12–13).

Thus Lark Creek Middle School was awarded the Schools for the 21st Century grant and also selected as one of the four sites to participate in the professional development center project. From its very inception as a PDS, Lark Creek Middle School would be pursuing a dual agenda—to restructure itself in accordance with the goals of Outcome-Based Education, as proposed in the Schools for the 21st Century grant, and to transform itself into a site for the career-long professional development of teachers, with special emphasis on the preparation of preservice teachers. This dual agenda provided the school's leadership with increased possibilities for both success and failure. On one hand, the Schools for the 21st Century grant gave the school additional money, staff development days, and resources not available to the other three sites of the professional development center. In addition, the school had spent several years developing both a philosophy related to Outcome-Based Education and a process for making site-based decisions. On the other hand, not everyone at the school understood the goals of the PSPDC project or how the Schools for the 21st Century grant, which they had bought into, related to the PSPDC project, to which they had not.

The University faced a similar dilemma, as very few faculty members participated in the preparation of the initial grant proposal. While there was a small group of interested faculty members, from the outset the PSPDC was seen by College of Education faculty as the project of a few rather than as a commitment of the entire college. The decision to focus on middle-level education meant that the new teacher education program was created alongside the existing elementary and secondary programs; the administration of the pilot program was handled primarily by PSPDC staff. This arrangement led to a form of "ad-hocracy" that enabled change to occur swiftly, while inevitably isolating the PSPDC from the mainstream of college life. The place of the professional development center within the college as a whole, and the relationship between the pilot teacher education program developed through the PSPDC and the regular teacher preparation program of the University of Washington, were to remain thorny issues.

LARK CREEK MIDDLE SCHOOL

Lark Creek Middle School is in a suburban community in the Puget Sound region. The school has a number of buildings connected by outdoor corridors and walkways, reminiscent of many California schools. To dash from class to class, students must brave the damp Puget Sound weather. To talk with each other, teachers must escape the confines of their corridors. Principal Gray contemplates a time when the very architecture of the building could be redesigned to foster a sense of community rather than to work against it. The school dedicated a room off the Instructional Resource Center as the Professional Development Center room, and it now features a PSPDC library of professional books and journals, several computers, round tables, comfortable chairs, and a blackboard. More teachers, however, still seem to congregate in a less formal faculty lounge off the library that houses the coffee machine, the thermofax machines, and a sofa.

One of the largest middle schools in the district, Lark Creek serves between 650 and 700 seventh and eighth grade students. The surrounding suburban community is predominantly white and middle class, though about 17% of Lark Creek students qualify for free or reduced-priced lunches. While students generally score higher than both national and district averages on standardized achievement tests, in 1986–87 approximately 20% of their students were failing core academic subjects.

Lark Creek Middle School provides a concrete example of school reform as "steady work." The initial incentive for reform came from both individual teachers' growing awareness in the early 1980s of the middle school movement and its philosophical commitment to team-teaching, and the district's mandate in 1984 that Lark Creek move toward school-based decision making. This mandate was accompanied by staff development opportunities. In 1984–85, Lark Creek received training in the district's school-based management program based on the school improvement process (SIP) model. The SIP team included teachers, administrators, parents, and students. Its goals were to acquire group process skills and to form a vision and specific goals for the school. The goal identified by the SIP team was "to raise academic achievement by developing each student's potential." With the support of a state grant for school-based management in 1986–87, and involvement in staff development opportunities through the Northwest Regional Educational Laboratory, the school continued to refine its goal of increasing academic success.

During this process, the faculty became interested in the model of Outcome-Based Education, and several staff members visited the Johnson City program (Vickery, 1988), attended conferences about Outcome-Based Education, and tried out mastery learning modules in their classrooms. The grant proposal to become a School for the 21st Century grew from the school's efforts to examine their school, to articulate a vision for the school as a whole, to investigate possible alternatives, and to reach consensus on the specific direction in which the school would head. The principal strongly supported the move toward Outcome-Based Education. These efforts to establish school-wide goals and processes for working together as a staff, as well as the emphasis on looking outward for new ideas and practices, were to serve Lark Creek well as a PDS.

THE UNIVERSITY OF WASHINGTON

No stranger to innovation in professional preparation programs, the University of Washington's College of Education had, in the 1970s, created the Northline Consortium, an award-winning program of teacher education based upon close collaboration with two school districts. Because of financial problems during the 1980s and increasing emphasis on research in the College of Education, the consortium dissolved, but a precedent had been set for closer ties between the schools and the university in the preparation of teachers.

In 1984, the Puget Sound Educational Consortium (PSEC) succeeded the Northline Consortium as a way to link 13 local school districts with the university. From its inception, the consortium had discussed the possibility of creating an educational development school, building on the work of John

Goodlad (1984). As one of its first activities under the leadership of Ann Lieberman, PSEC created a program in which a group of teachers from across the different districts met regularly to develop leadership skills, explore issues related to shared leadership and new roles for teachers, and learn about and carry out action research projects. Three Lark Creek teachers participated and all three would later play important roles within the PSPDC. In retrospect, one of these teacher leaders attributed her expanded definition of her role as a teacher and her interest in contributing to teacher education to her involvement with this teacher leadership group.

Another professional preparation program launched under the auspices of PSEC was the Danforth Principal Preparation program. The Danforth program, funded both by the university and the school districts, was to serve as an important precedent for the creation of an innovative teacher education program through a professional development center. The Danforth program also relied upon both university professors and clinical faculty to teach. The Puget Sound Educational Consortium helped provide a supportive context for the creation of a professional development center.

THE PUGET SOUND PROFESSIONAL DEVELOPMENT CENTER

In the spring of 1988, a committee of the Puget Sound Educational Consortium selected four school sites from four different districts to participate in the creation of a professional development center. The PSPDC began its year of planning in the Fall of 1988. The initial committee constituted to plan for the implementation of a PDS model consisted of the principal and a teacher from each of the four middle school sites, six faculty from the University of Washington College of Education, a representative from the Washington Education Association, a student teacher from the existing teacher education program at the University of Washington, an intern principal in the innovative Danforth Principal Preparation Program, the director of the Puget Sound Educational Consortium, and a representative from Washington state's Office of the Superintendent of Public Instruction.

The planning committee first developed a set of guiding beliefs underlying its vision of a professional development center. These beliefs included:

1. All members of the school community are learners.
2. The central purpose of a PDC is to assure the continued learning of all members of the school community.
3. Our PDC is committed to the exploration of new roles and responsibilities for educators, and new structures for education.

4. In our PDC, teacher leadership evolves over time and occurs within a context of colleagueship.
5. In our PDC, education is a team effort. Parents, students, university professors, teachers, principals, and other educators are all part of our educational team.
6. Central to the life of our PDC are dialogue and inquiry.
7. Time allocated for professional development is a legitimate expectation in our PDC.
8. In our PDC, school contexts must be created that foster innovation as a regular part of teaching.
9. All educators in our PDC share in the responsibility to create knowledge and to model good practice.
10. All educators in our PDC share in the responsibility to disseminate knowledge to audiences beyond the Center.
11. Our PDC is a multi-site center, unlimited by school buildings.

The long-range, essentially stable goals of the PSPDC are apparent in these guiding beliefs. They include: offering appropriate preservice professional preparation programs; providing opportunities for continuing professional growth; enhancing collaborative inquiry and innovation in education; and strengthening the ties among educational partners. While elaborating on the need for new roles and responsibilities for educators and the importance of collaboration and inquiry, these guiding beliefs do not specify a particular vision of teaching and learning, an absence that allowed partners with different underlying assumptions about teaching and learning to accept these beliefs.

The dual mission of the PSPDC focuses on both the career-long development of teachers and other school professionals and collaborative inquiry and innovation leading to school restructuring. While the Ford grant targeted preservice teacher education and called for the creation of clinical sites for field experiences, the founding group of the PSPDC held a much broader vision of its mission. However, several of the school sites continued to see preservice teacher education as the raison d'etre of the PSPDC and believed that their major responsibility lay in the creation of appropriate field placements for preservice teachers. This difference in perspective has remained a source of minor tension between university faculty and at least one of the PSPDC schools.

PRESERVICE EDUCATION IN THE PSPDC

After 1 year of planning, 12 students began the PSPDC pilot program of preservice teacher education for middle school teachers in the Fall of 1989. In its 4th year of implementation in 1992–93, this experimental program has continued to run as an off-shoot of the regular teacher education program at the University of Washington, serving approximately 15 students each year. Students in the PSPDC program must be admitted first to the regular teacher education program before applying for the PSPDC, and they continue to take a number of their required courses through the regular program.

The two major changes in the pilot PSPDC teacher education program involve (1) participation in a core seminar on teaching and learning in middle schools and (2) placement and supervision at a PSPDC site. The core seminar is a team-taught, interdisciplinary course focused around issues related to teaching and learning in the middle school; it replaces four required courses (general methods of teaching, crucial issues in education, educational psychology, and educational evaluation) in the regular program. In addition to the content from the four required courses, the seminar incorporates material on early adolescent development, middle school philosophy and organization, interdisciplinary planning and teaching, special education, and inter-professional collaboration. Three faculty members (from Curriculum and Instruction, Special Education, and Educational Psychology), a graduate student, and a middle school teacher from one of the four PSPDC sites form the teaching team for the seminar. From 1990 through 1993, a teacher from Lark Creek Middle School has served as the teaching associate on the team.

The seminar also connects with students' field experiences: many of the assignments require students to collect data at their school site. For example, students shadow both a regular and a special education student throughout the school day, collecting data on what their school day is like; these data become the basis for case studies the students will later write for the core seminar. In addition, teachers and supervisors from the four PSPDC sites occasionally teach the seminar.

For their field experiences, students are placed at one of the four PSPDC sites, often with a team of cooperating teachers who are collectively responsible for the student teacher's development. The program has tried to place student teams with a team of cooperating teachers. While the number of required credits for field experience remains stable across the regular and PSPDC programs, PSPDC students are encouraged to spend more time in the school. The students begin their field experiences when teachers return to work in late August or early September. Students are also actively encouraged by both university and school faculties to become involved in professional development activities at the school, district, and state levels, to attend any staff meetings or staff development days that precede the opening of the school year, and to attend colloquia, minicourses, workshops, or other professional development activities sponsored by the PSPDC.

One major difference between the PSPDC preservice program and the regular teacher education program involves the supervision of the student teachers. In the regular program, students are supervised by university supervisors, who are paid according to the number of students they evaluate. University supervisors, generally former teachers, visit students in schools, evaluate their teaching using the University of Washington Teacher Assessment System, and confer with cooperating teachers. Supervisors, who are assigned student teachers according to both grade level and geographical location, receive minimal training and have no formal connection to the teacher education faculty.

In the PSPDC model, student teachers are supervised and evaluated by an experienced teacher nominated by the school site. Supervisors meet weekly with the student teachers at their school to orient them and to provide on-going support and information. In addition, supervisors observe students' teaching and evaluate them using the same assessment system used in the regular program. The University of Washington pays the site the same stipend it would have paid a university supervisor, based on the number of students supervised; the schools then decide how to use this money to support the supervisor's work. In addition, three of the four PSPDC sites have reallocated one period a day to site supervisors for carrying out their responsibilities. Lark Creek is the one school that has been unable to provide a reduced teaching load for site supervisors; perhaps not coincidentally, Lark Creek has had a new site supervisor each year of the preservice program.

Supervisors also serve as an additional liason between the school site and the university. Members of the teaching team meet monthly with all four site-supervisors to discuss how students are doing in the field, to plan aspects of the seminar or field experiences, and to share information related to supervision and evaluation of preservice teachers.

While there is not yet a formal component of the PSPDC that addresses the induction of beginning teachers, several of the graduates of the PSPDC program have been hired on a part- or full-time basis after certification by the PSPDC schools. Two schools hired graduates as part-time substitutes during the 2nd year of the program to support the professional development activities of experienced teachers and several schools have hired PSPDC graduates.

An evaluation of the preservice component of the PSPDC revealed that student teachers generally felt very positively about their experiences in the PSPDC and experienced less of a gulf between the worlds of the school and university than students in the regular teacher education program. Student teachers mentioned the strengths of the site-supervision model and valued the chance to participate in on-going school reform efforts (Yerian & Grossman, 1993). One student who participated in the PSPDC pilot program at Lark Creek commented that site supervision

"was one of the best parts of the program . . . to have somebody out at
the site who can see you on a regular basis maybe and talk to you about
what's going on, what you're doing, what you're learning, and really
understand you as a person."

PROFESSIONAL DEVELOPMENT FOR SCHOOL AND UNIVERSITY FACULTIES

A second major component of the PSPDC concerns the professional development of experienced teachers. This has taken a number of different
forms, including workshops, study groups, fireside chats, a district-wide
colloquium for middle school teachers, action research projects, and conversations with the professor-in-residence at Lark Creek. One forum has
been a series of colloquia offered by individual PSPDC schools for all
members of the PSPDC and other middle schools in that district. The
PSPDC also offered a series of training workshops on topics such as peer
coaching, action research, and site-based decision making, to staff members at all four sites; during 1990–91, Lark Creek chose to continue with a
peer coaching workshop.

Less formal opportunities for professional development consist of
"fireside chats" or study groups. Teachers at Lark Creek with a common
interest in technology attended a series of chats with the dean of the College of Education and with graduate students in technology. These informal discussions eventually led to a task group that proposed ways to integrate technology into the school curriculum.

In 1990, the PSPDC received a grant from the Carnegie Foundation
related to its report on middle-level education, *Turning Points* (1989).
Grant recipients promised to work on implementing the recommendations of the *Turning Points* report. Each school selected a particular recommendation to focus on, with Lark Creek selecting the issue of interdisciplinary curriculum. In conjunction with this grant, 15 faculty members
and 3 student teachers attended a workshop on interdisciplinary curriculum run by a University of Washington graduate student. Teachers who
wanted to plan interdisciplinary units could apply for summer minigrants
from Carnegie funds for further curriculum development work.

NEW ROLES AND RESPONSIBILITIES

As part of its commitment to develop new responsibilities for educators,
the PSPDC created a number of new teacher leadership roles in both preservice and continuing professional education. Three primary roles in
teacher education exist for experienced teachers at PSPDC sites. They can
serve as cooperating teachers, as site-supervisor, or as Teaching Associate
for the core seminar, a clinical appointment with the University of Wash-

ington. The inclusion of roles in the preservice program under professional development activities reflects a guiding assumption of the PSPDC—that involvement in the preparation of new teachers can serve as professional development for experienced teachers.

While each of these roles offers the potential for reflection, and articulation and clarification of beliefs about teaching (Grossman, 1991; Grossman & Brantigan, 1992), additional opportunities exist for the professional development of experienced teachers who play a role in preservice education. In 1990–91, the PSPDC preservice program offered a two-part workshop on supervision of student teachers and issues related to diversity for cooperating teachers, site supervisors, and members of the teaching team. In 1991–92, additional workshops were held on cross-cultural communication and on meeting the needs of diverse students. The monthly meetings of site supervisors and members of the teaching team offer supervisors the chance to learn from each other, as they share common problems in working with student teachers and colleagues. They also participate in meetings on supervision held for all supervisors in the regular teacher education program.

Teachers at the PSPDC sites can also serve as the Teacher Leader Coordinator for their building, a leadership role that involves working with both faculty and administration to coordinate the efforts of the PSPDC (Romerdahl, 1991). Teacher Leader Coordinators must learn how to work with colleagues to accomplish a variety of tasks, to administer various professional development activities, and to work with the university to identify future directions.

A new role for University of Washington faculty—professor-in-residence, analogous to some of the new roles for teachers—has been created. A professor of Curriculum and Instruction has served in this role at Lark Creek for 3 years, spending up to 1 day a week there. When the role was newly conceived, he made himself available to teachers to talk about teaching or about questioning strategies, to have him observe in classrooms, or to propose action research projects. In 1991–92, Principal Gray hoped to make the professor-in-residence more visible to teachers and "to set conditions more intentionally" for matches to occur between the professor and teachers at the school. She would like to get the professor-in-residence, who is also a member of the PSPDC site committee, more involved in the big questions facing the school.

The core interdisciplinary seminar for the preservice program is perhaps the clearest instance of how engagement in PSPDC activities has contributed to the university faculty's professional development. As the content of the course goes well beyond the expertise of any individual, all instructors acquire new knowledge and perspectives from interactions in planning and teaching the class.

The PSPDC has also served as a site for the research of University of Washington faculty and graduate students. Much of this research has been related to the concept of professional development centers, including studies of teacher leadership and teacher learning within the professional development center (Bishop, in progress; Gehrke, 1992; Grossman, 1991; Grossman & Brantigan, 1992; Romerdahl, 1991), studies of perceptions of professional development centers (Grossman & Richert, 1991; Sagmiller, 1992), reflections on the work of a professor-in-residence (Hunkins, 1990), a study of team-teaching in the core seminar (McDaniel, 1992), and an evaluation of the preservice program (Yerian & Grossman, 1993). The PSPDC has also served as a site for internships for graduate students in education, social work, and school counseling.

ADMINISTRATION AND FUNDING OF THE PSPDC

Governance of the PSPDC takes place at both the central and local levels. Nathalie Gehrke has served as the director of the PSPDC since its inception, and played a critical role in its development. Her participation in collaborative projects with other schools and departments at the University has also broadened the focus of the PSPDC to include inter-professional collaboration.

The PSPDC Planning Committee made policy decisions regarding the larger issues facing the PSPDC, while site committees at each school made decisions about how those policies would be implemented at their sites. For example, site committees at each school decided how to compensate site supervisors and cooperating teachers, using the funds available to them. One site paid cooperating teachers a fixed stipend for their work, while another site used the money to hire substitutes, providing release time for cooperating teachers to meet with student teachers 1 morning a month.

Administering the preservice program has been complicated by the fact that the pilot middle school teacher education program existed as an offshoot of the larger teacher education program at the university. During the first year of implementation, a faculty member served as director of the PSPDC pilot teacher education program; in following years, a graduate student has served as program coordinator. Decisions regarding student teachers had to be negotiated between the PSPDC teaching team, including the director or coordinator of the preservice program, and the teacher education office at the University of Washington. Decisions regarding the pilot PSPDC program necessarily affected the administration of the larger program, as the two were not clearly distinct administrative units. For example, by using site-supervisors, the PSPDC program affected the number of university supervisors hired by the larger program; because student teachers in the PSPDC program were supervised by teachers at the school site, university supervisors had fewer students to supervise, which in turn affected their salaries. From its inception, the PSPDC preservice program blurred the administrative lines between the regular and pilot programs.

Funding for the PSPDC has come from a variety of sources including the University of Washington and each school district. The PSPDC has also benefited from grants from the Ford Foundation, the Carnegie Foundation, Metropolitan Life, the Stuart Foundation, and the Washington State Office of the Superintendent of Public Instruction. While each of these grants had a different agenda for reform, they all supported ongoing professional development of PSPDC teachers.

REFORMS AT WORK: CHANGING SCHOOL CULTURE

The changes made at Lark Creek most frequently mentioned by teachers there concern school culture. They cite greater collegiality, professional responsibility, and communication. Teachers involved with the preservice program consistently mentioned their new understanding of their role as teacher educators and the rewards of working with student teachers.

One teacher remarked on the increase in communication and cooperation among teachers, both within her department and in the school as a whole. She commented, "I hear people talking about ideas and if I have a problem I can approach people." Teachers spoke of increased camaraderie at the school as many began to share ideas. "I don't know of another school that talks as much about practice," explained another teacher. Teachers defined collegiality as the willingness to talk about teaching, and to share problems and ideas. A visit to Lark Creek reinforces the image of a collegial school. While the school's physical characteristics can hinder interaction, teachers nonetheless find opportunities to communicate and share ideas. Visitors might find teams of teachers working together to solve school problems, or walk in on a science teacher conferring with a science teacher from another PSPDC site about a new science curriculum.

Another change in the school culture involved teachers' expanded vision of their professional roles and their awareness of broader issues in education. Teachers believed that their colleagues have become "very aware of what's going on in education." One teacher commented that she had grown immensely through the opportunity to "look at education with different eyes," while others spoke positively of the constant flux of new ideas entering the building. A smaller group of teachers also spoke of their roles beyond the classroom and their desire to effect change in their district.

The student teachers at Lark Creek readily stated their sense of the positive and collegial culture of the school. They commented on "being included in all of the changes," and the excitement of being a participant in school reform efforts. One student teacher talked of the power of being part of the on-going renewal process at the school; "It's important that we know school reform can happen. It's not just theory." Another student echoed, "Lark Creek reaffirms that it can be done."

Structural Changes at Lark Creek

A number of structural changes have also taken place at Lark Creek. An instructional council, responsible for site-based decision making, was formed. In accordance with middle school philosophy, the staff was reorganized into interdisciplinary teams; all of the teachers and student teachers at the school have been placed on one of six teams, with each team responsible for teaching approximately 100 students. At least half of these teams appear to be functioning well, according to teachers and the principal, while others are still in the process of learning how to work effectively as teams. Instructional teams have become increasingly involved in making decisions regarding their work. For example, at a spring faculty meeting, the principal announced that students had been assigned to instructional teams, but teams would be responsible for scheduling those students into classes within the team. The principal also provided an example of budgetary decision making by teams, when the school received funding for an additional full time staff member to work with special education students. With the input of team members, the school as a whole decided to use the money to fund an assistant for each team, rather than funding one additional teacher. Teams can also identify problems facing the school and propose solutions. One team discussed problems with substitute teachers maintaining discipline and proposed a plan for dealing with the issue, that they then forwarded to the Instructional Council.

A structural change particular to PSPDC governance is the creation of a PSPDC site committee. This committee, composed of teachers from Lark Creek and a professor and graduate student from the university, makes decisions regarding the implementation of PSPDC projects at the school, the use of the PSPDC budget for preservice and continuing professional development activities, and recommendations to the PSPDC Steering Committee. It was the site committee who decided to use the additional money provided by the Carnegie Foundation's *Turning Points* grant to fund both a workshop on interdisciplinary education and a set of minigrants for teams of teachers to plan interdisciplinary curriculum units.

In some instances, structural changes provoked changes in school culture, as in the instance of the formation of instructional teams. Not surprisingly perhaps, the teachers who spoke most positively about changes in school culture appeared to be on well-functioning instructional teams. One teacher who reported feeling like a member of a team "in name only" was less positive about changes in school culture.

In addition to this reorganization, a number of teachers team-teach. In at least two instances, the walls between classrooms have been opened and a team composed of a social studies teacher and an English teacher coteach a group of 60 students. The student teachers, reinforced by their core seminar at the university, have adopted this emphasis on team-teaching. For example, three student teachers, all placed with the same instructional team, planned and team-taught an interdisciplinary unit on the environment during their student teaching experience at Lark Creek.

CHANGES IN PRESERVICE PREPARATION AT LARK CREEK

Another major change at Lark Creek concerns its role in the preparation of future teachers. During its first 4 years as a PDS, Lark Creek worked with 15 student teachers. In keeping with the principles of the PSPDC, the program placed most of these students with preexisting teams of cooperating teachers rather than with a single cooperating teacher. Teachers talked both of the improvement in the preparation of future teachers represented by the PSPDC pilot program and of the rewarding aspects of their own involvement. Most teachers felt that in comparison with their own professional preparations, the student teachers at Lark Creek were receiving "vastly improved" preparation. One of the biggest proponents of the PSPDC preservice program had been initially reluctant to take on a student teacher. He remarked, "I've been a teacher who likes to function alone. I don't like to team-teach. I didn't think I would like having a student teacher." This teacher now felt that the greatest rewards of his participation in the PSPDC have come from the student teachers, a sentiment echoed by another teacher as well; "The ultimate reward is working with the student teachers. They're so good. They know so much more than I did."

Working closely with student teachers has helped teachers expand their sense of a teacher's professional role. "Teachers really do have a responsibility to the profession. That's part of what we need to do. Find the best student teachers we can to replace us," said one cooperating teacher. Teachers also felt that they were learning from the student teachers; "I've learned from student teachers different ways to teach things. They're teaching me too," commented a veteran teacher.

The principal suggests that another major change has been the recognition that the preparation of future teachers is a school-wide responsibility, rather than just of a few cooperating teachers. She has tried to involve teachers in the preservice program, especially those who, because of their subject specialties, would not have direct classroom responsibility for student teachers. She gave the example of having students observe the classroom management techniques of a Home Economics teacher who excelled at creating a positive learning environment. According to Principal Gray, "student teachers have become a part of all that we do."

Student teachers participate in faculty meetings, as well as meetings of their instructional teams, and attend professional development activities along with experienced teachers. Three of the student teachers attended the workshop on integrated education and designed an interdisciplinary unit, that they later team-taught. The student teachers echo this sense of being welcomed and supported by the entire school. They commented, "people who don't work with us come up and give us advice. . . . People know what you're doing and if they have something you might use, they'll seek you out."

CHANGING TEACHING AND LEARNING

The most evident changes in teaching and learning occuring at Lark Creek have to do with the school's commitment to the philosophy of Outcome-Based Education (e.g. Spady and Marshall, 1991) and Glasser's control theory (Glasser, 1986). With the support of the school improvement funds and the Schools for the 21st Century grant, teachers at Lark Creek had been engaged in the process of redesigning the curriculum to fit an Outcome-Based Education model. The most apparent change is the adoption of a mastery approach to learning. Students at the middle school are expected to reach mastery level on their coursework, which has been operationalized as 80% or a B grade. They may redo work until it reaches this level. Students can then do extra work on projects to earn an A. To provide students with the opportunity to get extra help or to do extra enrichment work, an additional Mastery/Enrichment period was added to the schedule. During one Mastery/Enrichment period, for example, a seventh-grade boy explained the extension project he was working on for his social studies class, in which they were studying the Middle East; as part of his effort to earn an A, he was doing some research on Middle Eastern architecture.

If students do not achieve mastery, they are given an incomplete rather than a failing grade, and are encouraged to continue to work toward mastery. Since the program was implemented in 1988–89, D and E grades have dropped steadily, and A and B grades have risen, with close to 80% of students achieving As and Bs, up from 59–60% in 1987–88. These data support the principal's contention that students' grades have improved. However, the percentage of students with incompletes (15–17%) is close to the percentage of students who earned Ds and Es (17–20%) prior to the implementation of this approach. The principal is concerned about this core of what she calls "discouraged learners."

Teachers' reactions to these changes are generally positive, even among those who were initially skeptical of the concept of Outcome-Based Education. Teachers commented that students feel more successful under this approach and are beginning to take responsibility for their own learning. As one convert said, "Outcome-Based Education gives kids a chance to be successful. I didn't believe in Outcome-Based Education at first, but I think it's positive." On the other hand, at least one teacher expressed uneasiness about how Outcome-Based Education was driving the curriculum toward quantifiable objectives. This teacher saw Outcome-Based Education as a means to an end, rather than as an end in itself, and worried that the pressure to quantify student assessment—which this teacher felt is implicit in the approach the school has adopted—has resulted in more multiple-choice, true-false tests and less emphasis on the assessment of higher-order thinking skills. While the principal also expresses a desire to incorporate more higher-order thinking skills into the curriculum and to explore alternative forms of assessment, she argues that Outcome-Based Education has helped the school move toward a more "thinking" curriculum.

The school's adoption of Outcome-Based Education has brought them into some conflict with the district's high schools. The high school teachers feel that Lark Creek does not prepare students adequately for the demands of high school; in particular they feel that the mastery learning approach does students a disservice by teaching them they can turn in their work late, or do a sloppy job initially and later redo the assignment. This opinion was echoed by the seventh grader doing his project on Middle Eastern architecture. While he was doing well in middle school, he nonetheless worried aloud about whether or not he would be ready for high school—"Because at Lark Creek you can get credit for work no matter how late it is and high school isn't like that."

A second curricular change at Lark Creek Middle School involves teachers' preliminary work on integrated education. The school selected interdisciplinary curriculum as the focus of their participation in the Carnegie Foundation's *Turning Points* grant in 1990–91 and 15 of the teachers, including 3 student teachers, participated in the workshop on integrated education. Despite their interest in the approach, however, relatively few teachers have managed to incorporate interdisciplinary curricula into their classrooms.

A third area of curricular change is in the math department. In 1991–92, it began to pilot a new curriculum that placed greater emphasis on problem-solving and tried to respond to the new National Council of Teachers of Mathematics standards. This effort, while not explicitly connected to the school's mission as a PSPDC, represents the pervasive spirit of reform within the school as a whole.

As yet, there are few data on whether or not students are learning better under the new approach to curriculum and instruction. The principal would like to explore the use of alternative modes of assessment to discover if students are taking more responsibility for their work and if they feel more successful as learners. The school's interest in Glasser's control theory and in reality therapy has changed the way many teachers think about working with students. The principal comments that counselors have seen a change in students over the past few years; they report that now, very few students hold teachers responsible for their low grades. While the school's support for Glasser's work emphasizes their interest in encouraging students to take ownership of their own learning, some teachers worry that the mastery learning approach has left the teachers taking over much of the students' responsibility for achieving mastery or resorting to coercion to get students to finish up incompletes. The principal worries over the fine line between challenging students to produce quality work and coercion.

CHANGES AT THE COLLEGE OF EDUCATION

Since the creation of the PSPDC, the major change at the University of Washington has been the beginnings of the reform of the entire teacher education program. The PSPDC pilot program provided an alternative model to the regular teacher education program, provoking discussion of needed reforms in the larger program. In the 2nd year of implementation of the pilot program, a core of faculty began working on plans to reform teacher education; many of the faculty who have team-taught in the middle school core seminar are centrally involved with the reform efforts. In the 4th year of implementation of the PSPDC, the university identified six new profesional development sites at the elementary school level. Teachers from both the middle-level and the elementary PDSs serve on the teams that are charged with designing a new teacher education program.

Because the pilot program runs alongside the regular program, there have been no major changes in the university's elementary or secondary teacher education as a direct result of the PSPDC. However, faculty at the university who teach in both the pilot and regular programs reported changing the curriculum of their courses in the regular program as a result of their experiences with the core seminar. For example, the separate educational psychology and educational evaluation courses in the regular program, which are integrated in the core PSPDC seminar, have become more coordinated due to the efforts of a faculty member who teaches in both programs.

A second change resulting perhaps indirectly from the creation of a professional development center has been closer ties between the College of Education and other disciplines within the university that address the needs of children, such as public policy, social work, and nursing. The School of Social Work has placed social work interns at PSPDC schools, and the director of the PSPDC is part of an interdisciplinary effort to prepare professionals who work with children.

OBSTACLES TO CHANGE

As mentioned earlier, Lark Creek's evolution as a School for the 21st Century coincided with its selection as a Professional Development Center school. Lark Creek's involvement with the 6-year process of self-examination and school improvement provided participants both with a sense of school vision, based around the concepts of Outcome-Based Education and Glasser's control theory, and with the group process skills to work together as a faculty. At the same time, the dual agenda—to restructure in accordance with Outcome-Based Education and to become a site for career-long professional development—threatened at times to overwhelm teachers at the school. Teachers were also more familiar with the goals of the agenda to restructure than they were with the goals of the PSPDC. As the principal commented, the PSPDC mission at Lark Creek evolved slowly, in part because the school "was clearer about what we wanted from the Schools for the 21st Century grant." Given the time and energy needed to accomplish the goals of the Schools for the 21st Century grant, teachers sometimes resisted the pressure to become involved with the activities of the PSPDC as well. A number of teachers commented on "the unspoken pressure to be more involved," and several teachers reported feeling overwhelmed by all of the reform efforts.

In part, teachers felt torn between opportunities for professional development and their sense of responsibility to classroom teaching. One commented that they worried about how the PSPDC activities connected to "what I really do in the classroom." Others objected to being away from their classrooms too much in order to become involved with PSPDC activities. In each instance, teachers wanted to see the relationship between the new roles being offered to teachers and what they perceived as their major role—teaching middle grade students.

Not surprisingly, lack of time was mentioned over and over again as a barrier to involvement in the professional development center activities. Time is a particularly acute problem for a school that is trying to institutionalize both teaming, with the need for team planning time, and a mastery learning environment, that teachers perceive as requiring more of their time. Teachers talked not only of the need for more time to get involved with the various activities, but of the need for time to reflect on all of the changes taking place at their school.

The tension over the dual agenda facing the school was expressed most keenly by the teachers who were the least involved in the changes taking place. While teachers at Lark Creek were all aware and generally supportive of the goals of the Schools for the 21st Century grant, teachers were less aware of the school's mission as a professional development center. Many teachers continued to see preservice teacher education as the primary goal of the PSPDC. Teachers who were most closely affiliated with the preservice program, as cooperating teachers or supervisors, were the most positive about the PSPDC efforts.

Teacher leaders who played a central role in the creation of the PSPDC saw its mission as consistent with the direction in which the school was already headed; they tended to see the PSPDC as a means of helping them achieve the goals set out in the Schools for the 21st Century grant. The principal commented, "the goals of both are very similar." The PSPDC's focus on middle school was particularly important to her, as she saw the emphasis on middle-grades philosophy and curriculum fitting nicely into the goals already established by the school. Another teacher leader added that in some ways, the PSPDC mission, with its emphasis on continuing professional development, helped focus attention on changes for teachers, while the Schools for the 21st Century grant might have been perceived as primarily a change for students. Another teacher also saw the grants as interactive, but he saw the Schools for the 21st Century grant as "90% responsible for the changes in the school." While he believed that the PSPDC provided new structures and roles and assisted with staff development, he felt that Lark Creek had set its own agenda for restructuring prior to participation in the PSPDC.

Perhaps the concurrence of the two reform efforts can be usefully seen as both an obstacle and a conduit to change at Lark Creek. To the extent that teachers perceived the agendas as overlapping and the PSPDC project as a way of achieving the school's vision, the concurrence was positive. The lack of particular emphasis on a substantive direction of reform in the PSPDC guiding beliefs allowed Lark Creek to use the PSPDC as a way of building its own staff development programs in the areas of Outcome-Based Education and Glasser's theories. To the extent that teachers already felt overwhelmed by the efforts to restructure curriculum and teaching in pursuit of Outcome-Based Education, the PSPDC could be seen as an additional drain on the scarce resources of teacher time and energy.

The professional development activities on integrated curriculum initiated by the PSPDC illustrate the effect of multiple reform efforts. While the PSPDC site committee at Lark Creek had identified integrated curriculum as the *Turning Points* recommendation on which they would most like to work, there was no preexisting press for integrated curriculum among the teachers. In addition, no one made connections between the on-going curricular changes associated with the school's adoption of Outcome-Based Education and the concept of integrated curriculum. While the workshops were positively perceived by teachers, and a number of teams applied for minigrants to develop an integrated instructional unit, the activities did not ultimately seem to result in any real changes in curriculum at the school site.

While there are many possible interpretations for the lack of continuing work on integrated curriculum, one explanation is that many teachers saw the emphasis on integrated curriculum as simply another project, suggested initially by the university, that would demand considerable time and effort to implement. No one helped teachers see the relationship between the creation of integrated curriculum and the other goals toward which they were working, and some of the participants in the workshop did not understand how these activities related to the goals of the PSPDC.

Change has been no easier, and perhaps even more difficult, on the university side. From its inception, the professional development center has been cast as the on-going concern of relatively few faculty, rather than as the responsibility of the college as a whole, despite efforts by the dean and director to change this perception. The PSPDC has been seen as simply another project, rather than as an effort to change the way the college functions. The uncertain position of the PSPDC in relation to both the College of Education and to the larger Puget Sound Educational Consortium contributes to its peripheral status. Located physically within one of the four departments of the College of Education and administratively outside of the mainstream of both the college administration and the office of teacher education, the PSPDC remains on the sidelines of the college's organization.

Locating a professional development center within a research university suggests historical tensions as well (Clifford & Guthrie, 1988). Part of the demise of the earlier Northline Consortium had to do with the university's mandate that the College of Education become more research oriented. As the College turned its focus toward research, faculty who had invested heavily in teacher education and in collaboration with schools, felt unrewarded and unrecognized. While some of these same faculty became part of the initial planning group for the PSPDC, they brought with them a wariness born of bitter experience with the university reward structure. Junior faculty were warned of the dangers of becoming overly involved with the PSPDC. Despite assurances and administration support, the recent history of the college created a rocky environment for the PSPDC to take root.

LEARNING FROM EXPERIENCE

What do we learn from this case of a PDS? First we learn about the complexity of individual institutions and the impossibility of divorcing schools or universities from the multiple contexts in which they are embedded. As a PDS, Lark Creek exists within multiple worlds: the school site, the school district, the community, the Puget Sound Educational Consortium, and the larger PSPDC. Each of these contexts has a slightly different agenda, and efforts to restructure can be easily fragmented. While the school leaders understand the interrelationships among the different agendas, other members of the school community feel pulled in different directions. The teachers' feelings of being overwhelmed by reform efforts reflect their sense of fragmentation. Schools that are attempting to become professional development centers, or to restructure in other ways, will need to address the tendency to see reform efforts as detachable projects and to provide opportunities for all staff to understand the larger goals.

What is true for the school is no less true for the university. As the university struggled to expand the concept of PDSs to the larger teacher education program, the ad-hoc nature of the pilot program hindered its efforts to become part of the mainstream. The small size of the teacher education program and its emphasis on middle level education made it difficult simply to replicate the pilot program on a larger scale. Without the involvement of a critical mass of faculty members, the PSPDC was again seen as the project of a few, rather than as the work of many.

While the multiple contexts made reform difficult at times, it also made it possible. The Schools for the 21st Century program begun by the state of Washington, played a significant role in creating a fertile environment for the professional development of teachers. The state grant was critical to the process of establishing a specific agenda for change and fostering a dialogue about teaching and learning. The funding provided to the University of Washington by foundations also played an essential role in the very creation of the PSPDC; without the seed money provided by the Ford Foundation, the PSPDC might have remained a good idea, rather than a reality. The funding allowed the university to jump-start a collaborative program. Yet each of the grants also had its own agenda for reform. The Ford grant focused particularly on clinical schools for preservice education, Carnegie's *Turning Points* grant focused on reforming middle level education, while the Stuart grant emphasized training for interprofessional collaboration. While these agendas can be seen as complementary from a larger perspective, the teachers, who were seldom involved in writing the grants, were often hard pressed to see the connections

We also learn about the role of frameworks, such as Outcome-Based Education, within a partnership. The kinds of frameworks schools adopt to guide efforts at reform are critical to the on-going process. Frameworks provide a set of ideas around which teachers can struggle and a common language with which to discuss teaching and learning. The Outcome-Based Education framework adopted by Lark Creek served an important function in helping the school develop a common vision and agenda for change. Perhaps what is most striking about Lark Creek is the widespread use of a common language with which members talked about the activities of teaching, learning, and the process of reform.

However, the common language of the school was not necessarily shared by the other half of the partnership—the university. University faculty had not been a part of the discussions about Outcome-Based Education and did not share in the same understanding of the term held by Lark Creek teachers and administrators. What role should such frameworks play in the preparation of teachers within a PDS? To what extent should the school and university develop common philosophies with regard to teaching and learning? The general beliefs articulated by the PSPDC planning group did not specify any particular conception of teaching and learning; while everyone agreed that all members of a PDS would be learners, participants could still hold quite different beliefs about both what students, teachers, and faculty should learn and how they should learn it (Grossman & Richert, 1991).

Frank discussions of underlying assumptions about teaching, learning, and schooling need to occur within the context of a professional development center. When partners with differing underlying assumptions enter a collaborative relationship, they may tend to avoid these discussions and the conflict that might ensue. For example, within the PSPDC, the planning committee had to decide whether to accept elementary or secondary preservice teachers into the middle school program, a decision that rapidly turned into a discussion about the role of subject matter preparation in teaching. In agreeing to accept both secondary and elementary students into the program, the planning group essentially agreed to disagree about the issue of subject-matter preparation for middle level teachers. This issue, however, masked deeper philosophical disagreements about middle-level education that have yet to be resolved. Developing a common language for discussions of teaching and learning and creating a culture in which implicit assumptions of all partners can be identified and openly discussed are challenges facing PDSs.

Finally, we learn about the organizational complexity of collaborative arrangements between schools and universities. A small ad-hocracy wedged in the cracks of the college's formal organizational structure rapidly created the professional development center. Such ad-hocracies may be critical to innovative efforts within large bureaucratic institutions. Without substantive restructuring of the college, however, the very ad-hocracy that enabled the PSPDC to emerge swiftly as an entity may relegate it to the permanent periphery of university life. Dependent upon the good will, support, and hard work of relatively few key individuals, the PSPDC has yet to be institutionalized. New organizational arrangements must be created that address the special needs of a collaborative program of career-long professional development. Issues of funding, governance, and university and school culture must be central to the institutionalization of any professional development center.

NOTE

[1]This case study was commissioned by the National Center for Restructuring Education, Schools, and Teaching, Teachers College, Columbia University. It is based upon a wide variety of data sources. I interviewed teachers and administrators at the school, observed classes, and analyzed documents related to the creation of the PSPDC. This study has also drawn on other research, including an ethnography of the school written under the auspices of the PSPDC, a survey of teachers in 21st Century schools, and my own previous research as a means of triangulating findings.

Finally, this case is informed by my own active participation in the creation of the PSPDC first as assistant director, and subsequently as director of the pilot preservice program, and as part of the teaching team for the core seminar. My involvement in the PSPDC has provided me with a particular perspective—university-based, focused primarily on preservice issues—that has undoubtedly influenced my interpretation of the data. I have shared this case with PSPDC participants from both the school site and the university, including the principal and a teacher leader from Lark Creek, the director of the PSPDC, and an actively involved university faculty member, and have tried to incorporate their feedback and corrections. Nonetheless, I recognize that another writer might well tell a different story.

The names of the school and the principal are pseudonyms. Statements in quotation marks are direct quotations from interviews with teachers.

Acknowledgment. I would like to thank Nanna Brantigan, Linda Darling-Hammond, Ann Foley, Nathalie Gehrke, Ann Lieberman, Susan Nolen, and Ken Sirotnik for all of their generous advice and support.

REFERENCES

Bishop, J. E. (in progress). *Teacher supervision of preservice teachers: A naturalistic study of teachers' professional development.* Unpublished doctoral dissertation, University of Washington, Seattle.

Carnegie Council on Adolescent Development. (1989). *Turning points: Preparing American youth for the 21st century.* Washington D. C.: Author.

Carnegie Forum on Education and the Economy. (1986). *A nation prepared: Teachers for the 21st century.* Washington D. C.: Author.

Clifford, G. J., & Guthrie, J. W. (1988). *Ed school: A brief for professional education.* Chicago: University of Chicago Press.

Gehrke, N. (1992, April). Becoming a teacher leader in a professional development school. Paper presented at the annual meeting of the American Educational Research Association, San Francisco, CA.

Glasser, W. (1986). *Control theory in the classroom.* New York: Harper and Row.

Goodlad, J. I. (1984). *A place called school.* New York: McGraw-Hill.

Grossman, P. L. (1991). Teaching to learn. In A. Lieberman (Ed.), *The changing contexts of teaching: Ninety-first yearbook of the National Society for the Study of Education.* Chicago: National Society for the Study of Education.

Grossman, P. L., & Brantigan, N. S. (1992). The teacher as teacher educator: New roles in professional development schools. *Kappa Delta Pi, 28* (4), 116–121.

Grossman, P. L., & Richert, A. E. (1991, April). Necessary knowledge: Perspectives on teacher knowledge and teacher learning held by participants in two professional development centers. Paper presented at the annual meeting of the American Educational Research Association, Chicago, IL.

Holmes Group. (1986). *Tomorrow's teachers: A report of the Holmes Group.* East Lansing, MI: Author.

Hunkins, F. (1990, April). Collaborative inquiry: Establishing site-based research in a multisite professional development center. Paper presented at the annual meeting of the American Educational Research Association, Boston, MA.

McDaniel, J. E. (1992, April). "Why are we doing this?" Teacher educators' views on teaming in teacher education. Paper presented at the annual meeting of the American Educational Research Association, San Francisco, CA.

Romerdahl, N. S. (1991, April). Teacher leadership in a professional development school: A study of shared leadership. Paper presented at the annual meeting of the American Educational Research Association, Chicago, IL.

Sagmiller, K. (1992, April). Becoming a professional development school: An ethnographic study of transformation. Paper presented at the annual meeting of the American Educational Research Association, San Francisco, CA.

Spady, W. G., & Marshall, K. J. (1991). Beyond traditional outcome-based education. *Educational Leadership, 49* (2), 67–72

Vickery, T. R. (1988). Learning from an outcomes-driven school district. *Educational Leadership, 45* (5), 52–56.

Yerian, S., & Grossman, P. L. (1993). Emerging themes on the effectiveness of teacher preparation through professional development schools. Paper presented at the annual meeting of the American Educational Research Association, Atlanta, GA.

Chapter 4

PERMISSION, PERSISTENCE, AND RESISTANCE: LINKING HIGH SCHOOL RESTRUCTURING WITH TEACHER EDUCATION REFORM

Betty Lou Whitford

This chapter is about how the context of reform has encouraged the faculties of Fairdale High School and the Department of Secondary Education at the University of Louisville to begin connecting their work more systematically.[1]

Fairdale High School is located in a close-knit, predominantly white, working-class community in Jefferson County, Kentucky. While the majority of students live near the school, one of 20 comprehensive high schools in the district, about 30% of the 1,200 students are African American, bused from low income areas of Louisville 10–15 miles away. The higher education community is from the University of Louisville School of Education, particularly the Department of Secondary Education. One of eight School of Education departments, Secondary Education's 12 members prepare students for high school certification, offer several graduate programs, and participate in the School's Ed.D. program as well as the middle grades programs.

Among both faculties are innovators who have experimented for the past several years with new structures and programs. They have interacted often, each providing assistance with the other group's agenda. Both have learned a lot about change, collaboration, diversity, risk-taking, and the scarcity of resources to support education, not to mention the policies and politics that so influence how educational organizations operate and what children learn or fail to learn.

Because—and in spite of—these experiences, individuals on both faculties have persisted in their efforts to effect fundamental change. The high school's restructuring efforts have progressed to the point that many on the staff want to include the whole school. Similarly, the secondary education faculty is moving toward an entirely new program for preparing high school teachers, one that will be based in schools and linked to social service agencies and other community groups.

INITIATING CHANGE: SCHOOL DISTRICT CONTEXT

In 1975, the former Jefferson County and Louisville Independent districts underwent both merger and desegregation. Protests were sometimes violent, particularly in Fairdale, as the district's schools desegregated through a quickly devised busing plan based not on neighborhoods but on the initial of a child's last name.

Between 1975 and 1981, several superintendents came and went as the two former districts struggled to blend conflicting administrative styles and curriculum orientations. The former city system had a reputation for humanistic innovation (which some in the county called "1960s flakiness") while the former county district was known as orderly and structured (which some in the city called "oppressively bureaucratic").

In 1981, following a national search headed by University of Louisville School of Education Dean Raphael Nystrand, the district hired Donald Ingwerson, then superintendent of Orange County, California, schools. That year, he began what became a remarkably long tenure—12 years—for the top leader of an urban school district (93,000 students, 30% minority, 5,000 teachers, 160 schools). During Ingwerson's tenure, the district received much national attention as a leader in school restructuring.

Another significant event occurred in 1984, when the Gheens Foundation offered the school system $2.5 million over a 5-year period to support the professional development of the district's teachers and administrators. With the cooperation of the teachers' union, financial support from the Foundation, and a tenured professorship at the University of Louisville, the district successfully recruited Phillip Schlechty to develop a comprehensive plan for professional development.

Working with the top leadership of the district and an advisory committee composed of teacher, administrator, and university representatives, Schlechty's initial step was the establishment of the Jefferson County Public Schools Gheens Professional Development Academy. By 1988, the mission of the Academy was described as threefold:

1. Professional support for teachers and administrators with special attention to collegial interaction, intellectual and job variety, and honor and recognition for achievement
2. District leadership for "fundamentally restructuring schools"
3. Movement of the district "into a position of national leadership" in all phases of providing a quality work force. (Schlechty, Ingwerson, and Brooks, 1988, pp. 2–3)

To address this mission, the Academy staff began trying a number of reform strategies, including a small grants program called "Invitation to

Invention" and a confidential teacher assistance hotline. A more comprehensive effort began during the 1986–87 school year focused on creating professional development schools (PDSs). While this work was consistent with many of the recommendations of the Carnegie Task Force on Education and the Economy and of the Holmes Group, Schlechty et al. (1988) saw the effort as a "home-grown, local initiative" (p. 1). This work, called PDS in the district, began an intensive school restructuring process that continues to be supported, coordinated, and expanded through the JCPS Gheens Academy.

Planning to invent local PDSs began when the district leadership invited all schools to apply to become PDS planning sites. The faculty and administration of these schools were to work on dual goals: developing their schools as (1) exemplars of practice and (2) centers for the induction and continuing professional development of teachers and administrators.

At the time the invitation was issued to the district's schools, virtually no resources had been secured to support the work. The Gheens leadership made it clear that the participants might have to work on Saturdays and after school. Despite this condition, the faculties and principals of 24 schools voted to participate. Fairdale High School, with Marilyn Hohmann in her 1st year as principal, was one of seven high schools that came to participate in PDS.

PDS PLANNING

From January through March, 1987, 104 educators convened in three separate groups (elementary, middle, and high) for a series of 7 all-day seminars. Those participating included 2 teachers elected by the faculty of each school, the 24 building principals, 7 additional teachers selected by the union, 7 central office administrators, 9 University of Louisville professors, and 9 resource teachers from the Gheens Academy.

Large and small cross-role groups, facilitated by the resource teachers, worked as seminars focused on the nature of the problems facing educational reformers and what might be done to address them. Early discussions focused on the social and organizational structure of schools and the teaching occupation, the conditions of teaching and learning in schools, and barriers to desired conditions. Later discussions worked toward consensus on beliefs about schooling, learning, and professional practice; and how to create conditions that would support change—schools as cultures, professionalizing teaching, linking theory and practice, and promoting students as successful "knowledge workers." During the time between meetings, the representatives of the 24 schools held building-level sessions with their faculties to gain additional input and broaden involvement in the ideas.

By spring, 1987, Schlechty presented the group with a draft statement of a vision, six beliefs, and six sets of standards about exemplary practice derived from the 3 months of discussions. Following revisions, this statement was endorsed by the PDS planning groups in March, 1987. The resulting vision statement read, "The purpose of Professional Development Schools is to help the Jefferson County Public Schools to become a place where every leader is a teacher, every teacher is a leader and every student is a success" (Kyle, 1988, p. 28). Six beliefs were to guide the PDSs:

- Student success is the goal of all school activity.
- Students need to be challenged and need to learn to pursue difficult tasks and persist with tasks at which they are unsuccessful.
- Learning is an active process.
- Teachers are leaders, and principals are leaders of leaders.
- The business of the school district and the state is to assure that each school unit operates under optimal conditions and produces optimal results.
- Staff success results from motivated and competent people working in an environment that is committed to their success, continuing growth, and development. (Kyle, 1988, pp. 28–29)

The third section of the document specified 29 standards to be used by staff in a PDS to assess and continually improve their performance. These standards, presented in six categories, addressed shared vision, shared decision-making, success orientation, results orientation, flexibility and support. For example, one of the standards regarding shared vision specified that "all staff will hold a common definition of what constitutes successful student and staff performance" (Kyle, 1988, p. 28). One of the shared decision-making standards required that "those who are affected by and expected to help solve problems will be actively involved in identifying the problems and making decisions about how the problems should be solved" (Kyle, 1988, p. 29). Flexibility standards addressed the need for policies and procedures to expedite "goal enhancing decisions . . . made at the building level" as well as for flexible use of time and other resources (Kyle, 1988, p. 29).

After the PDS planning groups endorsed the document, the participants worked in school groups to decide how to involve their faculties in further consideration of "the standards document," as it came to be called. In April and May, PDS representatives conducted sessions for their own faculties during which the standards document was reviewed. Each of the 24 faculties was then asked to decide if they wished to continue being part of a restructuring effort based on the document. By faculty votes, all 24 schools decided to remain a part of the process. In May, the standards document was endorsed by the Board of Education. According to Schlechty et al. (1988), this document was intended to provide the PDS sites with standards for judging exemplary practice and objectives toward which the schools should work.

PDS GOAL I: EXEMPLARY PRACTICE

In early June, 1987, the PDS planners from the 24 schools reconvened for a week-long workshop. These sessions focused largely on ways to address the first of the two PDS goals, exemplary practice, in each building. Originally, the Gheens leadership envisioned working simultaneously on the dual goals of exemplary practice and exemplary induction and professional development, including links to teacher education. However, as planning proceeded during the spring, 1987,. sessions and into the summer, the groups focused more and more on exemplary practice. During the planning sessions, Schlechty would often say, "We have to know what we're inducting folks into before we can figure out what induction should look like."

As a result of the summer activities, the focus of the exemplary practice goal shifted to individual schools as planning became building-based and decentralized. Rather than giving schools a specific list of activities in which to engage, the Gheens leadership encouraged the staffs to invent their own ways of addressing the vision, beliefs, and standards. Rather than waiting for direction from Gheens, schools were encouraged to take charge and to call on the Gheens staff for assistance as needed. Many of the 24 schools responded very cautiously: The old top-down norms simply did not support bold action.

Marilyn Hohmann did not hesitate. In 1987, the Fairdale faculty held the first of what has become an annual out-of-town "advance" (rather than "retreat") to begin work in earnest with the faculty as a whole. At this first advance, the Steering Committee was created, a move consistent with the PDS standard about shared decision making. This committee, the first of its kind in the district, would become the chief decision-making body for the school.

INITIATING CHANGE: INSIDE FAIRDALE HIGH SCHOOL

Schools need to be safe and comfortable and uplifting and helpful and not cold, clinical experiences for kids. Somewhere along the way in American education, we forgot that these are children. And that was terrible.

What we do and how we treat people in this building are the keys to everything we do. Everything we do teaches. Everything I do teaches.

Genuinely sharing leadership with teachers means mistakes will be made. If the superintendent didn't take that into consideration, I'd be dead. But he does. And interestingly, you don't make that many mistakes. You make fewer actually because you have the wisdom of the group and the determination that if I own this baby, I'm going to make it work somehow.

In these statements, Marilyn Hohmann, who began her 7th year as Fairdale principal in the Fall of 1992, indicates some of her major commitments and beliefs: School should be a moral institution where people are treated decently. All adults in the building are teachers through the models they set for youngsters. Leadership should be shared. Decision making should be school based. And, these conditions require the support of the superintendent.

Reflecting these commitments, during the faculty's first summer planning meetings in 1987, Hohmann urged the faculty to establish a steering committee to govern the school. According to a school-produced booklet, this committee, composed of "elected teachers, students, administrators, support staff and parents," was created to function as

the shared decision-making instrument of change. The Steering Committee adopted inclusive operating procedures and established Task Forces to study, design and implement program changes, generated from staff brainstorming sessions. (Fairdale High School, 1988, p. 1)

Since 1987, adjustments and refinements in the structure and process have been made as district, union, and state policies have become more permissive and supportive of school-based, participatory decision making. In particular, parent involvement has increased. While in past years, the Steering Committee had been chaired by teachers, the 1992–1993 chair was a parent and former member of the district's school board.

This committee was the first of many changes since Hohmann's arrival in 1986. During her 1st year, Fairdale began participating in PDS planning. That decision formally committed the faculty to major reform guided by the vision, beliefs, and standards document. This formal commitment to change was extended in 1988 when Fairdale became affiliated with the Coalition of Essential Schools. By that decision, the faculty agreed to work on the Coalition's Nine Common Principles. (See Sizer, 1992, for a list of the principles.)

RESTRUCTURED RULES, ROLES, AND RELATIONSHIPS

Based on orientations such as shared leadership and Coalition principles such as increased personalization, Hohmann has encouraged faculty invention and experimentation within the rule, "Is it good for students?" The result has been the creation of several interdisciplinary teams, college-style arena scheduling where students select courses and teachers, faculty participation in hiring and budget decisions, an academic-technical magnet program, a new public safety program, and participation in the University of Louisville's teacher preparation program. Reflecting on this permission to be inventive, one teacher commented, "One of the best things about being here is getting to try things you've always wanted to try. We inspire each other to figure out how to work best with kids. We have lots of support for trying different things."

Two of the interdisciplinary teams, in particular, have received a lot of attention both inside the school and from visitors. One is the Bridge Team where 7 teachers work with a heterogeneous group of 130 ninth graders in a four-hour block. Guided by the Coalition's "student as worker, teacher as coach" metaphor, the team develops interdisciplinary units stressing problem solving and decision making, teamwork, social and organizational skills, student responsibility and success (Fairdale High School, 1988).

The team's classrooms are located together at the end of a hallway, though visitors may often find the rooms empty because of the team's frequent instructional activities outside the building. The Bridge Team teachers have common planning time and, according to one teacher, "We meet every day, sometimes twice a day, to plan, work out problems, review what happened, what worked and what didn't. We air differences and try to reach consensus." One student, commenting on her experiences on the Bridge Team, reported, "Those Bridge Team teachers, they won't let you fail. They were on my back constantly last year about doing my work. And even this year, when they see me in the hall, they are still after me."

Another highly visible team is called "U.S. is Us." The instructional focus of this team, available to juniors, is a course interweaving U.S. history and literature in six units guided by essential questions. Like the Bridge Team, students taking U.S. is Us are heterogeneously grouped.

Initially designed during a summer institute in 1986, team membership has since changed and the curriculum has evolved some. For example, last year the team instituted a "no fail" policy with a grading system that includes A, B, C and Incomplete. The policy of the team is that students are expected to work on assignments until they are completed. Along with this "success orientation," teachers also stress attention to individual needs, attendance, parent contact, and active student participation. Team teachers report that "this attention has yielded higher grades than those achieved by students in traditional classes taught by the same teachers" (Fairdale High School, 1988).

Many of the teachers with experience on teams agree with the view expressed by one teacher:

> Being on a team means more sharing, more learning from each other. The kids really benefit—they hear the same thing from all of us. And I've grown a lot from working closely with other teachers. But it's not easy. Being on a team is like a marriage without some of the good parts.

Most teachers are not in elaborate teaming situations, yet many in the building have significantly increased their contact with one another as well. For example, some special education and regular program teachers work together in a classroom where they have mixed their students. One special education teacher commented on the arrangement:

> It's been a big change for me. Where before I only had 40 kids to work with, I now have 80. But the kids are learning so much more. And I like to think that I might have had something to do with the fact that regular program students are also doing better.

Sometimes the increased cooperation is departmental, as in the Math Department where several teachers have reorganized their courses to take the new National Council of Teachers of Mathematics standards into account. A math teacher commented:

> We have really increased cooperation in the department. We are learning about new strategies from each other. But we still have a long way to go to get agreement on the best way to teach math.

At least one math teacher has drastically changed her teaching by creating a two-hour block course emphasizing cooperative learning strategies. A student comments on this class:

> She's not really like a mom, but sort of. I mean when I'm really in a bad mood, she won't mess with me. But I really learn a lot in there. She never goes on until she knows everyone understands.

Sometimes, teachers from different disciplines work together temporarily on special units or lessons. And many others continue to "solo." Even in this latter case, there is evidence that solo teaching does not necessarily mean sticking with traditional approaches. For example, one veteran credits Schlechty and Theodore Sizer, founder of the Coalition of Essential Schools to which Fairdale belongs, with returning him from burnout. He has abandoned lecturing and testing what kids memorize. Now his students spend much of their time working on various group projects and presenting the products of their work to their classmates. He explains the change:

In all my years in teaching, I'd never heard a central office administrator talk the way Schlechty did. He said we needed to reinvent American schooling and said there would be support for what we tried, that the superintendent supported it. Before that I'd only heard central office administrators tell us what to do. And I used to be a coach, so I understood what Sizer means by "student as worker, teacher as coach." When I lectured, after so many years, I got bored and the kids were bored. Now, they build so much confidence. That's one of my main goals now.

There is also evidence that this teacher's approach is an effective way to engage students in school work. In May, 1991, on the last day of school for the year, students in one of his classes were reading, discussing, and writing. They first read an essay written in the mid-1800s about why women should not be educated and then, in pairs, they composed a reaction. The teacher moved from pair to pair, listening to their arguments, asking questions, and commenting on their work. Such student engagement was also evident in many classrooms on the last day of school before the 1991 winter vacation.

Along with such changes in curriculum and organization have come alterations in the roles and responsibilities of teachers and administrators. For example, giving up lecturing means teachers have to be much more creative in order to plan engaging classroom assignments. School-wide responsibilities have also changed radically. Membership on the Steering Committee and task forces, open to all in the school, means many after-school meetings. All staff and faculty attending the meetings have voting privileges. These groups have decision-making responsibility for school-wide issues including programs, staffing, and budgets. Such responsibility is far more wide-ranging for teachers than ever before. One teacher expressed the change this way:

I've been here a hundred years and believe me, if we could spend money before, it was to buy paper clips or something. Now we decide if we want a VCR. And the other day, we interviewed 8 teachers for a position here. Before, the [school] board just assigned teachers. We've also hired assistant principals.

Making such decisions is very time consuming. Most teachers indicated they like the new authority, as this comment illustrates, "We're so used to being asked our opinion and participating in the decisions, if I went to another school, I'd expect the same thing and I probably wouldn't get it." Some expressed concern about doing more and more work with no salary increase as this teacher's comment reflects:

Sometimes when we have problems on the team, the administration handles it, but sometimes, we're told we [on the team] need to work it out. There's a lot of stress in such a situation, having to tell someone they aren't doing such a good job. That's very hard for one teacher to say to another teacher. I think that's what the administrators get the higher salaries for—handling the stressful situations.

These comments identify several challenging issues about the allocation of time, money, and other resources along with the restructured responsibilities, as Hohmann recognizes: "We desperately need more resources here. We write a lot of grants and we get support that way. But I don't think anyone really understands how demanding restructuring is on a school staff." It is important to point out that such comments from the staff are often accompanied by enthusiasm about how shared decision making has increased professionalism and ownership in what is happening in the school. While the day officially ends at 2:20, typically the parking lot is still full of cars at 4:00. And for many, work goes on well into the evening most weeks.

RESTRUCTURERS, REVIEWERS, RESISTERS

While many teachers are very involved in the changes at Fairdale, some are not. Some routinely engage in professional development while others resist change and the risks involved. Hohmann identifies three groups in the school that she calls restructurers, reviewers, and resisters:

Restructurers are really doing things differently, some are doing profoundly different things with kids. Reviewers watch and sit on the fence before they decide what they want to do. Sometimes, depending on the issue, reviewers become restructurers and the reverse. Resisters keep us on track. They keep us honest and balanced and don't let us think we know everything. You can't just push people aside. And, I see real change in the resisters. I see them headed in positive directions.

Despite these observations, she readily adds that change is difficult and uneven. Sometimes her patience wears thin and frustration shows, as these two comments illustrate:

It's disappointing to see some of your own folks turn completely around and fall back into unprofessional and immature practices. But you can't come back at them with the same low level and hope to keep people thinking about quality and good relationships. When you dig real deep, you can find a core that continue to hold the old attitudes that say our kids aren't motivated and parents don't care. That exists and keeps those teachers from looking deeply at their classroom strategies. How much talking and performing am I doing? If kids aren't inquirers and researchers, what are you going to do to change? Overall, we're getting improvement slowly. Some attitudes, though, won't change, and we won't get past that until some people leave.

We're drowning kids in our own verbal onslaughts. There are lots of times I want to do what most principals want to do and just walk out that door and raise holy hell with somebody because they may deserve it. But there has to be a respectful, collegial kind of confidence that teachers have that they are not going to get bashed, and you won't change the rules on them midstream. But there are some things I won't be collegial about. I won't tolerate people who aren't working well with kids.

Despite the frustrations and periods of low morale, no interviews—even the many conducted during February—indicate a longing for any "good old Fairdale days" when the principal made decisions with little teacher input. Still, for those who have taught at Fairdale for many years, their histories at the school and their professional biographies are important. Some on the staff are Fairdale graduates and have generations of Fairdale graduates among their families and friends. Some indicate that they hear a message in restructuring that says everything they did in the past was wrong.

Nevertheless, the dominant orientation emerging from the interviews is toward the present and future, a stance that is notable for a high school staff as experienced as Fairdale's. Almost 50% of the teachers have been at Fairdale for 10 years or more, while over 88% have taught that long in one school or another. About a third of the faculty have taught at Fairdale for 15 years or more, while 65% have taught that long overall.

It is also true that no one claims that Fairdale has resolved most problems and issues they face, or that their work together is free of stress and tension. Most of the restructurers are genuinely enthusiastic and proud of what they and their students are accomplishing. At the same time, they disagree among themselves about what to emphasize with their students. Others are more cautiously positive, showing a mix of support for some of the changes with concerns about attempting so much change at once. Indeed, the booklet given to visitors also conveys this duality. The cover announces "Fairdale High School, an Essential School Where Success Is No Longer a Secret." Inside, following the identification of Fairdale as a member of the Coalition is this title: "Facing the Essential Tensions: Restructuring from Where You Are."

PDS GOAL II: INDUCTION AND PROFESSIONAL DEVELOPMENT

When the local version of a PDS was being planned, the Gheens leadership envisioned working simultaneously on the dual goals of exemplary practice and exemplary induction and professional development, including links to teacher education. As planning proceeded, however, the groups focused almost exclusively on the exemplary practice goal.

In the fall of 1987 and winter of 1988, after some experimentation related to exemplary practice was underway in schools, the PDS planners turned their attention to the second goal about induction and professional development. However, unlike the vision, beliefs, and standards about exemplary practice, widespread consensus about what was needed to support induction and professional development in schools, particularly related to altered staff roles, proved much more difficult to attain.

Both the Gheens leadership and the directors of several school-university projects tried various strategies to create new staffing arrangements. In addition, several committees worked on various designs, including one developed by a joint union-district committee that recommended creating a limited number of beginning teacher positions in PDS sites.

Several schools, particularly middle schools, experimented with new induction and professional development roles for teachers. For example, one school received a small grant to support a "model teacher" who focused on professional development and the coordination of teacher education students. The university's middle grades program and all 8 PDS middle schools experimented with establishing student teacher positions on middle school teams (Whitford, Hovda, & Shelor, 1987, 1988). The university's center of excellence also funded several clinical instructor positions that, in various iterations, have brought experienced teachers into the university to assist with teacher education and supported induction and professional development positions based at Gheens. As of yet, these experiments, some of which are continuing, have not led to the creation of permanent positions within schools to support the second PDS goal. Several factors explain this situation.

School restructuring, as complex as it is, clearly falls under the auspices of schools and school systems. Induction, on the other hand, is much closer to the overlapping work of those in schools and teacher educators in universities. And while the union certainly has interest in school restructuring, induction directly relates to positions and jobs. Thus, induction is the issue around which most of the familiar turf battles and differences in educational philosophies between and among those in schools, universities, and union offices may be made more visible, more quickly.

Partly in reaction to the overlapping, complex interests involved in developing a new approach to induction, the Gheens leadership functionally split the second PDS goal into two separate agendas—professional development and induction. As the restructuring efforts proceeded, professional development happened and was encouraged to happen in at least two ways. One way was through planned seminars and workshops. Another was as a result of acting in new ways in schools.

Perhaps the most powerful professional development happened as those in PDS sites planned and experimented with innovative arrangements. As they talked about what they wanted to do, as they designed and refined, they encountered questions and problems. That prompted a great deal of professional reading and conversations with other educators. Thus, much professional development occurred in a learning-by-doing approach.

The Gheens staff augmented this by developing workshops and seminars around topics with which PDS sites had begun to experiment. For example, as schools worked with such strategies as shared decision making, teaming, cooperative learning, or authentic assessment, Gheens responded by providing more workshops and seminars on those topics. As a result of creating such experiences, the Gheens staff developed professionally as well. Further, the availability of the workshops encouraged other schools to learn about the strategies and try them out.

Many of the experiences provided by Gheens initially focused on those PDS faculties and principals who demonstrated the most initiative on and commitment to what the Gheens leadership came to call "the restructuring agenda." For example, both the Gheens leadership and many on the staff supported interdisciplinary teaming as an effective way to organize schools. Indeed, many at Gheens had extensive experience with such teams in local middle schools. Thus, schools experimenting with teaming could expect assistance and encouragement from the Gheens staff.

The Gheens staff developed their expertise with various components of the restructuring agenda in a number of ways. As a result of PDS planning and other work with some at the university, the staff could call on the university for assistance: At one point, 8 members of the Gheens staff were also doctoral students at the university. They also developed close ties with local businesses, particularly several operating with quality circles and other participatory management strategies. As a result, the district was able to gain access to several executive training programs.

In these ways, the Gheens reform agenda became focused primarily on school restructuring within which professional development was interwoven. As the schools involved in one or more aspects of restructuring went beyond the original 24 PDS sites, the Gheens staff began using the term "restructuring schools" rather than "PDS" to refer to this broader agenda. This emphasis was later formalized within the organizational structure of Gheens when the staff divided into teams—the "restructuring team" and the "induction team," with "staff development" placed in yet a third unit. Induction and staff development were increasingly viewed by the Gheens leadership as maintenance rather than development functions, seen primarily as ways to comply efficiently with state regulation and bureaucratic rules.

The separation of the induction goal from the restructuring goal can be accounted for in other ways as well. Since induction issues involve teacher preparation most directly, the more deliberative style of the university required a slower pace than the action orientation of those in schools. In addition, as the conversations among the PDS planners turned to induction, several issues arose.

One complicating factor was the existing Kentucky Teacher Internship Program (KTIP), a relatively new beginning teacher program with both supporters and detractors. Among the criticisms leveled at KTIP was that it is based on a narrow, mechanistic view of teaching characterized as direct instruction for student mastery of a "right answer" curriculum.

At the same time, the program had the support of union leadership, especially locally. One feature especially favored by the union was that each beginning teacher was assigned a mentor teacher who, for a salary bonus, would work with a novice at least 60 hours during the school year. The mentor was also a member of a three-person team who evaluated the novice's performance three times during the year and made a recommendation about certification. (The other two members were the principal and a university representative.) Currently, the KTIP evaluation system is under review. If the recommendations of the review team are accepted, significant changes more consistent with a constructivist and developmental view of teaching and learning are likely (Kyle, Dittmer, Fischetti, & Portes, 1992).

Other disagreements were evident between some of the PDS planners and some from the university. Nine School of Education teacher educators participated in the PDS planning sessions. Some of these individuals objected to the "knowledge worker" metaphor used in the vision, beliefs, and standards document. Some were also uncomfortable with the idea that induction was to focus on developing teachers for the local school system. In Schlechty's terms, novices needed to learn "the Jefferson County way."

This stance highlighted an issue about whether the university's teacher education mission should be focused on preparing teachers for the local school system or for schools generally. When effective practice is seen as generalizable and universal, this issue is rather insignificant. However, when effective practice is viewed as context-specific, a view many from the university hold, the issue becomes thornier.

Thus, while initially the PDS planners were committed to working toward dual goals—developing their schools as exemplars of practice and centers for the induction and continuing professional development of teachers and administrators—as discussions and experimentation proceeded, the participants focused more and more on exemplary practice. As one key administrator explained, "When we employ 5,000 teachers and are experiencing some enrollment decline, we aren't hiring large numbers of new teachers. So we just aren't very interested in putting a lot of resources into induction."

LINKING TEACHER EDUCATION WITH SCHOOL RESTRUCTURING

Despite the complexity of these and other induction issues, some at the university continued to strengthen connections with those in PDS sites that were most actively engaged in restructuring. At the high school level, Fairdale was the clear leader in attempting significant changes. University connections with Fairdale occurred in a variety of ways coincidental with as well as independent of PDS planning activities.

Some connections happened individually, independent of any intentions of policy makers or PDS planners as teachers and teacher educators met in courses or within local professional networks and found mutual interests. As a result of these relationships, for several years, some Fairdale teachers had worked with University of Louisville students in "field placements" attached to courses in the university's regular teacher education program.

Such placements in Jefferson County restructuring schools such as Fairdale were also encouraged by the School of Education's Center for the Collaborative Advancement of the Teaching Profession. The center also supported connections with restructuring schools through two experimental teacher education programs, one for elementary teachers and the other for secondary teachers. For several years, center funds provided some university faculty time, several part-time clinical instructor positions filled by teachers, and, in the case of the secondary program, tuition remission for students. While both programs operated in a number of schools in and out of Jefferson County, the center steering committee encouraged the directors of those programs to place students in Jefferson County's restructuring schools when possible. Fairdale routinely participated in the secondary program.

In other cases, the connections were made possible through outside funding. For example, for the first 2 years of a 3-year grant program, Fairdale was included in Ford Foundation funding used to support 7 local "clinical sites" selected from among the 24 schools originally involved in PDS planning. During the 1st year, funds supported joint planning sessions among the university and the schools as well as between the school district and the teachers union. During the 2nd year, each school, including Fairdale, received small grant assistance allocated through the Gheens Academy for school-based planning meetings. During the 3rd year, renewed Ford monies supported two teacher positions, neither of which went to Fairfield.

Just as inclusion in such grants is rewarding, being excluded is deflating. Since Fairdale teachers and university teacher educators working with them had been trying to find ways to better support on-site professional development (such as peer assistance within the math department) as well as increased involvement in the teacher education courses being taught on-site, some at Fairdale and the university were quite disappointed that Fairdale did not receive one of the Ford-funded positions during that 3rd year. From the perspective of one top school system administrator, since Fairdale had received support through other grants, this one should go to other schools.

From the perspective of others most involved in linking teacher education with school restructuring at Fairdale, this one additional teacher position for a year would have helped ease the pressure of work overload many were feeling. And, the decision symbolized to many inside the school that their efforts were not being properly recognized and supported. Such funding decisions are demoralizing for those feeling undersupported and overworked by the complexities of systemic reform. Yet, in the long run, if this type of work is to be institutionalized, one position for one year is not a solution.

TEACHER EDUCATION AT FAIRDALE

Within this context of district reform, the University of Louisville's Department of Secondary Education was operating an experimental teacher education program. Though the program placed students in Jefferson as well as other nearby county school systems, Fairdale was a key participant. Under a special arrangement with the state for 4 years, the program worked with four cohorts of 12–20 talented, second career liberal arts graduates.

Using a "teaching to learn" approach, an intensive summer of course work and student teaching were followed by most students being placed in paid, year-long, half-time teaching positions. In Jefferson County, these positions were in critical shortage areas such as chemistry and mathematics. Students in the program taught three of their own classes and took courses and attended teacher education seminars after school (Fischetti,

1990). Significantly, as Fischetti and Dittmer (1992) report, "Discipline dropped from #1 on their list of concerns long before they completed the program, and was replaced by a concern for developing alternative, student-centered curriculum that would engage their students" (p. 12).

Over the span of the program, several experimental positions were created at Fairdale. The most recent examples occurred during the 1991–92 school year when three Bridge Team teachers were program participants. Two were university students; the third was an experienced teacher who worked part-time with high school students and part-time with the teacher education program.

This program extended the collaboration between Fairdale and the university in several ways. First, each year of the program, Hohmann worked on the school-university team that interviewed applicants. Contacts made during these interviews led to the placement of several students at Fairdale. As Fischetti and Dittmer (1992) argue, this involvement also helped develop the trust needed between school and university personnel to share the risks involved in such an experiment. For example, since students were learning to teach by having their own classes, both school and university personnel shared simultaneous responsibility for the development of novice teachers. As Fischetti (1990) puts it, all participants were "learning to swim in deep water."

The year-long employment of university students at Fairdale regularly brought teacher educators into the building. These contacts led to many discussions among the members of both faculties and in some cases, led to extended collaboration in such areas as teaming and authentic assessment.

These contacts also led to others as Fairdale and university faculty members learned more about each others' activities and programs. For example, as Secondary Education faculty grew more aware of Fairdale activities, they encouraged graduate students from several different classes to assist with projects on both the Bridge Team and with the U.S. is Us program. And several doctoral students collected data at Fairdale, tracking the nature of change and the reactions of students. As a result, Fairdale faculty and students received some assistance, and the university faculty and students gained valuable insights into life in a restructuring school.

Fairdale teachers also gained professional expertise and confidence as they interacted with the novices from the university's experimental program. Fairdale students received attention from more adults, thus enabling some class activities that might not otherwise have been possible. Also, the university presence pushed teachers to reflect more on what they were doing and why, as university students asked questions.

Moreover, university teacher educators experienced much more directly the realities of teaching school —from hauling equipment around to dealing with fire alarms and pep rallies; from sharing classroom space to waiting for an available telephone; from helping teacher education students adjust their plans when high school students attended class irregularly to sharing thrilling teachable moments when lights suddenly went on in those same students' eyes.

The relations developed during the experimental program have also led to the placement of two regular program courses at Fairdale. One course focuses on teaching methods and the other on educational technology. For two years now, pairs of university teacher educators have combined these courses and cotaught them as a block to the same group of students. As part of the course work, the university students have worked in the classrooms of Fairdale teachers who, in turn, have led sessions in the university classroom.

During the fall of 1992, additional teacher education courses will be scheduled at Fairdale and Iroquois High School. Two courses, "Introduction to Education" and "Adolescent Growth and Development" will also be interwoven and cotaught by teams of university educators, this time from different School of Education departments. This meshing and coteaching of courses are further steps in the transition to an entirely new secondary teacher education program that will combine elements of the experimental program with substance and processes evolving from the teaching of these courses inside high schools, including links to health and human service agencies. Some teacher educators envision that eventually, formal teacher education in the evolving PDS sites such as Fairdale will be built around the experiences novices have working with youngsters in schools rather than through a predetermined series of discrete courses with supporting but disconnected and somewhat contrived experiences in schools.

EMERGING ISSUES

Educators at both Fairdale and the Department of Secondary Education are attempting fundamental change. As change occurs, issues are confronted both inside their organizations as well as in the way they interact.

At least two restructuring issues are producing tension inside Fairdale. One concerns the scope—and to some degree the pace—of change. In essence, this issue is about whether and when restructuring will encompass the entire school rather than somewhat disconnected pockets. In March, 1992, some restructurers believed a move to whole school teaming was likely for 1992–93. However, others had misgivings, and using their decision-making process, by late spring, it was clear that sufficient consensus on the whole school teaming plan had not developed. While Hohmann supported the plan, she seemed comfortable with the resulting compromise: "I think we reached a satisfactory compromise. Ninth and tenth graders will be teamed and we will have one team involving both eleventh and twelfth graders."

A second issue is more complex. During one faculty meeting about whole school teaming, it seemed that some resisted this change because they oppose change per se, while others who resisted this particular proposal have clearly been restructurers on other issues. While there is disagreement among the faculty about the sources of tension, in part it appears to be related to a second, more fundamental issue about how students' academic, social, and personal needs should be addressed and what levels of achievement should be expected and accepted. The emerging differences among the faculty on these issues of substance do not just separate restructurers from reviewers and resisters; divisions are evident among the restructurers as well.

For example, some in the school, particularly those on teams, stress what might be called a "generalist orientation," while others are more concerned about specific content. Teachers from both orientations are caring and nurturing toward students, while also stressing attendance, parent involvement, and student success. Both generalists and specialists among the restructurers also embrace the "student as worker, teacher as coach" metaphor.

The generalists, inclined as they are toward teaming, tend to use more interdisciplinary units of instruction. These units tend to stress social skills, decision making, and problem solving over any preferred core body of content. The specialists, particularly evident in the math department, place more emphasis than do generalists on students' achievement of specific, discipline-based content. One administrator explained the issue this way:

> This faculty is much more caring and nurturing than others I've seen. We bend over backwards to keep kids here, to not suspend, to not run kids away. In other schools, we push kids out. Here this faculty takes teaching every kid sincerely and seriously. It's the only place I've seen that. At the same time, some very caring teachers are hammering to get academic results and are concerned that others in the school believe that the socialization process is the goal. And if we don't get farther than that with the kids, that's okay. Well, I hope that's not accurate.

One restructurer, a specialist, stressed, "It hurts me to think that our kids think they're not smart because they aren't prepared and believe they can't achieve. This happens when content is not dealt with well." Others, including some teacher educators, worry about the appropriate balance between caring and academic achievement, as this comment illustrates:

> Are the kids being short-changed academically because they come to school with so many needs? I'm concerned that the academic work is not really at high school level. Are we just finding another way to pass poor kids? A lot of changes have been very positive. Kids are more involved in classes, maybe for the first time. But what's the next step? We need to push to the next level of quality with the curriculum.

As teaming arrangements proliferate and the work of those in schools intertwines, the nature of that work—its processes, goals, outcomes, and values—becomes more visible. Tensions about best practice within and among school and university faculties, kept sub rosa through isolation and disconnected through separation of work sites, are more exposed in a PDS. Learning how to take these differences into account in the context of a PDS can be highly stressful, especially when the norms of such new partnerships are emergent.

Indeed, as school and university educators attempt fundamental change, the prevailing pattern of rules, roles, and relationships inside each organization is being challenged. If such changes are institutionalized beyond the current experimental stages, the cultures of both will be altered to include more perspectives. In a PDS, this direction means that parents, students, universities, businesses, social agencies, and other outside groups will become more influential members of the school community.

The sources of pressure to change are internal and external to both Fairdale and the university. Inside each, while tensions develop around the pace and scope of change, new ideas also encourage others to be inventive. While there are resisters in both places, there is also support, particularly in the form of permission to experiment, from upper administrative levels. But uniformly, those most involved in the work of reform put in many long days, and uniformly they say they need more human and fiscal resources.

Outside groups have also influenced the directions the school and university are headed. In the case of Fairdale, both the locally invented PDS standards document and the Coalition's nine principles have provided direction and useful frames for reflection. At the university, the Holmes Group has provided visibility and additional leverage to connect teacher education with school restructuring more systematically. Other outside pressures will come to bear in the near future as the performance-based accountability stance of the Kentucky Education Reform Act of 1990 begins to affect curriculum and assessment of both high school students and prospective teachers.

At the same time, while externally developed frames are affecting the content of the changes, what both Fairdale and the Department of Secondary Education are inventing will be unique. This approach to reform can take local context into account and build ownership and commitment. It is also less risky than attempting to put an externally developed innovation into place. The adoption of externally developed programs often brings visibility and flexible resources that enhance participants' loyalties to the specific program. The risk is that these loyalties increase the likelihood that goal displacement will occur. In other words, that the goal—for some—might become implementing "the program" rather than viewing the ideas in the innovation as strategies to use, alter, and discard as necessary in the process of reinventing schooling and teacher education. Organizing change around principles or beliefs, such as those developed by the Coalition, the local PDS effort and the Holmes Group, provides the needed flexibility for local invention.

If teacher education continues to become more connected with school restructuring, other issues are likely to arise. An obvious practical issue concerns the many types of accountability described by Darling-Hammond and Snyder (1992). Since both school restructuring and teacher education reform are emerging and iterative rather than linearly planned responses, overall structures, including those affecting governance and performance standards are not "nailed down." Who will control what? For example, can the looser, consensus-driven style of school decision making of the type practiced at Fairdale blend with the more parliamentary style of universities? And, what role will new state and national performance standards for students, schools, teachers, teacher educators, and prospective teachers play?

A second issue is about time and other resources. Any dramatic change in funding policy is unlikely. That means more attention is needed on how to reallocate and redefine roles so that the additional work that restructuring brings can be handled within a reasonably long workday and shrinking budgets. It remains to be seen if the extra work is a necessary but temporary condition of change, or if resources eventually will be reallocated to sustain redefined roles.

A third issue concerns different types of expertise and knowledge. The university's claims to expertise are based largely on norms of disciplined ways of knowing such as knowledge of theory and research gained through scholarship. A good part of the expertise of those in schools is based on custom, tradition, and daily practice inside particular school cultures. Unlike university scholarship, much experienced-based knowledge is tacit and not easily articulated. Because of the isolation of teachers from one another, much of that knowledge also remains privately held rather than publicly debated. The status and prestige of those in universities relative to those in schools reinforce the view that publicly-held, "university" knowledge is superior to or better than school-based knowledge.

These conditions work against the best intentions of those who see collaboration within a PDS as a means of improving the education of teachers and public school students. Moving teacher education into a restructuring school does not guarantee collaboration or collegiality among teachers and teacher educators. Transplanting university courses to a restructuring school does not guarantee that teacher education or schooling will be transformed. In the short run, working in the same context increases the likelihood that connections can be made, resources and roles might be altered, and education occur in ever improving ways.

At the same time, if collaboration among teachers and teacher educators becomes more normative, debates about "best" practice are likely to increase. In such debates, attention must be given to capturing experience-based knowledge in ways that can be shared. Teacher-conducted action research is a promising strategy. Teaming is another way tacit, privately held knowledge can be made public so it can be reflected upon (Whitford & Kyle, 1992). In the meantime, however, university partners in collaborative ventures must be sensitive to the elitism in their claims to expertise or run the risk of limiting the appeal of much of their expertise to those in schools.

If the partners in school-university collaboration are to pursue a particular policy direction, such as linking teacher education with school restructuring as happens in a PDS, then as Whitford and Gaus (1988) have argued, they must come to see the relationship as a process of identifying problems and creating solutions through *interaction*. This perspective is not typical of school-university relations, partly because of the differences in claims to expertise. We are all familiar with accusations of "ivory tower idealism" and "trenches expediency" in the "ready, fire, aim" culture of schools and the "ready, ready, ready . . ." culture of universities.

These differences sometimes lead the university to an *interventionist* stance where experts bring solutions developed from outside research to a school in order to improve practice. From the perspective of many in schools, such an approach is often perceived as *interference*.

The issue is about more than who is right or who has better solutions. It is also about the basis of the judgment and how those in schools and universities interact as people. Given choices among intervention, interference, and interaction, only the last allows partners in a collaboration to treat each other as colleagues of equal status. Achieving such a relationship requires permission; that is, the authority to participate in making decisions affecting ones work, as is the case with Fairdale's steering committee. And, since collegiality also challenges long-standing patterns of school-university relations—those interconnected patterns of rules, roles and relationships—persistence is also required in order to work through the many ripple effects attempts at change create. But, at the core, such change is dependent on believing that the knowledge and expertise of those in schools and those in universities are both vital to solving educational problems.

NOTE

[1]This chapter was commissioned by the National Center for Restructuring Education, Schools, and Teaching (NCREST). It was initially presented at the annual meeting of the American Educational Research Association in San Francisco on April 22, 1992. A revised version of the case containing more detailed information about Fairdale's restructuring is forthcoming from NCREST. This research draws on both qualitative and quantitative data collected by two research teams I led with Ric Hovda (1984–87) and Gordon Ruscoe (1988–92). Oth er team members were Linda Shelor, Donna Gaus, Mary Esselman,Wynn Egginton, Kathleen Peixotto, Luis Canalas, Samantha Israel, and Donnie Lee.

A significant source of data is my own direct participation in most of what is described here. For example, as a professor in the Secondary Education Department, I worked with the Gheens Academy on the design of the PDS planning sessions and on the Steering Committee that shaped the initial 3 years of the Center for the Collaborative Advancement of the Teaching Profession.

Because I have lived so much of this case, I asked 19 local educators to review the initial draft for accuracy of the information included and logic of the interpretations offered. Of the 17 readers who responded, 14 reported that they found no inaccuracies and believed the analysis to be fair to those involved. Three readers pointed out data inadequacies and called for additional and more specific information, particularly about Fairdale and University of Louisville students.

Student data are certainly critical to judging the quality of educational reform, locally and elsewhere. As with other chapter-length treatments, this one presents only one slice of the complexity involved in systemic change. It is more about the wide range of events shaping the context of local educational reform than about how that context affects classrooms and students. Fortunately, other researchers, including some who critiqued this study, are focusing on other important aspects of the local reform efforts.

Three university readers offered several interpretations that differ significantly from those developed in the initial draft. Some of these have been added here in the appropriate sections as additional data. However, I doubt that each critic will be satisfied, and the story I tell remains largely my own.

REFERENCES

Darling-Hammond, L., & Snyder, J. (1992). Framing accountability: Creating learner-centered schools. In A. Lieberman (Ed.), *The changing contexts of teach-*

ing, 91st Yearbook of the National Society for the Study of Education, Chicago: University of Chicago Press, 11–36.

Fairdale High School. (1988). *An Essential School where success is no longer a secret.* School booklet.

Fischetti, J. C. (Session Organizer) (February, 1990). Of swimming lessons and deep water: The positive and negative tension between content coverage and student needs in intense post-baccalaureate programs. A paper presented at the annual meeting of the American Association of Colleges for Teacher Education, Chicago.

Fischetti, J. C., & Dittmer, A. E. (1992). Using an alternative certification program to develop school/university collaboration. Unpublished manuscript. University of Louisville.

Kyle, R. M. J. (1988). *Innovation in education.* A progress report on the JCPS/Gheens Professional Development Academy. Louisville, KY: The Gheens Foundation.

Kyle, D. W., Dittmer, A. E., Fischetti, J. C., & Portes, P. (1992). *Aligning the Kentucky Teacher Internship Program with the Kentucky Education Reform Act.* A report to the Kentucky Department of Education. Louisville, KY: University of Louisville.

Schlechty, P. C., Ingwerson, D. W., & Brooks, T. I. (1988). Inventing Professional Development Schools. Louisville, KY: JCPS/Gheens Professional Development Academy. Manuscript later published in *Educational Leadership, 46*(3), 28–31.

Sizer, T. R. (1992). *Horace's school: Redesigning the American high school.* New York: Houghton Mifflin.

Whitford, B. L., & Gaus, D. M. (November, 1988). Collaboration for action and inquiry: Some effects of an ethnographic stance. Paper presented at the annual meeting of the American Educational Studies Association, Toronto.

Whitford, B. L., Hovda, R. A., & Shelor, L. G. (December, 1987). *Progress report on goal 1.1: Establish Professional Development Schools, benchmarks 2.1-2.4 to the Kentucky Council on Higher Education,* University of Louisville: Center for the Collaborative Advancement of the Teaching Profession.

Whitford, B. L., Hovda, R. A., & Shelor, L. G. (March, 1988). *Using research knowledge to improve teacher education: Training principals to become teacher educators.* Progress report no. 3 on OERI contract no. 400-85-1058, U.S. Department of Education. Louisville, KY: University of Louisville.

Whitford, B. L., & Kyle, D. W. (1992). Interdisciplinary teaming as staff development: Initiating change in a middle school. In W. T. Pink & A. A. Hyde (Eds.), *Effective staff development for school change.* Norwood, NJ: Ablex, 111–138.

Chapter 5

PERILS AND POTENTIALS: A TALE OF TWO PROFESSIONAL DEVELOPMENT SCHOOLS

Jon Snyder

In the Spring of 1988, Teachers College, of Columbia University; two schools within New York City's Community School District Three (Public School 87 and Intermediate School 44); and the United Federation of Teachers agreed to pursue funding from the Ford Foundation to plan a Professional Development School (PDS). By the following January, the collaborators began meeting with an established planning committee consisting of school, district, union, and college representatives. The basic thrust of their work was to improve the professional education of teachers with an initial emphasis on creating new and improved school-based experiences for preservice teachers. The goals were to alter: (1) the nature of preservice teachers' experiences, (2) the induction of beginning teachers into the profession, (3) the ongoing professional development of school and college educators, (4) the relationship of college and school based work, and (5) the caliber and use of educational research. The PDS was to be collaboratively developed and involve all members of the educational community in the continuing education of teachers. The planning committee stated, "The plan will be built using the experience and knowledge of teachers and the experience and knowledge of professors of education. A partnership between these two groups of educators is the foundation of our work" (Snyder, 1992). The remainder of this chapter provides an overview of the struggles and successes of the two PDS models that resulted from this collaboration.[1] Chapter 6 provides an in-depth look at one particular component of the model that emerged at I.S. 44.

PROJECT DESCRIPTION

Despite differences of opinion and perspectives, the need to "feel one another out," and some open distrust of the project at the schools, by June of 1989, a year after initial agreement to work together, the group had begun designing two models for preservice teacher preparation—a P.S. 87/TC PDS for students preparing to teach in elementary schools and an I.S. 44/TC PDS in the secondary subject matter areas of math, science, art, English, and social studies. Both models were 2-year graduate programs with the 1st year consisting of 2 semesters of student teaching along with the existing academic work. The most noticeable changes from the previous non-PDS program were that: (1) secondary school subject matter teacher education programs would be doubling student teaching time (previously, only the elementary program required 2 semesters of student teaching); and (2) cooperating teachers from the schools would be taking a more active role in designing and delivering the college coursework, especially in the seminars that accompany student teaching. For instance, in the new elementary plan, student teaching and the concomitant seminar would constitute 40% of the required academic credits for a master's degree. The student teaching experience would consist of 2 semesters at the school site in two different classrooms at two different grade levels. Also during the 1st year, cooperating teachers would be required to take an existing Teachers College course in supervision. The course would be cotaught by a TC faculty member and a teacher from each of the two schools and be held at the school site.

At the conclusion of the 1st year, the student teachers would be eligible for certification but would not receive their master's degrees. In the 2nd year of the program, they would be teacher-interns. In the elementary model the teacher-intern would be working with two teachers in a team teaching arrangement, all three working with two "classes" in a variety of innovative grouping modes. In the intermediate school model, the intern would have one teacher as a mentor but would observe and participate in a number of other classes within his or her discipline. Near the conclusion of the intern experience, the teacher interns would assume full teaching responsibilities for a 6-week period during which their mentor teacher would be freed for self-designed professional development activities. In both schools, seminars for the teacher interns were to be organized and run by school faculty. These would be credit-bearing "courses" taught by a mentor teacher with adjunct status at the college. In addition, the plans called for school teachers to team with college teachers in presenting the seminar accompanying student teaching.

In the 3rd year of the program, the interns would become full-fledged teachers in other District Three schools. Here, they would be mentored by the teachers with whom they were paired for their intern year. In its entirety, the 3-year teacher education process incorporated the following ideas about what beginning teachers need to experience in order to teach more effectively:

- more extended time in classrooms with intense supervision and guided reflection;
- opportunities to observe and work with more than one group of students;
- opportunities to observe and work with more than one approach to teaching;
- team teaching;
- professional collaboration;
- and improved linkages between college and school experiences.

SITE CONTEXTS

Three different school sites and cultures came together to plan and implement this PDS project: Teachers College, P.S. 87 Elementary School, and I.S. 44 Middle School. To understand the successes of the effort, the barriers it faced, and the factors that allowed barriers to be overcome, requires an introduction to each of them.

THE COLLEGE

Teachers College (TC) is located in the Morningside Heights area of Manhattan in New York City. The Heights, which travel brochures call "The Acropolis of the New World," is home to Columbia University and its related schools: Barnard College, Union Theological Seminary, Manhattan School of Music, Jewish Theological Seminary of America, and Teachers College. TC is bordered on three sides by institutions of higher learning and housing for its students and professors. On the fourth is the steep precipice dividing Morningside Heights from Harlem.

Three TC contextual themes significantly affected the process and ultimate outcomes of the project: mixed perceptions of status, TC's poor reputation with schools, and organization of teacher education programs. Within the world educational community, TC is a high status institution. Students from all over the world flock to what Time Magazine once labeled the "Mecca of progressive education." This status was not lost on the school people involved. An I.S. 44 participant remarked:

> Coming in, I thought "TC knows how to get things done. If TC is going to invest all this time and energy into the project, they will get the money." We'll play this game of going around and asking for it, but in the end, TC will find the money. After all, they were TC. It's like kids raising money for a field trip. They get what they can and then the adults make sure it happens.

The initial perception was that TC teacher educators had greater power, and the institution had greater willingness, to support the project than they actually did. When TC could or would not live up to the perception, its support of the project was questioned and it was accused of undermining the group's efforts, leaving a residue of bitterness: "In terms of making something happen, I thought TC could do it, but they can't."

The second contextual theme was TC's poor reputation with New York City public schools. School people around the city often referred to TC as "the relic on the hill" and "the dinosaur." One TC participant noted, "TC's got a bad history in this city. And anybody who denies that is playing ostrich. . . . We are not, in most people's view, 'of this city.'"

The third contextual theme revolved around the organization of teacher education programs in different departments within the college. Elementary teacher education is housed in a single program in a single department. As the former chairperson of that department noted, "Teacher education has been seen as central to this department and the program has been seen as central . . . to our mission." But secondary teacher education is housed in a variety of departments and programs based on subject matter. Thus, there are secondary teacher education programs in art, music, English, math, science, and social studies.

Unlike the elementary program, teacher education, especially preservice teacher education, has not been seen as central to the mission of discipline based secondary programs. Until very recently, students in some secondary programs were "Forced to go out and find their own placements" and were not provided any college supervision. In describing the director of one of the secondary programs, a secondary teacher educator said, "He'll tell you. We are not about creating a preservice program. . . . He has no interest in supervision. He puts the kids out there into a school and they never get seen by anybody at Teachers College." In general, "Teacher education has been seen as sort of something you have to do on the side." Secondary programs, "were staffed with subject matter people and they were the people who got tenure and the teacher education people were adjuncts." Additionally, even in pockets of commitment, the emphasis of the secondary programs was on high schools. Therefore, the selection of a middle school as a PDS site also proved a barrier to participation for those programs.

Not surprisingly, most secondary programs were not interested in entering the PDS project. An influential discipline based educator at TC publicly commented, "The issue is this is not my priority in life. . . . I just don't think we should get involved. . . . We would have to restructure how I do what I do."

THE SCHOOLS

Both P.S. 87 and I.S. 44 are located in Manhattan's gentrifying Upper West Side where spacious, luxuriously renovated Brownstones nestle near dilapidated, crowded, and crumbling tenement houses. Small neighborhood shops and a once sizable Hispanic community have been "pushed uptown" by ice cream parlors, restaurants, boutiques, and the forty-one women's apparel shops in the ten blocks immediately south of the schools. The PDS Committee said of the neighborhood:

> Slums and ghettoized housing projects exist within a few short blocks of some of the most expensive real estate in America. This economic and racial diversity is a source of both concern and pride to its residents, many of whom, rich and poor, share the fact that their parents or grandparents were born in another country. Theirs is a complex interaction for which the term "melting pot" is much too simple. Suffice it to say that life on the Upper West Side is never easy and never dull. (Snyder, 1992)

P.S. 87.   Constructed egg crate style in 1954, P.S. 87 serves approximately 1,100 students in kindergarten through fifth grades with a professional faculty of 58 teachers. The school's distinctly progressive educational vision is captured by a poster outside the principal's office. It is a picture of the "P.S. 87 Pizza" divided equally into key ingredients of: (1) integrated curriculum, (2) diversity valued, (3) heterogeneous grouping, (4) respect for feelings, (5) active learning, and (6) academic excellence. With few exceptions, the staff agrees with these principles and strives to achieve them.

Their success in doing so is partially validated by the 400 students on the waiting list for the 1989–90 school year. Coupled with the baby boomlet of the neighborhood's new inhabitants, these "choice" students have significantly raised the enrollment. The school was bursting at the seams. Aside from the effects of what one administrator called "chaotically cramming kids into cubbies and scheduling nightmares," the size of the school affected the project in that there was no room at the P.S. 87 inn for the project coordinator. His physical location at TC exacerbated the issue of just whose project this was while hindering communication with the school site.

While neither lily white nor universally wealthy, the student population at P.S. 87 is decidedly whiter and wealthier than other schools in the district. As of 1990, 40% of P.S. 87 students qualified for free or reduced lunch while 82% of the students across the street at I.S. 44 qualified. Table 6.1 compares the ethnic population of the two schools.

Table 6.1. Student Ethnicity by School

Ethnic Group	P.S. 87 (%)	I.S. 44 (%)
European-American	48	16
Latino-American	23	39
African-American	22	42
Asian-American	7	3

The PDS Project presented the positive aspects of this heterogeneity: "A partnership with these schools is a partnership with schools which represent urban schools as they can be: schools where children from many races and cultures and from families with varying amounts of money learn to live and work together" (Snyder, 1992). At the same time, however, P.S. 87's clientele and reputation for excellence were a mixed blessing. Jealousy of the school within the district fueled the flame of the elitist argument leveled against TC. Additionally, other schools in the city, and some potential funders, found it puzzling because P.S. 87 was neither in need of fixing nor representative of a "real city school."

The school's excellent reputation was in no small measure attributable to its principal who personally tacked advertisements for the school around the neighborhood, actively recruited families of color into the school, made visits to daycare centers, and instituted the weekly parent tours. She found "loopholes" in the hiring system to hand-pick teachers, relegated several tenured teachers to "fill-in" status, and saw to it that parents and the press remained actively informed and engaged in school activities. She stamped the school with progressivism because she believes, "There is no subject matter that is as critical as the well being of the individual child." She was also highly supportive of the project, so much so that one TC participant commented, "She sees the PDS as her legacy to P.S. 87."

The 1st year of the project was the principal's 9th at P.S. 87 and in that time, she had "welded a team together." She makes no bones about her dominant style, laughing heartily, "I like to have a large hand in shaping anything that I care about."

The centrality of the principal's leadership affected the functioning of the PDS Project in at least four ways. First, P.S. 87 had an established, long running, and well-functioning program for its students. This freed the school and its committee members to think about—and share their considerable expertise concerning—the larger issues of teacher education and professionalism. Second, she had recruited strong teachers who were encouraged to grow professionally and to speak out. Noted one teacher:

> We're used to running our mouths at P.S. 87 and being heard a lot. And
> being valued. . . . I will say this for her, no matter what her final decision
> is about an issue, there is a lot of staff input. . . . And maybe that's the
> thing that makes the difference. I don't find us to be an especially threat-
> ened bunch. . . . We're not used to being talked down to.

Third, the principal actively exerted leadership to maintain the
school's commitment to the project. She had a strong hand in helping the
informal teacher leaders of the school volunteer for the committee and
kept important elements of the school informed and involved. Finally, her
voice on the committee itself was a powerful one, partially because she
was not afraid to say what she felt needed to be said: "I think part of my
role—at least I take on the role—is to verbalize what maybe other people
are too frightened or too tactful to say. . . . Maybe because I just feel
someone's got to say it and it might as well be me."

In summary, P.S. 87 entered the PDS project with an excellent reputation. It was headed by a strong central leader who had put together "her
team." Key "unassailable teacher leaders" on that team were enlisted very
early in the project to support its efforts. Finally, the staff had a high sense
of self and school esteem, power, and intensity.

I.S. 44.   I.S. 44, also housed in a egg crate school building, serves approximately 950 students in grades 6 through 9 with 83 professional staff members. Among the significant contextual issues at I.S. 44 were: (1) the middle school theme, (2) administrative structure, (3) internal dissension, and
distrust of outsiders. At least initially, these issues proved problematical
for the PDS project.

The middle school theme has two components: the effects of discipline
driven organization and the perceived nature of the teaching force. The
traditional Balkanization of education into disciplines in middle schools
resulted in the same departmentalization, communication, and fragmentation issues that affected the secondary programs at TC.

At least initially, the nature of the middle school teaching force was
viewed with skepticism:

> There's a different mentality in elementary school than there is in junior
> high school. I think the best teachers are elementary school teachers. They
> are interested in learning and they are interested in teaching and they view
> themselves as teachers of children. Once you get to junior high school, I
> think people view themselves as sort of like high school teachers. High
> school teachers wish they were college teachers and college teachers
> know nothing at all about teaching or at least don't use whatever they
> know about teaching if they do. They are the worst. . . . People here

view themselves as teachers of subjects, not teachers of children. [I.S. 44] Junior high teachers are the teachers in this system who feel the worst of all teachers. Most of them really want to be in high school. . . . Also, [they are] very concerned that somebody is going to do something to them that's bad. . . . Middle school teachers are the step child of the education system. [UFT representative]

The second contextual factor affecting the PDS project was that I.S. 44 itself had broken into three distinctive mini-schools the year immediately preceding the initiation of the PDS project. In addition, it housed two "alternative programs" with semi-autonomous status in relation to I.S. 44 proper. There were, in effect, five "new" schools within the physical plant. In short, the PDS project entered a school in the very early struggles of a major restructuring effort—an effort designed to bring about many of the same goals to which the PDS aspired. However, the need for, as well as the trauma of, change created a problematic environment for introducing a PDS.

The third contextual factor affecting the project was internal dissension and distrust of outsiders. As the PDS coordinator observed, "There was traditional animosity at I.S. 44." At the beginning of the project, internal distrust and dissension were key components of the relationships, values, and expectations of the school culture. Some participants felt the history of tension and lack of respect had led the school to automatically assume malevolence. Said one P.S. 87 participant, "I.S. 44 is suspicious of everything." Internally they described themselves as possessing, "wariness of outsiders from past negative experiences—university people with no classroom experience, programs that don't work, people telling us what to do." Another participating teacher commented: "Someone is always trying to pull a fast one and we don't find out until we get involved."

The "assumption of malevolence" and distrust affected the school, the other participants' view of I.S. 44, and the project itself. One of the ramifications at the school level was the presence of internal factions. Said one teacher leader of another, "He's stupid, deliberately obtuse . . . you can't trust what he says. . . . The last person he talks to is his opinion." Said another, "There are people who have been around for . . . 25 years who have absolutely no interest in examining what they do. And they have been doing it the same way for 22 years anyway. And that will never change."

One of the effects bickering had on internal teacher relations was a felt need to "keep an eye on one's back." Said one teacher, "You know, everybody is watching his own back and no one is looking out for the student and no one is looking out for the rest of the staff." Related to this was concern that someone else was "getting something I'm not." The same teacher quoted above commented, "Everybody is jealous of somebody else's power. And that's what I see more than anything else." This type of attitude reinforced stereotypes about New York City public school teachers. An I.S. 44 participant commented, "New York City teachers don't want to do much of anything. There is a lot of burn-out in New York City. The system reinforces it. There is not really much you can do." The PDS coordinator described the typical New York City teacher as someone who, "In some fundamental way, that he doesn't quite understand, is both ashamed of himself and angry, and depressed. . . . There's a certain resentfulness that's oozing out of this typical figure."

PROJECT IMPLEMENTATION

To the amazement of even some of its most ardent supporters, by the end of its 3rd year, both PDS models had evolved in synch with their original plans. As originally designed in both models, all prospective teachers had 2 semesters of student teaching. In the elementary model, groups of two student teachers were placed in existing teams creating seven, four-person teaching teams. During the 2nd year, three of the teaching teams also had an intern—a credentialed 1st year teacher with 4 days of teaching responsibilities and 1 day for structured reflection and completion of college Master's Degree requirements. Near the end of the experience, the interns assumed full teaching responsibility for 3 weeks rather than for 6 weeks as originally planned.

At the middle school, student teachers were placed in one of three configurations: the traditional one student teacher–one cooperating teacher format; two student teachers with one cooperating teacher; and one student teacher with two cooperating teachers. During the 2nd year of the program, the middle school had one credentialed 1st year teaching intern, but also emphasized a modified "1 year internship." This consisted of student teaching in the school for the entire public school year. When the college was in session, the five 1-year interns spent from 15–30 hours a week in the school. When the college was not in session, they spent all day everyday in the school.

Cooperating teachers attended the cotaught supervision class held at the school and received district staff development money for planning both their teaming experiences and their work with student teachers. During the 2nd year, teachers cotaught TC seminars and mentored interns. The four teachers who had interns utilized the 3 weeks when the intern assumed full classroom responsibilities for self-designed professional development such as action research, library research, and curriculum development.

In addition, both school sites made highly successful additions to the original plans. At P.S. 87, one significant addition was a pre-student teaching workshop, designed and taught by school educators, for the 20+ TC student teachers at the school. Another addition was a school-university "faculty switch." A TC professor was released from one of her courses to spend time at the school while two teachers from P.S. 87 became adjunct instructors for a team-taught course at TC. The most significant addition to the plans at I.S. 44 was the intersection of the school's movement towards interdisciplinary team teaching with one TC participant's desire for an intensive school site experience for multidisciplinary teams of student teachers. The product of this intersection of interests was the "January Experience" (see chapter 6). Each day for the entire month of January, 1991, multidisciplinary teams of student teachers worked with multidisciplinary teams of teachers to plan and implement a cross-cutting curricular theme. This month-long experience in interdisciplinary, team-taught education involved 17 I.S. 44 teachers, 14 student teachers, 4 school administrators, 1 TC faculty member, and nearly 300 junior high school students (Snyder and Schwartz, 1991).

PROJECT OUTCOMES

Both the elementary and middle school models wrought changes in the major PDS agenda areas. Preservice education was changed by increasing student teaching time and credits received, increasing the role of school-based educators in the academic offerings at TC, and holding course work at the schools. Fundamentally, each of these changes improved linkages between school and college, and thus, increased connections between theory and practice for all project participants.

The induction of beginning teachers was changed by the internship for 1st-year teachers complete with individual mentoring and on-site seminars for collaborative discussion of common problems. The internship provided a guided entry for inexperienced teachers with the requisite professional and emotional support for interns to grow into their potential by building on their strengths.

The professional growth of experienced teachers was changed by creating formats for collaboration, such as teaching teams at P.S. 87, interdisciplinary team teaching at I.S. 44, and school-college teaching teams. These PDS-spawned collaborations led to new forms of reflection on practice (e.g., formal and informal research opportunities) as well as curriculum development. *All* collaborating educators, no matter their depth of experience or whether school or university based, reported creating totally new curriculum units—some for the first time in years. In addition, the PDS offered experienced teachers new and altered roles and responsibilities, such as teaching college courses and mentoring interns.

The professional growth of college-based educators was also changed by the new collaborative formats. These formats increased the amount of time professors spent in schools, created better working relationships between college and school educators, and enhanced the college educators' understanding of the language and value of practitioner wisdom.

Finally, the nature of research began to show signs of changes. At I.S. 44, for instance, one teacher completed an action research investigation comparing hands-on and rote learning while another teacher worked with TC personnel to document the January Experience (see chapter 6). At the elementary school, two teachers wrote a history of the PDS project from a teacher's perspective, and another did library research on cooperative learning and teaching.

OVERCOMING BARRIERS

The road to the positive outcomes of the project was not altogether smooth. This section will discuss three of the more thorny, overarching problems that initially inhibited the collaboration: conflicting fundamental interests, intra-institutional issues, and who is improving whom. The adjustments and strategies that were used to traverse the perilous terrain of change will also be discussed.

CONFLICTING FUNDAMENTAL INTERESTS

The participants in the collaboration had different responsibilities, interests, and perspectives arising from their roles in the educational enterprise. These differences meant they had overlapping, but still separate, fundamental interests that, across the board, were both altruistic and essential to schools. Differing fundamental interests were related to different identifications of the problem and different notions of who and what should change to make things better.

College Educators. The fundamental interests of TC college educators were their students, that is, their student teachers, and the generation of knowledge and theory. In the words of TC participants,

> The student teachers are the primary benefactors. . . . They are the reason we're all doing this. . . . In our initial debate . . . some people felt that the primary benefactor had to be the kids in the classroom. And I feel the primary benefactors have to be the student teachers. . . . If this

becomes too overbearing or conflictual for the student teacher, it's not worth doing.

The scholarly enterprise for professors of education at the moment, is in the most fundamental ways, to determine the conceptualization of the field. That is, the world views, the philosophies, the ethics, the words that we use to describe it.

TC's image of the professional teacher, arising from its fundamental interests, revolved around career-long education. A professional teacher was one who learned from teaching: "The emphasis should be on learning from teaching rather than learning how to teach" (Zumwalt, 1988, p. 170). Since preservice teacher education can only be an introduction to this career-long process of learning from teaching, what needed to change were the schools and their support for continued professional growth. Said one TC participant, "What we're really asking for is the district to assume some responsibility for the induction [and development] of teachers."

School Educators—Teachers. The fundamental interest of the teachers in the project was their students, the children: "I'm in it for the kids. . . . When you talk about the professionalization of teachers . . . you talk about kids. Because the profession of teaching is the business of teaching children, not teaching walls or something." With a fundamental interest in "kids," a professional is one who has learned "how to teach" them. Thus a PDS should teach how to teach better: "One of the primary goals [of a PDS] is to provide a basis for new teachers in the system to equip them with the necessary skills they need to teach." While one never stops learning how to teach, one should have a pretty good notion of how to teach upon entering the classroom. Thus, it was teacher preparation, the college, that needed to change. As a teacher bluntly put it, "We want more changes in the university."

School Educators—Principals. The fundamental interest of the principals was to keep their staff "alive" and in the school. One principal commented, "It's also exciting to me as the principal of the school because . . . when you bring in new ideas that stretch people and keep people growing, then you keep your school alive and you keep your faculty there." For the principals, a key element of a teaching profession was new roles for teachers that allowed them to remain in the classroom. The role the principals had in mind was teacher preparation. Since colleges historically have been responsible for teacher education, it was the college that would have to change to provide mentoring roles and opportunities for professional growth to challenge experienced teachers, helping them grow while remaining in the classroom.

There was also a second, more concrete interest for the principals. When asked what involvement in the project would bring to his school, the middle school principal answered: "Well, it would certainly be helpful to have . . . an extra four people on my faculty."

District Administration.   Perhaps because of a role with diffuse constituencies that demands working with teachers from hiring to retiring, the district representative, more than any other participant, consistently articulated a broader set of interests. For instance, she felt the purpose of a PDS was:

> To train student teachers and expose them to . . . master teachers. . . . Secondly, that the staff of master teachers would be able to share what they have, not only theoretically, but practically to . . . students in the university as adjunct professors. . . . That is a wonderful way for those teachers . . . to stretch . . . a great opportunity for them. And finally, knowing that teachers do drop out of teaching and fail the first year, I thought having that internship year . . . was ingenious.

Because the district was held accountable primarily for student outcomes, their definition of a professional teacher was one who improved results. To attain this required both better prepared beginning teachers and the continuous development of experienced teachers. Once again it was the college that would have to change to improve teacher preparation and to provide new growth opportunities for experienced teachers.

Union.   The fundamental interest of the union was teachers as a collective group, not the success of these programs in two schools or of several interns. While there are internal conflicts within the union regarding how best to meet the needs of teachers as a collective, the bottom line for the union bargaining staff, as stated to the group by the coordinator of negotiations, was money. A professional was one who made a professional salary, thus enhancing recruitment and retention:

> Teaching will be a profession only when the regular teaching salary structure raises.

> Our competition is at entry level salaries. . . . The reason there is an impending teacher shortage is the abysmal salary. . . . There is currently a long ramp to professional pay. We should all be advocates of better pay because that is what is going to help recruitment and retention to the profession—not working conditions. . . . Economic competition is the basis of my efforts. It is economics that pulls people into careers.

clearly they were learning, understanding, and acquiring knowledge. That so many youngsters viewed their classroom project activities as fun, rather than work, attests to the imaginative planning of the teaching teams, for perhaps youngsters learn best when they are not aware that they are being taught. They said that "It was a fun project, we were never doing the same thing every day," and "It was fun . . . and hard too." In agreement, others wrote, "I really enjoyed it . . . why? . . . because now I will know all the information that I need to know when I am bigger," and "The project was fun and so were the teachers"; "it was so much fun . . . it wasn't like plain ordinary school."

Two variations on this theme were "I feel so good that I had fun . . . and I am proud of myself for doing a good job," and "It was fun to do interesting things, and I felt as if I was in a new world for 3 weeks."

On the Downside. But not all the youngsters felt this way: it was clearly overwhelming for a few. There were mixed reviews from a few students about the project being over. For the youngsters who reported at the end feeling glad it was over, generally the theme was that they had been working very hard during the project and had found the increased expectations demanding. Responding to how they felt about it being over, these children wrote: "Glad so that I don't have to be going to the library all the time"; "Glad because now we can relax a little more"; and "It was so much fun, but so much confusion." One child explained "It's not that I don't want to learn, it was just too much." Another made it even more explicit, "I liked the student teachers we worked with, and the topic, but some work was brain tiring."

On Working in Groups. One experience common to all the youngsters in the program was a new classroom organization and an emphasis on cooperative learning. Even though some chidren were used to perhaps one of their subject classrooms being organized cooperatively, this became the norm in January. Moreover, the preponderance of project work meant that they collaborated as a group on one piece of work over several days, and this also was unusual. As with the individual attention theme, feelings of students and teachers coincided about the advantages of working in groups. Slavin (1989) wrote "cooperative learning makes life more pleasant for teachers as well as for students. Students love to work together and their enthusiasm makes teaching more fun" (pg. 3), and this was how most of the youngsters felt. They wrote: "I liked working in groups . . . together as a team"; "The classes were fun because you worked in groups"; and "I liked it because I learned with my friend. . . . my group helped me a lot."

Working in groups is a natural way of functioning. Students were allowed to talk, a basic need in itself. It allowed them to get to know each other better, especially when the composition of the group was varied, because ordinarily youngsters, like adults, tend to stay within their cliques. Cooperative learning groups made it almost impossible during January for any child to get educationally lost as they do, not uncommonly, in traditional classroom organization. Clearly, along with appreciating the extra help from the adults—the teacher team—the youngsters responded well to working alongside each other. The children told us that collaboration and cooperation felt good to them too in this context that is traditionally fueled by competition.

On the Student Teachers. The children knew, of course, that the extra teachers were student teachers and would be there just for the January Experience. Since they seemed to function like teachers in general as far as they themselves were concerned, most drew no distinction between them and other teachers. Earlier their appreciation of getting help was discussed, but it was more than that. Everyone seemed to get to know each other immediately and they genuinely liked the student teachers, in addition to respecting them. Teachers know that it is impossible to fool kids. They like and respect someone when that someone has been involved in something of significance to them, a significance that goes well beyond the answering of an occasional question. In schools, "The caliber of the people is the most important thing you have to work with, not the procedures or handbooks or regulations or curriculum guides" (Darling-Hammond, 1988, pg. 15). For these youngsters, it was clear that the student teachers were of high caliber. It is a tribute to the student teachers, as well as to the program design, that so many established such good relationships with the youngsters in such a short time. The youngsters were unstinting in their praise in this regard: "I liked the extra teachers, it was pretty fun sometimes"; "I hope the teachers come back"; and "They all helped me with my work." Others continuing this theme wrote: "they gave you ideas"; "they were young and new and funner"; and "I will miss the student teachers."

THE CONCLUSION

We asked about the program's value, as an indication from the childen's point of view if they recognized whether or not it was worth repeating. Their comments yielded a positive consensus, in such summaries as: "it was the best project I ever had"; and "It was the best project of the year." One hoped that "we do something like this again," whereas another shared "I liked it, but things don't last forever." One youngster may have summed it all up with her grandiloquent "Thank you."

The essence of the union's definition of a profession was money and the status it brings in this society. Thus, schools, the district, and the college all had to change so that resources and status were reallocated to school teachers.

Conflict Resolution.   The differences delineated above often led to conflicts. Principals wanted special status for their teachers and interns that involved differentiated staffing and salary patterns. The union would have nothing to do with it: "We have no interest in cheapening the profession and that is what you are asking us to do. . . . You cannot raise the profession of teaching by arguing that practitioners of teaching should be paid less at any level." When the principals were looking out for their schools and salivating at what they could do with the extra teachers, a TC participant responded, "For you the PDS is a school. For me, it is an idea with visiting rights."

TC had a fundamental interest in building theory: "A scholarly point of view . . . may necessitate . . . for a while we forget the empirical data . . . the children, the classroom, the 50-minute period. What we are really trying to do is to theorize." Teachers, whose professional lives may currently be bound by, and whose fundamental interest in even participating in the project, was "the children, the classroom, the 50-minute period," were not particularly pleased to hear that they may "need to be forgotten for a while." Conversely, TC personnel were not pleased when the needs of their students were subjugated to the needs of children. For instance, some teachers, because of a fundamental interest in their students, saw student teachers less as learners in need of time and support than as helping hands in the classroom. Of greater concern to TC was the fact that, on occasion, student teachers were placed in dysfunctional classrooms because the teacher needed help.

In short, all the participants had a difficult time transcending their historical roles, responsibilities, and perspectives. Wrote one TC participant:

> It was exceedingly difficult for everyone to give up representing the traditional interests of their own group in the conversation and to find one common, new, voice, that of the PDS. For example, for a TC secondary science person, the primary interest was in finding classrooms and teachers for useful placements for science student teachers. Only when being a PDS member became a new and distinct role, a role that was not an extension of a TC professor but a completely separate role, could a different way of thinking emerge. Adopting a new role fully meant both understanding that some college ways are inappropriate to PDS ways, and a willingness to put aside one's primary stance. If not done, the process would have continued to be a jockeying for ownership, rather than a collaboration out of which could spring an entirely new idea.

"An entirely new idea" only emerged when the conflicts were allowed to surface, and the differences between everyone's interests and needs were explored. Until common underlying needs could be established through constructive conflict resolution, the committee was unable to craft and articulate a common goal. Because the group had not confronted their differences early and often, it had neither crafted nor articulated a common goal nor a common strategy to move in a mutually acceptable direction. As a teacher commented, "If we ever get anything off the ground it will be a miracle . . . everybody has such different conceptions of what we are." Second, the project had become trapped in a specific strategy rather than liberated by a common vision. The original unifying common goal of reinventing teacher education had gotten lost in specific strategies driven by competing conceptions of what was wrong and should be changed. With no common goal, strategies can become inflexible ends in themselves. Thus, when strategies meet obstacles, alternate means to circumvent the obstacles are less likely to be explored. The group tends to focus on work rather than on what works (Lieberman, 1992). In this manner, lack of a common goal inhibited creative problem solving and led to stalemates.

Midway through the 3rd year, however, the group exhibited a significant attitudinal change. The fundamental attitude changed to "let's get on with it and quit blaming everyone else." This was especially true among the school teachers:

> Whoa, hold it a minute. When I hear this many we's and they's it tells me we've set up a competitive win-lose situation. We're all the same "we" here. . . . Let's quit placing blame and start figuring out what we can do.
>   We just got tired of rehashing the same problems and complaints, so we ignored the disorganization and just went ahead on the collaborative part between us which wasn't new for us but which we got better at.

This focusing on one's own fundamental interest paradoxically reinvigorated flagging commonality. Late in the 3rd year of the project, an entire meeting of the executive committee was spent discussing a statement each member had prepared indicating immediate priorities and long range goals of the program. There was still some of the "college is not changing" attitude (e.g., "At what point do we see what's going on up there? At what point do we get involved in analyzing and restructuring TC?"). However, there was fundamental agreement. The immediate priority was to "keep the collaboration alive, no matter how limited, until the economy gets better." The long range goal continued to be "significant mentoring for 1st year teachers." The change was that "significant mentoring" no longer meant solely the initial plan for a 2-year internship. Instead, there were principles underlying "significant mentoring" that should be incorporated rather than a specific strategy. Said one teacher, "It has to focus on the collaborative element. It has its difficulties, but it has made for consideration of all sorts of essential restructuring of the school and TC." Thus, the group agreed that "Induction of new teachers is our goal," but were willing to move toward that goal in a variety of ways building upon what had been successful to that point—collaboration at P.S. 87 and the January Experience at I.S. 44.

INTRA-INSTITUTIONAL ISSUES

A PDS attempts to change behavioral and programmatic regularities (Sarason, 1982) in numerous educational institutions. In so doing, it will come up against the inertia of the status quo that inhibits any movement in directions away from "what is." An institution's inertia is not static, but rather a large mass moving in a particular direction. The problem for a PDS is not just to create the momentum it itself needs, but also to take on institutional constraints accelerating methodically in its path. The small mass of the PDS must pick up a good deal of velocity to avoid being sent reeling when it inevitably collides with the larger mass and velocity of the status quo.

For all participants, a major conflict in the PDS process was to change themselves and their institutions: "I think what's absolutely clear, is that . . . more than half the energy is expended with your own peers and your own institution . . . and then the rest is expended in the collaborative effort." In effect, internal clashes with the status quo prevented all the institutions involved in the project from fully "living up to their commitments." Thus, follow-through was difficult and suspicion aroused—even when initial distrust had been allayed.

Union. For the union, the clearest example of an existing position inhibiting change concerned salaries for interns. The original intention of the group was to put together a package (e.g., tuition remission, stipend, and housing at TC) close to a regular 1st year teacher's salary. When all was said and done, however, the coordinator of negotiations (CN) for the union very clearly said this was not acceptable:

> Any project must fit in with the contract and other rules and regulations the Board and the union have negotiated. . . . We have a very modest bottom line. . . . We are very open to programs such as this, provided that the working conditions and pay of participants meet the standards of the contract. That's it.

While supporting the project with words, the union's decision meant that this was now a very expensive program, which inhibited political and policy support; made it more difficult for the project to happen, even in a pilot;

and limited the notion of an internship as a step in a professional career ladder. When the CN was confronted with the idea that her position might indicate a lack of support for the PDS she angrily responded: "I am mystified by this conversation. . . . We have been committed from the start—otherwise we wouldn't have been here. If we were opposed to this plan, you wouldn't have a plan. You wouldn't have anybody in those schools."

College. TC's most inhibiting position was its reward structure. At TC, as at most research universities, publish or perish is more than a cliché, it is an oppressive reality. TC expects its professors to do research, teach, and provide service. Like most postsecondary research institutions, however, TC's professors are rewarded primarily for research, secondarily for teaching, and least of all for the service component of their roles (Soder, 1990). This inhibited the labor intensive process of collaboration:

> Instead of sitting in these meetings all day, we could be doing our research and writing, which is what we need to get the perks from our job. . . . I mean we're on the edge of collapse all the time.
>   This gets back to what we're rewarded for. You know, it's hard to write if you're in a classroom. You need the privacy of your office to write. . . . We get the biggest rewards from writing. . . . You don't do that by staying continuously in schools.

PDS-type projects are construed as service. Aside from the condescension inherent in the service notion, participants were not, therefore, particularly well rewarded for their efforts with schools. TC nominally supported the PDS Project and wanted its faculty to help develop a model PDS, yet primarily continued to reward faculty for doing other jobs. The institutional demands of the PDS on TC then, were to: expand reward structures beyond research, redefine research, define collaborative work with schools as a form of teaching, or elevate the value given to service.

Schools. For principals, the essence of the issue was an "I will remain the boss" position that conflicted with support of a program that through enriching teachers and teaching changed the nature of principal/teacher interactions. One principal spoke of the discrepancy in personal terms:

> It's one thing to say . . . I am one among equals instead of the one at the head. It's another thing to think what is my job going to be if all this happened?

As with TC participants, rewards were a major inhibitor for school participants as well. Teachers defined themselves as good teachers because they gave their all to children which meant being with children constantly. Two of the major rewards they received were the pleasure of being with children, and the ability, when in their classrooms, to be the sole adult responsible for constructing classroom reality. A PDS demanded a new role for teachers—one for which most were neither emotionally nor professionally prepared. As one teacher explained:

> I would prefer a one-on-one, having an assistant teacher. I think that it would be much easier to have a student [she paused, recognizing that the vision of the group was that an internship was not simply another year of student teaching] to have another person with one teacher rather than two. . . . I really am not all that certain I want to do this.

When reminded that one of the rewards for participating was the 6-week period for professional development opportunities, she exclaimed, "No way I'm leaving my kids for 6 weeks!"

The effects of the reward structure at I.S. 44 were notable in that concern over inequitable influence and outcomes led to a highly vocal concern about "What's in it for us?" A teacher commented: "The questions . . . the I.S. 44 faculty were having . . . related to how they were going to be compensated for this. What were they going to get out of it?"

As a result of these concerns, rewards were consciously built into the I.S. 44 plan. An entire afternoon session of the planning group was given to developing a list of "what's in it for I.S. 44." The report from that session stated:

> Because of the substantial opposition to the program we have to present up front all the inducements of the project. From the I.S. 44 perspective there are four of them: (1) reduced class load, (2) reduced class size, (3) pay for objects/materials, (4) a room set aside. (Snyder, 1992)

The core inducement seemed to be less time with fewer children. The list did not include the notion that teacher preparation and induction requires the perspective of practicing teachers. Early emphasis on rewards may have backfired:

> What's in it for them? Less time with kids. Great. [Sarcastically]. . . . It's very sad. It's like saying to a doctor, "Oh, you're going into your profession so you won't have to see patients." It's bizarre. . . . But that's how we're selling it and that's who you're going to attract. [P.S. 87]

Other participants were a bit softer in their concerns, questioning whether a professional teacher should be in the classroom all the time:

In so far that we are falling into the same trap that everybody is always falling into which is to set up a reward system . . . which consists of getting people out of the classroom, then you can only say guilty as charged. . . . I think the other response however . . . is that most people . . . ought to be out of the classroom a little more. Where is it described that everyone has to be 5 hours a day in the room with children. Or that the optimal experience for teaching is to be locked up for 5 hours a day? [Coordinator]

There was a fear that a differentiated career ladder was just another escalator out of teaching—what administration now is for people. I think that's a real dilemma. . . . I guess what I come down to is that if you really want to do the kind of things you want to do with kids, you need a little time away. [TC]

A second problematical element of the emphasis on rewards at I.S. 44 was resentment of those receiving those rewards: "Those not involved will be damn jealous of two adults in one classroom!" "People are miffed because some people are getting something the others aren't." The resentment of nonparticipating faculty towards participating faculty at I.S. 44 was publicly acknowledged in a committee discussion regarding pay for committee meeting time outside of the school day. "It would be a mistake because there are already questions about vested interests and what people's motives are." "It seems self-serving to serve on a committee and vote ourselves pay. . . . I don't want to add fuel to their fire."

When rewards were not systematically built into the project, their absence made it difficult for participants to engage as fully as they might have liked. As a result their support for the program was questioned and trust suffered. When rewards were built into the project, as they were at I.S. 44, they were perceived by some as being the "wrong" rewards, attracting the "wrong" type of participant, and creating resentment. It seemed that with reward structures, the PDS could not win for losing.

OVERCOMING THE OBSTACLES

The discrepancies between institutional rhetoric and actual support do not, by themselves, demonstrate the impossibility of a PDS. Rather, they indicate the inherent institutional difficulties in establishing one. The essence of each internal clash was that the institutions supported the project in rhetoric, but had difficulty relinquishing existing positions that legislated against the kinds of changes needed to implement the group's vision of a PDS. Institutions tended to maintain existing positions rather than inventing ones required by the new set of needs created by a PDS.

Given the size of the educational institutions involved and the interplay of educational with social and economic issues, this particular PDS project did not radically change the college, the schools, the district, or the union overnight. Nevertheless, significant inroads to organizational change were made. The indisputable first step was always an acceptance of the need, and a commitment, to change oneself and one's own institution. In short, the key change piece was to recognize that we have seen the problem and we are it. A story told by a TC participant captures her painfully poignant moment of acceptance and commitment. She had attended a lecture by a university professor who was demanding changes in the way public schools are organized. When the professor was asked if the colleges weren't perpetuating the system, his answer, according to the TC participant, was very odd.

> He said, "Don't try to change universities. . . . Universities are not going to change. Don't do it." And I thought to myself . . . he ought to be challenged on that. . . . He ought to be told, "Look, for God's sake, if you believe in your point, then don't go out of your home institution and insist that these people over there change. Get your act together and work within your own institution to make those changes and let the people in that institution work to make their business change." . . . I think he is wrong. . . . He ought to be devoting equal effort to . . . working within his own institution and dealing with the political realities, political problems, and the personal angst that that's going to cause him in his own house. And I guess that's—I guess I'm talking to myself right now too. I mean, we haven't done anything here. [sad laughter]

Every significant outcome of the project began with the personal angst of taking on one's own institution. The union representative, following the conflict over the intern's salary, alone in his office one late Friday afternoon, commented: "Teaching has changed in so many ways over the years and we're aware of that. We have to look at our structure and how we have to move on from here." The result of his soul searching was that he was instrumental in persuading the union to use its state mentoring funding to pay for the interns so that the project could continue. Rather than let calcified positions present road blocks to change, he steered a course through those road blocks and furthered the movement to better education for all students.

One of the participating elementary teachers had never been particularly keen on taking in an intern. She had regretted agreeing to the idea during the entire 2 years between when the internship was proposed and an intern arrived in her class. "I don't want to give up my kids. I enjoy teaching. That's why I do it. I don't think I can give up the thing that gives me such a buzz." Nevertheless she accepted an intern in her class. "At first it was really hard but . . . I realized that now I could get to do all the fun things with kids that I never had time for before—and I can't believe how good it makes me feel to help the intern grow." As the end of the year approached and she thought about what to do when the intern assumed full teaching responsibilities, she wondered, "I guess I could leave the classroom, but where would I go?" It turned out that she enjoyed and profited from her time away. She became so involved in writing the history of the project that she found herself "hiding out" in offices at TC to avoid phone calls from the principal requesting her presence back at the school. At the end of the experience she wrote, "The release time for professional development is one of the key reasons to team and is an integral part of the whole program."

The TC professor who participated in the faculty switch was not personally enamored of the idea. She knew there would be pressure for her to model lessons with children, which she considered demeaning to those who teach all day everyday. In addition, the "Biggest downside to this [PDS work] has been my increasing disconnectedness with my students." Nevertheless, with a sigh, she consented: "It is time for the college to come through with something besides generous talk." During her day and a half on-site, the college professor coordinated all PDS activities at the school, counseled in crisis situations (e.g., a personality clash between an intern and a mentor teacher, a troubled cooperating teacher), oversaw the planning meetings, and in general, participated in P.S. 87 school life (e.g., made candles with a fourth grade class, ate lima bean soup made by a kindergarten class). Despite painful moments, the trial switch was enough of a success that the college institutionalized the change by providing funding for the switches to continue.

THE PERILS OF COLLABORATION: WHO'S IMPROVING WHOM?

In an ideal state, the power to reinvent teaching, schooling, and teacher education is located in neither the university nor the school but in the collaborative synergy of the two (Cochran-Smith, 1991). In this ideal state, each party has knowledge and each party's knowledge is equally respected. Reality, however, reflects the tendency for individuals to think that everyone's knowledge is equal, but some is more equal—usually one's own. Collaboration activates these perceptions of power and power relationships. Since altering power and power relations may be at the heart of restructuring education (Hargreaves, 1991), it is not surprising the PDS project found them problematical. The barriers the PDS faced in this regard can be analyzed by exploring three models of educational change: the school improvement program model (SIP), the inverse school improvement program model (flip-SIP), and the PDS model (PDS).

SIP.   Historically, college participation in schools has been on a SIP model. In general, the purpose of a SIP is to "save a school." SIPs are based upon a deficit model of development (Dillon-Peterson, 1981; Griffin, 1983), and adjustments in the current system rather than the creation of a new system (Jones & Maloy, 1988). The SIP model has been the approach used by colleges to "inservice" teachers and clearly contains status elements (Lieberman & Miller, 1990). There is something "wrong" with the school/teachers, the college "experts" have the answers, and, for a price, will provide the benefits of their wisdom. In a SIP, the university owns the knowledge that counts. Thus, the perception is they both control and reap the rewards of such projects.

SIPs have been neither popular nor particularly effective with school teachers. They reflect, however, a strain that runs deep in both schools and colleges. With limited exceptions, SIP was the attitude brought by secondary teacher ed programs at TC and it was the expectation of the school people.

As a result of these SIP orientations, there was, early in the project, an oft expressed fear that TC would have more influence than the school people. There was a concern that TC would impose its will on the schools: "Will we have to follow TC's philosophy? Is a TC supervisor going to tell me that I should do thus and so?" asked one elementary teacher. The summary given by a teacher of a faculty meeting discussing participation in the project was, "This is just another case of the ivory tower coming down to tell us our business." These concerns were exacerbated by the process by which the project began: TC initiated the project and TC selected the participating schools.

It took time to overcome the trust and status issues related to the SIP approach to change, but eventually, most of the school people came to believe that the college people really did respect them, really did want to improve the college with their support. The greatest accomplishments the participants spoke of the 1st year of the project were in the areas of reducing mistrust and status differences:

> I think one thing is an incredible level of trust that has been built between teachers in the two schools and several faculty members on the project. The level of communication and trust that I now see, I hadn't even hoped for. . . . And that is just very gratifying. [They] make me feel that I have really been accepted as a colaborer. [TC]

> I was a little wary and I'm not by nature. I mean I don't assume people are out for no good. . . . But I wasn't sure what the college's role was going to be in all this. . . . But I must say I've been very pleased with the attitudes of the college personnel. I think they really listen. I think they're

open to suggestions. I like the . . . feeling . . . of everybody working
toward the same end in the same way. . . . We've become like family.
[P.S. 87]

Flip-SIP.   The inverse school improvement model, or flip-SIP, is the
notion that the school people own all the knowledge that counts and that
the college people are the ones in need of saving. In the flip-SIP approach,
the traditionally lower status group in the collaboration wishes to establish an environment where they are the high status partners. When this
occurs, the negative outcomes of the school improvement model are
inverted. The schools become arrogant, treat the college with derision,
blame the college for not doing what the schools (who now own all the
important knowledge) tell them to do, and fail to make their own needed
changes. The university becomes bitter, defensive, and fails to hear the
value in the school's wisdom.

As the school people became increasingly aware of the limitations of
power and commitment of TC, the flip-SIP factor became increasingly vir-
ulent. It was the college that was deficient, that was at the root of all evil,
and that had, basically, nothing of value to offer. Since the enabling grant
framed the project as a change in preservice teacher education, and since
teacher education historically has been a college responsibility, some
school people came to believe they were being called in to change the college. In effect, the school people seemed to feel the onus of change was on
TC, and they, the school people, should be paid consultants to straighten
out preservice teacher education. When the college did not change as
rapidly as the school people told them to, it was seen as being recalcitrant.
For instance, when not all of the college courses were taught by school
people, one commented:

> The shift was supposed to be that practitioners would be doing teacher
> education. . . . The reading methods course should be taught by those
> teaching reading in the schools, writing process should be taught by those
> teaching writing process in the schools. . . . I don't see any of that real
> change piece spelled out. . . . The real involvement of the school in the
> preparation and teaching of the students.

In a discussion centered around the phrase in a grant proposal, "The
cooperating teacher is the pivotal figure in the design of our program,"
school people argued that it was not strong enough language. One teacher
stated, "We need to focus more on the role of the cooperating teacher as
the only real educator of student teachers." While several TC participants
stewed, one of the more gentle TC souls questioned, "One of the things
that seems to be missing here is the role of TC faculty. . . . Is there any

role for TC faculty?" A principal responded quickly, "No." A more mag-
nanimous teacher acquiesced somewhat, "If they want to facilitate our
planning, that's OK."

In the SIP change model it is the college that may refuse to accept the
responsibility for changing itself. In the flip-SIP it is the school that may
not take that essential first step toward significant collaborative change. In
addition, whether SIP or flip-SIP is operating, the same destructive notion
of quid pro quo justice results. That is, great concern is aroused over who
is doing the changing and who is getting the most rewards. In both, there
always seems to be present an informal but very conscious change and
reward score board. The problem is that different institutions keep score
differently. Thus, each institution always feels they are changing more
than the other, while the other is always receiving more rewards.

In a particularly perceptive quote, a particpant summarized the problems with the process of strict equity accounting:

> It's kind of like a marriage . . . where equity is tallied. In the marriages
> where people keep equity charts, there is always alot of bickering. And it's
> never fair. It never comes out fair. . . . The same is true in families with
> kids. You did it this time, now he has to do it. So that everything has to be
> even. That never works because it's impossible to keep the tally marks
> even. Where you have people who have a sense of equality . . . and of
> the equal status that we all have, then you are able to do the job that needs
> to be done, or share a skill that you have, at a time that is necessary and
> acknowledge disappointments and hopes. . . . When we keep bringing
> up those equity issues and trying to keep tally marks even, we are always
> going to run into problems.

Unlike a SIP or flip-SIP model, a PDS is based upon (1) respect of the
importance of the school environment and the professionalization of
teaching (Holmes Group, 1986; 1990), and (2) the necessity of inventing
new systems (Schlechty, Ingwerson, & Brooks, 1988). In a PDS, both
school and university own significant knowledge but neither's knowledge
alone is sufficient to the task of reinventing teacher education. The crucial
distinction between the SIP models and the PDS is the premise that something is wrong with one party that an outside expert must fix versus working with inside experts in all parties to invent a new system.

THE PDS DIFFERENCE

When participants openly confronted their differing fundamental interests, accepted the need to change their own institutions and committed

themselves to doing so, all collaborating parties were afforded equal esteem and all knowledge was valued. Collaboration could begin and proved successful.

> I'm learning a lot, a tremendous amount. . . . The nice thing about the meetings is that most issues are really explored very carefully . . . and basically I feel that everyone feels that they had a voice. . . . The university, the UFT, teachers, administrators—we've got all of us working together toward one common goal. [P.S. 87]

> What I do know though, and this is real, is that I enjoy working with them a lot. I really do like it. I like the outcomes from our work together . . . and I find more real pleasure and satisfaction in the group work that we do together than . . . I do in other parts of my work and life. [TC] .

Successful collaboration led to positive outcomes for the schools and for the college:

> It has helped the school restructure itself. . . . The committee has accomplished very good channels of communication with . . . the staff in this school—in the way the feedback went, the reporting and openness of the committee members to meet and to honor people's concerns and questions. [P.S. 87]

> I think that the knowledge that they [teachers] have and the knowledge that they can construct with the students [TC's student teachers] is part of the knowledge base of teacher education. . . . I think what we get in interacting with experienced practitioners are new ways to look at what we're looking at through a research perspective that is not only useful in terms of our work with prospective teachers, but useful in terms of the way we do our research: the way we interpret our findings; the way we conceive our research questions; what we think are the important agendas to pursue. [TC]

> I have learned alot in the process. [Pause] I don't think my listening skills are always what they should be. . . . To watch the teachers . . . with all their energies and concerns . . . is really an inspiration . . . to shut-up and listen. [TC]

As collaboration began to click and school and college had some initial victories in the slow and arduous task of change, success brought increased self-respect, especially for the school teachers:

> I am very struck by the change in all the teachers. . . . In fact, it's proba-
> bly the most dramatic change I've seen. . . . One of the things the teach-
> ers needed to learn was a sense of their own value, not as teachers—God
> knows they have that. They know they're good doing that. But as people
> with ideas and points of view that are valuable. [Project Coordinator]

As teachers recognized, and became recognized for, the talents and
intellect they brought to the table, all the institutions began to present less
of a group front. "What's happened over time is that the lines in any
debate or discussion over a particular thing . . . initially broke down in
terms of affiliation. I think now it's more mixed up." The resulting
broader debate opened issues and solutions and tapped the best the group
had to offer rather than simply restatements and reenactments of institutional and/or role positions. In a sense, increased self-esteem made all the
participating institutions more professional:

> The professionalism of the teachers in these schools has certainly been
> heightened. . . . It's always been too bad that great teachers [and teacher
> educators] always feel that they needed to leave the profession in order to
> be respected and . . . that moving up was the way to go. This project has
> shown teachers [and teacher educators] . . . that remaining in the class-
> room . . . is indeed a very, very important part of our profession. [District]

The project, on occasion, operated with the assumptions of a PDS
model—a change effort designed, with everyone's expert input, to
enhance teacher professionalism through creating an entirely new system
of teacher education. When it did, conflicts were more likely to be con-
structively resolved, relationships strengthened, productivity of the
group increased, the self-esteem of members grew, and the group gained
greater influence in their home organizations. In short, the project began
to achieve some of its potential and nothing succeeds like success.

Change was difficult and continues to be so. The PDS Project has not
changed the world of teacher education or professionalized the career of
teaching. It has taken much time, much energy, and it has not always been
fun. Often, struggling with the politics of problems and the funding of
solutions overshadowed the problems and solutions themselves. In only 3
years, however, significant chunks of a college and two schools have
changed and the potential and motivation for greater change remains
high. Perhaps it is as one participant said, "I always think everything is
possible. To think something impossible, if it is the right thing to do,
defines what you will fight for." It is as if, even if the ultimate vision might
yet prove illusory, their work together has convinced them of the elegant
power of the idea and the moral imperative of attempting to realize it. In

the words of a teacher, such attempts to realize new visions of teaching and learning "are rare opportunities of hope."

NOTE

[1]This case study is the result of 3 years of documentation. The author functioned, often simultaneously, as a reseacher, a documentor, a participant, and a confidant. Data was collected from a variety of sources and procedures including: (1) document review (i.e., proposals, minutes and agendas to meetings, yearly progress reports); (2) tapes of formal meetings; (3) observational field notes of formal and informal interactions; (4) observations of classrooms; (5) three sets of interviews with participants; and (6) countless casual conversations. A subtle form of data collection arose from sharing my attempts at writing about the project with participants. The resulting negotiation of meaning and language was immensely valuable to the author, and hopefully to project participants.

REFERENCES

Cochran-Smith, M. (1991). Reinventing student teaching. *Journal of Teacher Education, 42*(2), March–April, 1991, 104–118.

Dillon-Peterson, B. (Ed.) (1981). *Staff Development/Organization Development*. Alexandria, VA: Association for Supervision and Curriculum Development.

Griffin, G. (Ed.) (1983). *Staff Development*. Chicago: National Society for the Study of Education.

Hargreaves, A. (1991). Restructuring Restructuring: Postmodernity and the Prospects for Educational Change. Paper presented at the Annual Conference of the American Educational Research Association, Chicago, IL, April 3–7, 1991.

Holmes Group. (1986). *Tomorrow's Teachers: A Report of the Holmes Group*. East Lansing, MI: Author.

Holmes Group. (1990). *Tomorrow's Schools*. East Lansing, MI: Author.

Jones, B., & Maloy, M. (1988). *Partnerships for Improving Schools*. New York: Greenwood Press.

Lieberman, A. (1992). Personal conversation.

Lieberman, A., & Miller, L. (1990). Teacher development in professional practice schools. *Teachers College Record 92*(1), 105–122.

Sarason, S. (1982). *The Culture of the School and the Problem of Change*. Boston: Allyn and Bacon.

Schlechty, P., Ingwerson, D., & Brooks, T. (1988). Inventing professional development schools. *Educational Leadership* (November, 1988), 28–31.

Snyder, J. (1992). Documentation of the First Three Years of the District Three/United Federation of Teachers/Teachers College Professional Development School Project. Report to the Ford Foundation, January, 1992.

Snyder, J., & Schwartz, F. (1991). *IS 44 Professional Development School*. Report to the New York Community Trust, February, 1991.

Soder, R. (1990). Viewing the non-distant past: How faculty members feel when the reward structure changes. *Phi Delta Kappan 71*(9), 702–709.

Zumwalt, K. (1988). Are we improving or undermining teaching? In L. Tanner (Ed.). *Critical Issues in Curriculum,* Eighty-seventh Yearbook of the National Society for the Study of Education, Part 1, 148–174. Chicago: University of Chicago Press.

Chapter 6

PROFESSIONAL DEVELOPMENT IN ACTION: AN IDEA WITH VISITING RIGHTS

Jean Lythcott and Frank Schwartz

A youngster said, "I felt as if I was in a new world for 4 weeks." "To me it was like a present, not just a program, this rich thing that I got to partake of," reported a student teacher. A cooperating teacher and team leader commented, "I saw kids in a different light . . . kids could express themselves more because the setting was different." Another student teacher smiled wistfully, saying, "It was just so great; no one wanted it to end."

These were typical comments from participants in a unique program instituted for the first time in January, 1991, at Intermediate School 44 on Manhattan's Upper West Side in New York City. The program was invented within the Professional Development School (PDS) relationship described in chapter 5. Directly involved were over 300 youngsters, 17 school faculty and 1 intern, 3 school administrators, 14 student teachers, and 1 college faculty member. The college people were at the school all day, every day, for the duration of the project. The student teachers, graduate students in secondary education programs at Columbia University's Teachers College, were grouped into four teams in which each member represented a different discipline; a typical team involved a student teacher from the English, social studies, mathematics, and science preservice programs. Each of these teams was placed with, and combined with, a team of teachers from I.S. 44, teams in which members also represented different subject areas. The I.S. 44 teacher teams involved a specified group of youngsters that each team member taught, for example the seventh grade of the science mini-school. It should be mentioned that I.S. 44 is a regular urban public school with a very wide range of students and with many youngsters having a school history of significant learning problems. No youngster, however, was excluded in order to make the project appear to function more effectively. The four teacher teams were asked simply to invent, enact, and reflect on an interdisciplinary unit of study for their youngsters during the month of January. We call this program the January Experience.

Here we describe the first actualization of the program design, through the stories of the teachers, student teachers, and children who were a part of it, because for all who may be persuaded of the usefulness of such a program for themselves, beginning is the major step. The program design is a complexity of elements that securely frame the work and yet provide sufficient space to allow, even to require, individual and collective creativity. A full description of the program design requires more than the scope of this piece allows. Below we describe some of the key features that illuminate the stories that we tell here.

DESIGN FEATURES

The design features are the combination of interdisciplinary curriculum, combined multidisciplinary teams of practicing and student teachers, with a team locus for all decision-making with the timing of it—the College Intersession. Its spirit is one of risk taking within a network of supportive mechanisms. Key to its acceptance by the PDS committee was the active direction of it in the school by members of the PDS committee who were college and school faculty members. Moreover, as a program, it promised important experiences for the education of entering teachers, for the professional growth of school faculty, for the education of youngsters, for restructuring the organization of school ways, and for a restructuring at TC involving teacher education at the secondary level. In this sense, and from a retrospective view, The January Experience is a prototypical PDS program.

Toward this promise, the January Experience was designed to break with the norms of traditions, to create a discontinuity, to present a situation so new as to create the possibility of, even to require, new ways of functioning, a situation so different that a sense of risk, adventure, and creation permeate the whole. It is a framework for change, a challenge to take the risk of reaching toward an ideal, to "dream dreams about teaching not imagined before," as a student teacher expressed it. It is a context within which teachers can make new meanings about children and schooling, and create new ways to foster important learning experiences for childen. Rules are few, but decisions are many. The framing context is the professional model of learner-centered teaching, of personal and collective initiative, responsibility, and accountability, a model at odds with the bureaucratic model of external rules, presciptions, and evaluation (Darling-Hammond, 1990).

Instead of presenting student teachers with the typical classroom and school images that frame their preconceptions the January Experience is designed to create the possibility that preconceptions be suspended, or shut down, as organizers of thought and action so that the learning of new conceptions is more probable. Understanding that making the familiar unfamiliar is to take risks, this process is accompanied by several support mechanisms. The facilitating presence of a college faculty member at school every day, all day, for the duration of the project, a school faculty member in the role of facilitator, in-school seminars for student teachers and open to school personnel, the basic team concept, and the blessing of the administration, all create the network of support as teams engage the risks inherent in the January Experience.

Several design factors, each and together, create the discontinuity, they are:

1. interdisciplinary teaching as opposed to the traditional pigeon hole structure of discipline-driven organization in secondary schools and colleges;
2. multidisciplinary teaming instead of the lone teacher isolated in her room;
3. in-class team teaching among two to five adults per classroom; and
4. a change from old modes of assessment as work on interdisciplinary projects span several class periods.

Perhaps the most central feature of the design is its use of interdisciplinary teaching and multidisciplinary teams such as the teaming of student teachers. Student teachers naturally connect with each other, both in the powerful feelings of beginners and in the conversational connections of being TC students in a TC course. It is a design factor that assumes that, given the opportunity to have their needs met, the need to connect, to share the flush of success and the responsibility for failures, and to seek support in daring to reach toward some ideal, the tradition of isolation will be overcome. Putting people together in groups, however, does not guarantee that they will make significant work together. Interdisciplinarity particularly requires that teammates talk and have a basis for compelling conversation in the planning stages. During January, although the student teachers are at school all day, every day, they are not bound by the schedule. In a design that affords them the time to talk with each other a lot during the school day, there is a possibility that they will seek, evermore avidly, to function together as an inventive, instructional, and reflective team. In this way, the in-class aspect of teaching becomes one of three phases of professional practice rather than the only phase that counts.

A second piece of the team design factor ia a volunteer multidisciplinary team of practicing teachers, each of whom is a counterpart discipline specialist to a student teacher. These paired specialists form the core of the team-to-team connection since they have the immediate conversational connection of subject matter. The team driven relationship between practicing teacher and student teacher forms another discontinuity with tradition. Rather than the lone mentor/apprentice model of student teaching, this design fosters significant team work in which everyone contributes some important knowledge in the making and honing of inventions for interdisciplinary classroom practice. The practicing teachers in these teams do not function as traditional cooperating teachers sitting in the backs of rooms, making notes about a student teachers' performances, and tactfully telling them afterwards what they did wrong. There is no tacitly assumed "right way" to do the January Experience; so, everyone helps everyone else to hone their practice.

The third piece of the team design feature is that teams of beginners and practicing teachers are combined. For those practicing teachers who have already found ways to connect with each other, the combined teaming validates, extends, and supports such activity. For practicing teachers who have had no practical experience in either team teaching or interdisciplinary teaching, their student teacher team is a center around which they can begin to work together, around which they can begin conversations with each other about children, content, and their own work. The presence of multiple voices and visions, and the possibility of multiple personal relationships, provide many permutations and combinations for creative work and for learning. We believe that the combined team size of six to eight people, half student teachers and half practicing teachers, generates a synergistic effect. With the combined team structure of this size, what emerges is more than the sum of the parts of the team. Teachers gain support from their team and the support makes taking risks easier the next time.

Because there were three well-defined participating groups in the program—the practicing teachers, the student teachers, and the youngsters—there are, as in 'Roshomon,' three sides to every story. The first is that of the school faculty and it characterizes the general setting and framework of the program. The second is the student teachers and it is the longest side because they are a prime focus of our PDS work to date. The third, perhaps most important, side is from the youngsters, for, if they did not benefit, then other gains would constitute little more than an engaging illusion.

THE SCHOOL FACULTY STORY

This teachers'-eye view is based on individual and small group conversations, random observations, and interviews with the 16 practicing teachers who were team teachers in the experience.

THE BEGINNINGS

Armed with a design, a willingness, and a climate of administrative support, the teacher who was the PDS liason between the committee and the school disseminated the description of the January Experience to the staff at I.S. 44. By this time, some teachers were already teaming in some way, were undertaking interdisciplinary activity, and were involved with the general PDS activity. Several responded eagerly to the new program, though most chose not to be involved. Through the PDS, funding was solicited for summer work that would involve teams of teachers brainstorming and planning an interdisciplinary theme in preparation for the January Experience. The New York Community Trust provided this funding. Nine selected teachers and an administrator met, discussed, and resolved key issues in choosing a useful theme and then started planning. The nine worked together for 2 weeks and reported gaining new respect for each other, feeling rewarded by their selection, and empowered to change the school schedule to create more productive time. Buoyed by this collaborative activity, by September there were several teams primed for the onset of the January Experience. By October, four teacher teams had identified possible themes for the interdisciplinary unit of study, "The Bridges of New York City," "The Industrial Revolution," "Animals of Mexico: Myth and Reality," and "Endangered Species" and had requested student teacher teams for the program. Two of these teams had teachers who had worked in the summer project, but not necessarily together. Another team had faculty who had spent the summer exploring a new theme independently, the fourth was a team of two faculty who had already had much experience working together.

The participants were taking a risk by choosing to do things differently. January was clearly going to be some break with the norm, if only from the points of view of interdisciplinarity and the use of a group of volunteer student teachers in some way for full and consecutive school days for the month. The teams were set. One team was the teachers in the Discovery Program on the second floor. This is an innovative program for 24 gifted, but learning disabled, seventh and eighth graders. Some of the teachers in The Computer School, a semi-independent alternative school of about 130 youngsters that is housed on the basement floor, formed a team. The other two teams came from one of the thematic mini-schools, the Science School, housing about 90 youngsters in each of grades 6, 7, and 8 with teachers who worked mostly, but not exclusively, with one of those grades. Some of these teachers had begun to form teams, meeting together both formally and informally. Two groups of teachers in the science mini-school had volunteered for the project; one group encompassed all of the teachers who interacted with a group of youngsters, the other group was comprised of only some of the subject area teachers of a particular grade.

Team members were looking forward to the stretch, but some wariness existed. This was a TC course, the TC faculty member was going to be at school for the whole time. Why? Were they going to be under a supervisory, evaluatory eye with someone making notes about what they were doing wrong? College faculty often do not truly know about the real life of school, the day to day realities, and those issues that come up that interfere with the best laid plans. What were the expectations of the college? This was going to be a student teaching program but a very different one than the traditional model. There were no real rules, no specified objectives, no paper work to follow. How were they expected to meet expectations when none were explicitly articulated? Suppose things didn't go as well as anticipated, would the administration be upset? What does it mean to have a project derived from the PDS concept? Having one student teacher can create extra work and some disruption, but in this program each team of teachers would be working with four student teachers. How would we keep track of all of them? What would the student teachers from the prestigious, perhaps even elitist institution, be like? Would they fit in with a city school, with regular city children?

The student teachers finally arrived at the school, with the professor, to meet the teams, to say "Hello," and to set up a schedule of planning sessions. But very soon afterwards, after a couple of meetings, the college supervisor stopped coming. This was somewhat of a relief because she had some good ideas but everyone had seemed to defer to her in meetings. In fact everyone left the teachers to get on with it, by themselves. Planning resulted in some firm decisions, a lot of suggestions, and a little dissatisfaction in the selections from the ideas proposed. The four teams went their separate ways as each team decided the best time for them to get together. All of the student teachers did come to school to see the classes and the youngsters at some time and they seemed knowledgeable and likeable.

One team chose to retain the Bridges of New York City theme and the student teachers went off doing research together. Several key experiences were fixed: they would build bridges themselves, they would take field trips to the bridges, they would role play a mock hearing about whether or not to build the Brooklyn Bridge, they would investigate the map of Manhattan and discover why bridges were built where they are. A block of time each day was given to the program for the three classes of children involved and it was decided that the program would take precedence over the subject assigned by the schedule during those time periods. The student teachers were going to be taking charge of some projects right away and would generally move together as a team from class to class.

The Animals of Mexico: Myth and Reality theme didn't appeal to the student teachers in that team. Several alternatives were explored and eventually the theme became The Biomes of Mexico. The student teachers took ownership of that theme immediately, naming three biomes to be investigated: rain forest, desert, and ocean, one biome per class of children. Exploration of the ecological connections would be a major issue and field trips to the American Museum of Natural History would be a piece. But they would also read "The Lorax," write poetry, and explore these biomes through art. A time block for three classes of children was created. Each student teacher was placed with an individual practicing teacher and one class of youngsters, and student teachers would begin "taking charge" almost immediately. Once per week the three groups of children would be reorganized into three new groups in order to share knowledge about their biome with peers from the other groups.

The Industrial Revolution theme was dropped and that team discussion topic became the Middle East. The theme would be explored in all subject areas in all classes for the month; the three classes of youngsters would keep to their usual schedule. Plans were made for specific subject area explorations and projects, travel brochures in social studies, Arabian Nights and writing serial stories, geometric shapes in mathematics, science experiments to illustrate alchemy, Islamic art, and the like. The student teachers would be assigned to work with their own subject area teacher much of the time, but would also work in classes of different subject areas, sometimes in teams. Creating a new schedule for each of the four student teachers overlaid on the existing schedule was dificult, but it was finally worked out so each had a full weekly schedule. The student teachers would begin by observing and helping the practicing teacher with the planned projects.

The Endangered Species theme was selected and maintained. The whole month would be given over to the interdisciplinary theme in all core periods for the 25 youngsters—even though this meant stopping the reading and exploration of a classic mid-stream. Flexibility was the plan. Student teachers were encouraged to observe for a few days or to begin in-class work immediately, to teach in or out of their discipline, to enact as a team, a pair, or solo. There would be a strong out-of-school element with field trips to various places. Each person was responsible for trying to invent some learning experience that would be challenging and meaningful for the youngsters in the context of "Endangered Species" to bring to the team discussion.

In some ways there was a lot of planning, but many details were missing. It became difficult for the student teachers to meet at school because their end of semester exams were coming up, and they already had a full load of course work and job. But during the holiday breather the pieces would come together, phone numbers had been exchanged, and at least the first opening activities were more or less organized.

THE EXPERIENCE IN PROCESS

Wary participation marked the mood on opening day, January 3rd, a Thursday. "I'm wondering if we can pull this off," a team leader confided on Wednesday morning. "You mean after all the meetings, planning, preparing materials . . . ?" "Oh we're ready, but can it work?" The program marked a radical change, and this was a risky business. The volunteer teachers were "charged" as one put it by the project's basic concept of interdisciplinarity. They were impressed by both the academic qualifications and the cordial personalities of the student teachers and their supervisor. And they were looking forward to "doing something different" to brighten the dull January lull that frequently follows a spirited holiday season. According to Kerekes, "An interdisciplinary unit is best implemented at a time when students' interest in school is traditionally at a low point . . . by changing the pace and raising the interest level, students become involved almost without realizing it" (Kerekes, 1987, pg. 12). It seemed like a perfect time and opportunity to do something new.

Yet the anxiety was tangible. The teachers were to be classroom mentors, in something they hadn't done before, and with a team of student teachers who had also not worked together and hardly knew each other—good grounds then for a colossal mess. Getting off on the right foot was going to be crucial. Would everyone show up? So many details required attention: where to hang coats, handing out keys to the lounges and bathrooms, signing in with security, lunch logistics, finding 14 new "teachers" a home, a place to sit, and a place for the in-school seminar—all in an already crowded school, where most of the faculty were not involved in the program.

The mess did not materialize. Teachers were free to focus on the classroom as the facilitators handled the logistics. The 1st day sailed along smoothly, and Friday was also fine. Professional interactions were constructive and genial. The revised and flexible scheduling revealed no irreparable glitches, people ended up where they were supposed to be. The student teachers and the kids were actually getting to know each other. Nonparticipating teachers were not upset by a suddenly busy teachers' lounge and the disruption of their familiar routine. By Wednesday, the 9th, it was clear that the progam was not only going to fly, but also that there was something special in the air. "How are things?" was greeted not with equivocal okays, shrugs, and controlled resentment. Rather "By George, I think we've got it!" quipped one teacher, and "Fine!", "Yes!" voiced others. A happy hum seemed to accompany the busyness about the place.

In one team, there had been an almost immediate difficulty with a student teacher who seemed so distracted and disabled with the assigned class that the youngsters were quite unhappy. The message was delivered and the resident college facilitator immediately joined that team and spent a lot of time working one-on-one with the student teacher—the teacher team was relieved and impressed. Decisions were made in the youngsters' best interests, and the student teacher gained a lot of support from the full team in working through some of the difficulties. Communications flew around the school, to, from, and between students, student teachers, facilitators, and school faculty. As a result, a couple of misunderstandings were cleared up before there was time for them to interfere or fester. Word went out that challenge was in the air, ground was being broken, and everyone was doing just fine. People wanted to hear how about the other teams and to share ideas. Erstwhile uninterested teachers began to tap into the project, to converse, to listen, and in some cases to join in by offering their classrooms for project work as well.

Changes in Plans.   The on-going conversation among and between the four teams, and through the facilitators, fostered evolutionary changes in plans. From the interdisciplinary aspect, two teams had gelled as whole groups immediately, and could be seen regularly in knots of interdisciplinary activity both in and out of class. Another team that had begun more as a model of student teacher/mentor pairs began to reformulate to create more explicit team and discipline connections, and to identify some time periods to conjoin two or more disciplines. The fourth team, which also began with the traditional discipline pair model remained in that organization but decided to reduce the emphasis of work that had somehow become quite discipline specific during the first 10 days in favor of including the other disciplines in more explicit ways.

From the aspect of time, in the two teams where specified time blocks had been given to the project, the plan remained essentially static, although in one other class, periods were used for project work on occasion. In one of the teams where the project occupied the whole schedule, people began to use the time in more in-class interdisciplinary collaborations and to allow more planning and reflecting time for the student teachers. In the other, the evolution involved student teachers becoming increasingly autonomous in the classroom.

Student teachers in all models had in-school time for talking together. Cooperating teachers with their full day schedules did not have the same time availability, but team conversations were squeezed in when possible. Some teachers and administrators attended one or another of the in-school seminars that were held for both the student teachers and any school personnel who wanted to join in. In three teams, student teachers had significant time every day for planning and reflecting. As the days went along, student teachers became completely commited to this activity and none thought anymore of leaving school a little early or arriving a little late if they were not scheduled into the classroom. In one team the amount of time given to planning and reflecting continued to increase as the student teachers requested it.

Classroom Organization and Activity.   In classrooms there was a lot of activity; they were not sit and listen classes. The teachers' roles changed remarkably, especially when team teaching involved several student teachers and a cooperating teacher. It was often hard to find the teachers midst the zeal of childen working. In each room youngsters were talking with each other, and with the teacher team members, they were writing together, making things together, and solving problems together. Word about cooperative learning had trickled into the school through workshops and readings. A small percentage of middle school teachers can and do, create and manage small group activities, and in fact a few classrooms at I.S. 44 were already organized in this way. Why don't more middle school teachers use it on a regular basis? The problem is not the concept but the complex logistics of its implementation. Most teachers with classes of around 30 in a full progam of 120 or more students find the challenge so demanding and daunting that they avoid it.

Our program broke the ice for many. "There were more small group activities," reported a teacher. Another voiced appreciation of the program, saying, "Kids had more opportunities to stimulate each other academically, and to learn by doing." This was reflected particularly in the sudden increase in the number of well-planned, worthwhile field trips— the January cold did nothing to squelch the enthusiasm of learning in the field.

With all this innovation going on, it was important that the program included the freedom to make mistakes and to try again. Although lots of people were visiting classes, no one was hovering around the door to complain, or to find fault, rather there was a sensitive facilitation. Even though not everything had gone perfectly by any means—this was a real school with real children after all—the evident trust enabled teachers' confidence to increase. It was simply worth it to try to do these new things because the youngsters were responding and stretching academically. Our classrooms became transformed, "The kids seemed to find this approach refreshing," and "Students saw fresh faces with great amounts of energy," were two comments. For example, the bridge team had assigned 19th century social roles, such as "ferry owner," "steel worker," and "commissioner" to everyone in each class in preparation for the mock hearing about whether or not to build the Brooklyn Bridge. Groups of "ferry owners,""shop keepers," "steel workers," and so on prepared their speeches, elected group representatives to deliver the speeches at the hearing, and edited them to perfection. The kids were expected to create the rules for the hearing and to hold the class to them. The hearings themselves were surprisingly well conducted. They were scheduled in when the students were ready regardless of what subject was printed on the schedule. In the Middle East theme, teams of youngsters were assigned a country and they created a travel brochure of places to go and things to see. The brochure included the money and conversion to dollars in one or another country. More than one parent was impressed by youngsters' knowledge of this complicated region. Also in this team, children were learning to do several mid-east dances—shyly or enthusiatically, they were dancing. In the Endangered Species group, creative writing had taken them to thinking about themselves being endangered, and several periods were involved in having them experience that perspective, trying to work with their thumbs taped to their palms, and inventing stories about an animal who saved their life. In the Biomes of Mexico, a "Jeopardy" type of game was invented in which in each classroom three teams of seven or so youngsters from each biome group would have to share their knowledge and cooperate to arrive at the answer. It was extraordinary to see youngsters crawling along the table tops to be closer to the conversation in the group and to offer their own input into the team decision. Different work was going on, creativity seemed rampant, and interdisciplinarity became the spur to increasingly innovative active learning tasks and learner-directed teaching.

Teachers agreed that one major benefit of the cooperative learning activites was the capacity to meet the needs of individual youngsters and to get to know them better. Teachers said: "We could give them more time and attention," and "The extra teachers allowed for better communication, cooperation, and rapport between students and teachers." The presence of teams of adults, allowing the many small group activities, may be especially suited for the middle school population. While it is difficult to respond to every youngster's needs on a regular basis, a diverse teaching team creating a variety of activities involving all subject areas, seemed to accomodate a high percentage of them.

A New Perspective on Mentoring.   It was clear that the teachers were not playing a traditional role with the student teachers. This was not a program in which "experts" mentored "apprentices"; rather everyone was learning together. The student teachers were only at the school for the month, so this was not a case of them sitting and taking notes while "real teachers" taught. They quickly took charge of the instruction, being completely involved from day one. Released from a self-conscious mentor role, cooperating teachers began to focus on what they themselves had been able to achieve in doing things differently, and to build on those. Rather than explicitly focusing on what student teachers were learning about teaching, they assumed that that was going on and they simply talked, analyzed, invented, modified, and shared in conversation with them as one set of colleagues to another—a new model for student teaching. The student teachers were in some ways the proverbial extra pair of hands in the classroom, to help make the new activities work. But they were much more than this—their knowledge was valuable in that they actually created some of the most innovative ideas for activities. Typical comments were: "Having the extra support gave me the confidence to experiment more"; and "We could achieve more because the student teachers were so helpful"; but also "The personalities and knowledge of the student teachers were a big factor that influenced content."

Interdisciplinarity.   The interdisciplinary aspect had encouraged teachers to recognize, in increasing depth and possibility, the value of other disciplines with respect to their own. Everyone seemed to be involved in at least thinking about instruction and knowledge in other disciplines. A flexibility, and a reduction in a sense of ownership over times, spaces, and kids grew. For instance, in the Middle East team there was a peculiar timeliness as the country engaged itself in the Gulf War—Desert Storm, a war that took many family members of the students into active combat. Two, non-English, class periods were readily allotted to focus on reading the newspapers and writing letters to soldiers in the Gulf. Many other examples of the program needs being given priority over the subject-scheduled class time occurred. But rather than comments that might have been expected about students missing math, or English, teachers grew into a deeper understanding of child-centered instruction as the old centers of power, the time and spaces of the schedule, crumbled. "It was a great experience for me to develop lessons in other content areas and to see how other teachers planned and taught these lessons," reported one seasoned teacher, and "The program made me more conscious of the social aspects of science," said another.

The Climax

The project bubbled to a climax; the team synergy generated something too large to remain confined to individual classrooms. A project observer wrote:

> During the 3rd week in January, the school was awash with student products from the interdisciplinary rooms. The project flooded the entire

school community. The basement was plastered with collages of biomes of Mexico. The cafeteria was the scene of a Middle Eastern feast and belly dancing. Bridges spanned from classroom to classroom, and students argued out of school and into the evening about whose bridge had appropriately applied physics and should be chosen by the students' Bridge Commission as the design to be built. Endangered species were alive and well on the second floor and a letter writing campaign added significant heft to local mail pouches (Snyder & Schwartz, 1991, pg. 8).

Toward the end of the program, the issue of assessment resurfaced. In one team the search for a proper and useful way of evaluating these interdisciplinary projects occupied large and heated segments of the team discussion. This became for most teams, however, mostly a cooperating teacher task.

The Conclusion

In the days after the program ended, teachers had suggestions for improvement of the program. One suggestion was that the goals for the student teachers be more clearly defined. The goals for this program would be necessarily different from a regular student teaching experience and some felt that this aspect required clarification. For some, then, the requirement of external expectations as a defining feature of educational activity still remained after the month of working differently.

The most common suggestion was that there be more planning time among cooperating teachers with the student teachers both before, but especially during, the project. "We needed more time before the program started, and while the program was in progress . . . things became so busy that there wasn't time to plan," proffered one teacher. Others agreed. It is clear that the feelings were that more could have done, and that working along with the student teachers was somehow a key issue. Needing the student teachers in the planning process makes clear that they were not just another pair of hands to lighten the classroom load, but rather had brought something necessary to the program in the creation phase, and had operated as a fulcrum for change. It also illustrates that a new model of interaction between experienced and entering teachers had been operative. Doubling the number of people thinking about and acting for the education of specific classes of children seemed to have generated a geometrically progressive effect in energy and outcome.

"Should we do it again?" produced a clear consensus from the participating teachers that it had been valuable and that it should be repeated. The following comments specify such a summary. "It's the kind of program that could keep me here!" one of the newer teachers commented. "In my opinion it was so worthwhile that I suggest that we have it twice a year, at the end of each semester. I gained a tremendous feeling while team planning and team teaching, as we did with this project," was a view of a veteran.

This is a success story. Regardless of the extra work, the occasional failure, and the general disruption, school faculty were so convinced of its worth that they recommended it be done again. School practices for teachers had changed in important ways during the experience, mostly in terms of the nature of the organization and goals in their own classrooms, but also in collaborative work with other teachers, experienced and beginners. And the support network held so that problems were solved and conflicts were resolved, although not completely, at least sufficiently that changes not only occurred, but evolved.

THE STUDENT TEACHER STORY

This story emerges from written reflections during and at the end of the course, from on-going conversation, and from post-school experience interviews with the 14 student teachers. The student teachers' personal comments are extensive because, of course, they were writing as a part of the course work. They tell of their learning about children and their capacities, and of their learning to work as collaborative professionals. They also testify to the robustness of the traditional teacher icon to shape actions regardless of context.

The design of the January Experience was intended to enable student teachers to make themselves into professional practitioners for a short period of time. Inventing and planning and post-classroom reflection were to be raised for them to the same status as in-class interactions with the children. As student teachers they were expected to learn significant and new understandings.

THE BEGINNINGS

After the PDS committee had approved the concept of the January Experience, the elective course was developed formally, approved, and its description disseminated throughout the secondary teacher education programs at TC. It appealed to a number of faculty there, but not all, and its inclusion into degree programs was feasible in some but not all cases. The potential student teachers were graduate students, usually working while attending TC and were enrolled in very different course schedules. There was no time when students in each of the secondary teacher education progams could come together, and so they were not reachable as a collective unit. Faculty members in different programs spread the word of this new, additional, and elective student teaching opportunity by either posting the written description, describing it verbally, or announcing it as an intriguing elective and sending students directly to the course instructor. Students also disseminated information by word of mouth. Four students were already functioning in the school as student teachers under the PDS auspice, and they were expected to join the teams. Others were motivated to enroll in an extra student teaching course, and to spend the college Intersession, normally vacation time, all day, every day in an intermediate school, for a variety of reasons. As one explained "The interdisciplinary aspects sounded interesting and I also wanted as much time in an academic classroom as possible before student teaching." Another said "The idea of working as a team appealed to me as a way for all of us to get our feet wet without drowning so to speak." In contrast one "wanted to finish [i.e. graduate] earlier, and it was a way of condensing the whole year." Several shared that they "thought it would be a nice change, something different, something new."

Some 16 student teachers applied, and in the end 14 entered the program: 4 each from social studies, English, and science, and 2 from mathematics. Four multidisciplinary teams were formed by having the student teachers select one of the themes already identified by the teachers. This process worked smoothly.

In November, the student teachers went in teams to the school to meet with their counterpart teacher teams, to see the school, and to begin the planning process. From this point, and after the professor left them to their own devices to make decisions, each collaboration developed uniquely. Their response to the collaborative process was individual and varied. They were either active participants or quite passive, working from the outset as integral team members or in a typically isolated fashion, leaping in to learn new information as a part of the planning process or withdrawing from the discomfort of handling unfamiliar themes in the unfamiliar collaborative context. Most responded energetically to the new context. They commented: "We kept planning, we spent all our time planning, there was a whole lot of planning time involved, more than I expected." and "We all went together to the New York Public Library reading up on bridges since that was our theme; we couldn't go in knowing nothing about bridges!" Others described the beginning in different ways,

> When I first signed up the theme was the Industrial Revolution, then it was on the Middle East in the Middle Ages, and I didn't know anything about that so I went to the library and tried to find some books before we even went to I.S. 44, because I didn't want to seem like an idiot once I got there!

When we met with the teachers they said that Animals in Mexico was the original idea, but that it was open to change. We could have made it whatever we wanted. At one of the earlier meetings he [a teacher counterpart] was encouraging us to think big and not worry about what was realistic, basically to get rid of the editor on your shoulder and let your ideas fly at first.

For one the beginning was less dramatic, "I acted somewhat passively from the beginning. Planning was done at team meetings, I think we were told more or less what to do; I mean there was some opportunity for input, but we were presented with what would happen."

It had a scary quality for one who, "did not feel confident or competent to offer many suggestions in a field of teaching that I knew little about." and another, seemingly bewildered, kept asking himself "How can I plug into something I know nothing about?" although he had been present at all meetings in which the theme was selected.

The level of involvement was not theme related. Those given an active role in theme choice did not all become active decision makers, those given a fixed theme to work with were not all passive decision makers. Some who had already student taught were active while others were very passive; so, it did not seem to be experience related. Not all members of a given team were either passive or active and thus it seemed to be an individual rather than a collective issue. There is a possibility that, for some, the traditional teacher icon of the isolated adult was so powerful that it made working, talking, and planning with a group of other teachers seem inappropriate. How many times they met, how they communicated, how they planned, divided the work, and organized action was idiosyncratic to person and team. The press of final exams in December, however, curtailed organized teaming at the school for everyone. Asked at least to stay in touch with each other and their teacher team actively over the holidays, they did.

THE EXPERIENCE IN PROCESS

Buoyant but a little anxious, the fourteen tumbled into school midst the press of the youngsters for the opening day of the project. They met the professor standing with the security guard at the visitor sign-in book and then went to 'their' classrooms to meet the teacher team. Information about keys, lunch, meeting rooms, bathroom, coat closets, where the course readings were to be kept, and where the seminars would be, kept flowing in from one source or another. They were absorbed into the community as quickly as they came. Counselled to be sensitive that their presence en masse had the potential to be disruptive of familiar routines in the teachers' lounges and the cafeteria, where most faculty were not a part of the project, and also feeling most secure in the actual classrooms anyway, they were not immediately visible in the school. A journal entry of the first day reads "This school must welcome us, or be comfortable with us—at least tolerate us—the gang will affect spaces, the lounge activity and etc., there's 15 of us, we'll have to find a way to ease in, to find a niche." As the days went along, however, they could be seen more and more knotted in avid conversation, eager, smiling, telling their stories, asking for advice, floating ideas for spontaneous responses, in the lounges, the teachers' cafeteria, and in the hallways. A journal entry 10 days into the project concerns an incident in the second floor faculty lounge. Eight student teachers and the college faculty member were conversing, occupying almost all of the chair space in the room, when a school faculty member not involved in the project came in, only to leave shortly thereafter. One of the student teachers raised the earlier issue of the potential problem of taking over the faculty lounge, and all understood that the student teachers had truly settled in and owned their place as teachers. Moreover, the whole school seemed warm and supportive.

Student Teachers and Children.   The issue of immediate interest to most student teachers was the children, and most were meeting them as individuals from the 1st day. How and what they felt about, and what they knew about these diverse inner city children, as learners, was of enormous interest from a course point of view. All had stories to tell about children, and those stories were usually about individuals, so that very few were stories of unnamed, faceless children hidden in a collective title, such as "the second period class," or "these kids." Interactions with the youngsters mostly yielded genuine delight, and discovery. The discovery that these were interested, talented, and interesting children was a true surprise to many of the student teachers. Since surprise is evidence that expectations need to be reframed, each such incident was an opportunity for a student teacher to learn. Finding out early that the youngsters were interesting people, was key to the strong close relationships student teachers formed with them. They wrote or said:

> I realized that I was not looking forward to this trip and felt somewhat
> guilty about that. I was not looking forward to shepherding the kids
> through the streets, to the subway, on the subway, etc.. I remembered
> watching teachers do this and always feeling that I would hate to be in
> their position. But to the contrary, it turned out to be a wonderful day. The
> weather was clear and sunny, the zoo was very quiet, and the kids were a
> pleasure, interested, polite with our guide, asking intelligent questions.

When our guide left us he complimented our kids on their behavior. He was absolutely right. They managed to be exhuberant young adolescents without being obnoxious.

We formed a mock debate over building the Brooklyn Bridge, a mock hearing. There was a commission of kids that had to keep order. The kids were GREAT! And I was very surprised and happy that one group at least decided NOT to build the bridge—they didn't go along with the history and the norms.

Another day, the teacher suggested that they write their thoughts on the Middle East, on the pending war. I really liked to see this because they would sit down and 80% of the class would actually get into it! It was so exciting to see, I really loved that. A lot of them would bring them up and show them—even though we said that they didn't have to share them with us. Some of them wrote stuff that you didn't want to read. It was so funny because one day when they were writing in their journals, she said "OK, we're going to read them now," and half the class said "Wait, wait, wait, just let us write a bit longer." That was great, I like to see when kids are interested.

Couple these successsful activities with the kids' overwhelming enjoyment of the personalized attention afforded by the student teachers and it became apparent that the kids were willing to participate in their own learning. In fact they seemed to prefer it! One period was spent with the students providing the information and insights necessary to solve the problems. Ironically, the so-called "difficult group" was the most engaged! In fact, I was quite surprised to find that on a Friday, during the last period, half the class remained after the bell to find the solution to one of the problems presented. Clearly these students enjoy being challenged.

There was this girl, T., we had asked the kids to imagine that they had been dropped blindfolded into their biome, and to write how they would know where they were without being able to see anything. Some wrote about hearing a particular bird sing, some about the soil on their feet, or the feel of the air. Anyway she read her piece out loud, everyone was hushed as she read, it was a lovely piece, and then it was over. About 20 seconds of silence lasted and then A. said "So what, you think you a poet or somethin?" What do you make of that, A. . . . putting her down like that?

Y'know I'd never taught in a school before, and this was a New York City public school and you're asking for it if you go there. But I can say this now—I'm doing better, I'm really making an effort to see each kid as an individual not as a mass, a group, a class—which I did before.

Most of the student teachers reported really enjoying the children, but not all. One wrote:

Mostly they were horrible to me, well really just a few of them were horrible, but it felt like them all. I knew they didn't want to go to the museum, I wasn't sure why we were going and I was afraid that they'd touch something and break it. It was awful, I was not very effective, and it did not go well.

Why is it that experiences would be so different? It would appear that, when student teachers replaced a focus on self and teacher activities with a focus on meeting and getting to know individual children and their learning activities, the program worked for them. It was true, in this small number, that although not all the passive planners reported being upset by children, none of those who were active decison makers in the planning stages did. Active creative work inventing activities for youngsters to do so that they could come to an understanding, had the effect of moving student teachers' consciousness from their self to the youngsters, and enabled student teachers to remake themselves into learner-centered professionals. The very few who did not successfully connect with the children as whole people and who did not actively take on the task of inventing learning activities were those who also retained the teacher icon of the isolated person in power.

Student Teachers and Teaming. The other issue of import for the student teachers was teaming. In some teams student teachers taught mostly within their discipline, in others they also taught in other disciplines. There was no experience that was typical for the student teachers. In the busyness of a full school day, the practicing teacher teams and their team connection with the student teacher team generally became more loose. Although the planning and reflecting connection became mostly a matter of a few hurried comments with one practicing team member before school, at lunch, or between classes, all teams had at least one scheduled session together per week.

The extent and depth of collaborative work varied considerably. Team work was a planning and reflecting activity for all groups, but team teaching in the classroom characterized all in-class activities for one group, most in another, an increasing number in the third, and none for the fourth. In one team they moved as a unit of four in everything from the very beginning. Most student teachers made themselves into a collaborative team readily, for others this was not intuitive. Some sought advice about how better to team with their peers, and took the advice. Others seemed to be satisfied with whatever loose nexus of connection they had created, and did not change during the program. A few of the student teachers even sought to cloak themselves in the mantle of the icon of the isolate, fitting comfortably into a plan that allowed that activity, seeking no deeper collaboration. One, falling through the safety net of team, required extensive counselling and support from the "supervisor," an intervention requested by the practicing teacher team. Another, suddenly apprehensive about "being evaluated as a teacher," early in the program reported anxiously that a teammate in "his" classroom spent the whole time sitting in the back of the room making notes, and worried that teaming was not synonymous with collaboration.

As the days went along, however, it was clear that all the student teacher teams grew tighter. Everyone was engaged in avid conversation with teammates, spending lots of time inventing and reflecting, putting in-class time with the youngsters as just one of the three phases of professional practice that serves the needs of the children. The more the student teachers gelled as a team the greater the risks they took toward making important learning experiences for their "kids." Most propelled themselves into decision making and into owning the project for themselves and their students. Most increasingly trusted the value of their own ideas and conversation. The student teachers generally began to rely more and more upon themselves as a team. In the Bridge team, for example, during the second week, one student teacher had suggested that playing "Bridge Over Troubled Waters," the '60s Simon and Garfunkel classic, would be an interesting mechanism for exploring the metaphorical dimension of bridges. The initial response from the team was negative, even derisive—"These kids will laugh us out of the classroom with that music!" They worked with it, however, brought it to the classroom, and reported being elated both by a fruitful discussion and by the fact that when they played it the second time the youngsters were singing along with the music.

For some the concept of team deepened from the initial joint planning. At first tasks were parcelled out to a community of support and strength within which partners could dare to stretch and contribute, and both make and use a piece of the safety net. One had noted simply that "Team teaching provided us with a great support network!," whereas others elaborated in some detail:

> That first experience of being in front of a class with my peers was extremely supportive. We could watch each other flounder together and then we could talk about it together. I think that this was the best, . . . working with other people and seeing what perspective, discipline they were coming from.
>
> Team teaching proved to be much more difficult, but coincidentally much more rewarding, than I anticipated. Having at least four supporting teachers in any given classroom at any given time was comforting. Not only was it worthwhile to share the fruits of our success, but we were also able to spread the blame for our failures. Personally I felt confident going

into greater depth in a variety of subjects knowing the responsibility for continuing the class discussion would fall upon the shoulders of one of my cooperating teachers should I falter.

We weren't team teaching in the sense that each had a set piece, a responsibility, we were rather cooperating and helping each other. Decisions were made cooperatively as we gained confidence and the cooperating teacher gave up ownership. I mean we talked all the time about lessons and about the kids. I felt I was constantly learning from the cooperating teachers, in that sense they were my teachers . . . but I never felt the distance . . . y'know, you know everything and I know nothing. . . . I mean we were collaborating constantly.

For some, then, being part of a team was such a powerful discontinuity with the traditional icon that discovering the joys of working collaboratively as a professional had a profound effect. They felt supported and nurtured as they reached for learner-centered practice. For them, it was the nurture provided by collaboration, pre, post, and in class, that mattered not so much the content around which the collaboration occurred. For other student teachers, the aspect of interdisciplinarity, the content of the collaboration, was as important as team collaboration in their construction of a new teacher icon. One recalled that for her:

Working together cooperatively as teammates was an aspect that we took for granted rather than something to work on. Initially, our lack of communication rendered us disabled as a team and left us each to work solely with our cooperating teachers. After approximately 5 days into the program it came to our attention that we could redirect ourselves and work on making subject-to-subject connections with teammates.

She then described a team-taught lesson conjoining two disciplines that she created with a teammate "that worked fabulously" and allowed her to see her subject in a new dimension

One student teacher described an incident with a particular student in a class activity about the wooden bridges they were building. She was trying to enable the student to solve the problem, began to feel inadequate, called over the science student teacher, and observed the interaction as the child responded to the analogy provided. She wrote "My three peers often had the insights I needed to understand my new role as a teacher." Others had also thought about the effects of interdisciplinary work; one said:

Teachers are not used to working together. For an interdisciplinary course to work teachers need to work together—to not feel ownership of children, time periods, classes and materials, to accomodate and to eliminate feelings of competition and insecurities among cohorts. But this is not easy to change. School is structured in a way that does not allow teachers to see and talk to each other, and often teachers are not even allowed to talk about kids and classrooms in the faculty lounge. Rooms are too small to allow for two classes to meet together with two teachers; separate schedules and different grade levels all make collaborating difficult . . . to ask what comes first interdisciplinary teaching or collaboration, is like asking what came first the chicken or the egg. They are so interrelated I think it would be difficult for one to happen without the other.

As a preliminary conclusion, it seems that those who went beyond feeling supported by team to reflecting about interdisciplinary learning were moved to adopt a learning orientation themselves. The practice of these student teachers became a knowledge-building activity. They became interested in how particular children behaved differently from one content area to another, why and how a single discipline skews one's view of the whole child, and how working in a discipline other than their own changed their view of teaching.

For two student teachers, however, the January Experience was not the knowledge-building activity that the design sought. For one student teacher the whole program had been an exercise in amiably suppressing feelings of discontent with teammates and what they created together. He said,

The one thing that bothered me at first, and still bothers me, was that we were always trying to make class fun for kids, and I don't agree with that. I mean life is learning that you have to do stuff you don't want to do, it's not always fun. I think you prepare a class, and they do what they are supposed to do, and if they behave themselves then I might think of rewarding them with a fun class or a field trip. But I don't usually make a fuss, and I just went along with it. It was okay, and they did some great things, but I just don't agree with it, that's all.

Since this was not evident until the end of the program, a learning opportunity had been lost. This student teacher had preconceptions about youngsters, classrooms, learning, teaching, and his subject that remained unchallenged by the January Experience. Interdisciplinary teaming, even among peers and under the compelling circumstances of this project, is no guarantee that people will take the risk to learn otherwise. Clearly we can do work with the seminar activities that might better enable everyone to name their views and to open them for discussion.

For another, it had been frustrating in the extreme to be caught in a team whose decisions conflicted with personal preferences. This student teacher, although experienced with conflict resolution mechanisms in another setting, in this context of school and teacher teams made no attempt to raise and resolve this personal conflict in team discussion. The suppression created anger and frustration, and disabled even routine action. In fact the program seemed to create a crisis much more rapidly for this student teacher than a more typical student teaching experience might have. The ever-present example of thriving peers, in the same school, with the same youngsters, seemed to sharpen the sense of personal failure. One worries about losing potentially inspiring teachers, especially for urban youngsters, and we shall work hard to create ever more surely a supportive experience for everyone. But not everyone can or should try to make such a person of themselves. It may be that the January Experience is such a powerful discontinuity that instead of functioning to free everyone to make themselves as learner-centered teachers of urban children in public schools, for a very few it becomes itself the source of a disabling degree of frustration, anxiety, anger, and distress. If this does turn out to be the case, it could be an additionally useful function of this PDS experience in the education and preparation of new teachers, and a function that we should seek to understand.

THE CONCLUSION

At the end of the program, most student teachers were sorry to leave their children behind. Even those who had experienced some sort of distress reported feeling that the program had been valuable, and suggested that it be continued. All suggested, more or less strongly, that ways be found for everything to occur earlier, from notifying students in different TC programs, selecting and identifying the teams, planning, and having the readings and related seminars. A few felt that student teachers should be party to selecting the theme. Most had become completely comfortable in the teacher-as-professional role, and only two retained a need for a set of more explicit and detailed goals and objectives, "guidelines" they called them, for who should do what, where, and when.

The student teachers' unanimous recommendation that it be continued without major design changes attests to the worth they found or perceived. There were major changes in student teaching practices during the program, the most important being that when given the opportunity to do so, they reached into themselves to invent, enact, and analyze tasks by which children would learn, instead of seeking to follow some prescribed set of classroom "dos" and "don'ts." They interacted with their experienced teacher team members as colleagues rather than as the keeper of the rules, or the evaluator of their performance. Problems that arose derailed neither the project nor the animus of adventure, and were solved usually via team discussion or by calling on the college facilitator for advice or intervention. And most of them learned. Their acts and their thoughts evidenced learning about childen, about learning, about interdisciplinarity, and about ways to teach, that were consistent with the course goals.

THE CHILDREN'S STORY

We asked the students to write answers to some questions about the program in the days after it ended. Their involvement, the quality of their work, their pride and enthusiasm, and their enjoyment were evident daily, but we wanted them to tell us what they thought. To the extent that these responses represent a valid evaluation method, it was he,rteningly clear that our youngsters' learning experiences were dramatically enhanced and enriched. Their remarks, synthesized below, offer a powerfully persuasive argument for the educational potential of a PDS relationship.

THE EXPERIENCE IN PROCESS

The youngsters, in all models, moved as a group in their usual fashion from class to class and room to room most of the time, although what occurred in those rooms was quite different from the norm. They did go outside of school much more often in all teams. In one team, however, there was an interesting commitment to restructuring the grouping. Every Friday, new groups of youngsters were created comprised of some students from all classes involved. During these times, they were involved in an activity that was designed to have them share what they were learning in their regular group. In one model, the culminating activity was a whole morning spent in the school cafeteria sharing what they learned with all the other children, team teachers and student teachers, administrators, and some parents. In two models the program was "kicked off" by a combined session of all the youngsters, teachers, and student teachers. In some models the time spent in one activity exceeded the period time of the schedule, as double periods were created, or three scheduled periods were reorganized into two longer periods.

On Getting Help. Foremost in the minds of the children was the "help they got" it seemed. This was the most prevalent theme in their responses and may be considered to be the other side of the individual attention coin noted by the teachers. Individual attention is especially beneficial to middle schoolers so that their differences can be addressed. Their development is so rapid and varied that many individual concerns go unnoticed in the traditional large group classroom setting. One continual challenge confronting teachers is discovering means to increase academic expectations for youngsters without simultaneously increasing individual frustrations. Part of the resolution to the challenge, in this progam, was the increase in person power that allowed someone to be in touch with and respond to the individual children. They told us that "Having the extra teachers was nice. The reason why? . . . they all helped me with my work" and that "I like having extra people to help because more than one person can get help from a teacher." Another "felt happy to have two or three teachers in the class . . . they were very nice" and was echoed by "It was a lot easier to get help." They really appreciated the extra and personal attention that was provided, attention both from their regular teacher and from the student teachers. For these childen, it did not seem to matter to them what the help was about, in which subject, in what project, with what skill, or with what problem, only that it was there.

For a few students, however, this sudden increase in the number of adults in the room drastically changed the classroom ecology in ways that made them both initially uncomfortable and later pleased. One student addressed this directly: "I felt like I couldn't hide . . . 'cause there was always a teacher looking over my shoulder. . . . I'm sort of glad this happened." Another student, during the project, had described that the usual state of affairs in the classroom was "it's one of them against all of us" whereas during the January Experience the odds had decreased considerably.

On Having Fun. The second general theme that emerged from the youngsters responses was that it had been fun. That they were having fun, and were enjoying school in January, had been abundantly evident, perhaps never more so than when they were skillfully persuaded by the belly-dancer to join hands and dance—90 youngsters, laughing, snaking around the cafeteria, tapping their feet, and singing along with her. We had seen them designing bridges on paper and then making their designs come alive with straws; we had seen them hunting information about specific animals and delighting in confirmation of what they knew with what they saw in the exhibits in the museum; we had seen them discovering the meaning of "opposing thumb" as they made concerted efforts to do things with their thumbs taped to their palms. They worked with advanced software, created Islamic art, avidly calculated percentages and charted graphs, wrote letters to a business leader and to soldiers, and did experiments that mimicked the alchemical search for gold. They became avid journal writers. They had spent days completing whole projects, reworking, and improving, asking for advice and for helpful assessment. They had stood, almost everyone, in front of their peers, sharing with obvious pride some meaning they had made. Not only were they having fun but

THE FINALE

In addition to the educational worthiness of the program, the experience was a rather wonderful fruition of the mutual trust and respect developed during years of school-college collaboration in PDS activity. If a project of this nature and scope had been attempted without the long and intense PDS activity preceding it, before the basic foundation of communication and trust was established, and if that spirit of trust and support had not been nurtured throughout the duration of the program it might well have been a disaster.

As it was, cooperating teachers felt that they owned their programs. They did not feel that they were being constantly critiqued by either school administration or college faculty. They felt comfortable including student teachers in all phases of planning and implementing and entrusting them with as much responsibility as was feasible. Enough favorable feelings had developed that both groups felt secure in taking the kind of professional risks so essential in this kind of innovative program. The faculty of Columbia University's Teachers College felt confident that they were allied with capable school professionals who shared the basic philosophy of fulfilling the educational needs of youngsters. School administrators were totally supportive of the program, in every detail of logistics and teacher and student need. Student teachers knew that they were involved in a satisfying, challenging, and empowering experience and rapidly sought to strengthen those components in the program. They were working side-by-side as full, albeit novice, participants to invent, enact, and reflect on child-centered instruction.

Of course the youngsters sensed this uplifting spirit of doing and learning, as they sense any underlying spirit in a school. They worked hard and long, and they worked together. So we were all buoyed by the shared wave of positive interpersonal interactions that enabled us to think, work and achieve together.

In the beginning, we wondered if the design would work as anticipated and questions were raised about how we would know if it had worked or not. As a PDS program concept, success would mean that the design enabled gains in all goal areas at the same time, though not necessarily to the same degree. Even for the first effort, had it "worked" in one arena but not in all, it would have been an indication to go back to the drawing board. But it was also clear that the first attempt might be plagued by unforseen difficulties. Success for the first effort, then, lay in answers to four questions:

1. Would it work in a way that enabled people in all groups to recognize a value to themselves and to commit to a second effort?

2. Would there be any recognizable change in school and classroom practices enabling important learning by the youngsters during the experience—would the teams take the available risks?
3. Would we be able to diffuse the difficulties that emerged and solve problems that arose before they shaped the outcomes—would the support network hold and be sufficient?
4. Would there be any evidence of knowledge gained by the student teachers in keeping with the course goals?

In our own terms, then, it was a success. Everyone recognized the program's value and urged that it continue, the teams took the available risks and new practices emerged during January, the support network held, and it was evident that individual student teachers had constructed knowledge for themselves. Each of the teams generated for themselves a new way of enacting curriculum with children. It is clear that teams risked restructuring the schedule of time, space and teachers, as well as the subject matter, and to a lesser extent, the class grouping of youngsters. Team planning, team reflecting, and in-class team interactions were instrumental in driving the evolution of the models toward interdisciplinary work and child-centered instruction.

POSTSCRIPT

The 2nd and 3rd years' experiences have now come and gone. We continued our sucesses and went beyond them. We began earlier and, no longer worried about whether it would fly or not, honed the experience more surely as one in which both teacher planning and teacher learning are key issues. The same faculty members were involved again, but in revisiting the idea created new January Experiences with new themes for themselves and their student teacher team. There were more people and more disciplines involved in '92: two new mini-schools at I.S. 44 including several teachers, 2 administrators and 120 more childen joined in, two new departments at TC, Art and Special Education encouraged student teachers to enroll, and we had six teams at work. People made more connections within and beyond the school in '92: some I.S. 44 teachers made more active connection with colleagues in other teams and one teacher even led a team other than her own on a field trip to chip garnets from rocks in Central Park; four TC faculty and the dean visited I.S. 44 during the experience; one team of youngsters spent the morning in a nearby elementary school teaching the little ones how to juggle, something they had gained from the January Experience, and these same youngsters, through writing letters to the media, brought a major television network to the school for the morning of their major juggling performance; yet another team took the books that they had made in their "Family" project to TC to give an exhibition of them. There was an increased reach toward learner-centered practice in one team as 99 youngsters completed and presented a portfolio of their work in art, science, English, mathematics and social studies to be assessed by the combined team in the final days of January.

We have continued to write and talk about our work. One writing project, close to completion, distills understandings about the "student teaching" aspect of The January Experience and involves the four student teachers of a team as collaborative authors. A group of about a dozen or so I.S. 44 teachers have been in conversation with other TC faculty on the subject of creating closer collaboration and involvement in each other's work and creating a new "June" Experience. Our PDS relationship has expanded to include another intermediate school in the district and several interested faculty from that school have been visiting the idea of the January Experience with us. We become increasingly convinced of the capacity of the January Experience to enable colleges and schools to remake themselves so youngsters experience school as a place in which they want and are able to grow.

REFERENCES

Darling-Hammond, L. (1988). The futures of teaching *Educational Leadership, 46,* 4–10.

Darling-Hammond, L. (1990). Teacher professionalism: Why and how, in *Schools as collaborative cultures: Creating the future now.* A. Lieberman (Ed.) New York: Falmer Press

Kerekes, J. (1987). The interdisciplinary unit . . . It's here to stay! *Educational Leadership, 18,* 12–14.

Slavin, R. E. (1989). Here to stay—Or gone tomorrow? *Educational Leadership, 47,* 3

Snyder, J., & Schwartz, F. (1991). A report to The New York Community Trust. New York: Teachers College, Columbia University.

Chapter 7

THE LOS ANGELES PROFESSIONAL PRACTICE SCHOOL: A STUDY OF MUTUAL IMPACT

Johanna K. Lemlech, Hillary Hertzog-Foliart, and Arlene Hackl

How likely is it that teachers and teacher educators, jointly, will assume responsibility for structuring a school-within-a-school to model professional practice? Can norms of colleagueship, openness, and trust be developed between campus-based educators and inner city teachers to accomplish the aims of restructuring? Will teachers assume responsibility for making decisions related to teaching and learning processes, school environments, use and management of resources, and assessment of teacher and student performance? How does change (restructuring) happen? How will faculty in a school-within-a-school relate to their faculty as a whole? How can student teachers contribute to the project? Will there be reciprocal effects on the practices of project teachers and university teacher educators? Will fundamental beliefs about teaching be altered as a consequence of collaboration? Will changes in teaching practices, beliefs, and a sense of professionalism occur as a consequence of structural change?

Each of these questions has arisen and become the focus of a current restructuring project at the Norwood-University of Southern California Professional Practice School (PPS). Begun in the 1990–91 academic year, the PPS is funded by the American Federation of Teachers (AFT) union and the Exxon Corporation. The aims of the project, as conceived by the AFT, are to improve instructional programs for children, to provide a professional environment for the education of student teachers, and to promote inquiry on teaching (Levine, 1988). The Los Angeles site was selected by the AFT because of (1) the USC Collegial Teacher Education Program, that prepares preservice teachers to establish collegial relationships and assume teacher leadership, and (2) the established relationship between the university and the elementary school.

This case study reports through participant perceptions a slice of the chronological history of the ongoing project. It begins with descriptions of the school and university, continues with how the project began, and then describes the major issues that have arisen and how the author-participants from the school and university perceive those issues.

THE LOS ANGELES PROFESSIONAL PRACTICE SCHOOL

NORWOOD STREET SCHOOL

Norwood is a Los Angeles inner city elementary school serving a 99% Hispanic population of 1,300 students in grades K through 6. The school is situated a mile from the USC campus near downtown Los Angeles. Overcrowding has resulted in the school being organized on a year-round schedule with four "tracks" of classrooms that function on a rotating vacation schedule. As a result, only 75% of the faculty and students are present at any given time. Administration of the school is the responsibility of a principal and assistant principal. Chapter I, bilingual, and state school improvement compensatory education funding allow for a large support staff including program coordinators, resource specialists, classroom aides, school nurse, psychologist, and social services specialist. Free breakfast and lunch programs are widely participated in by students. A large percentage of the faculty are emergency-credentialed bilingual or probationary teachers.

USC COLLEGIAL TEACHER PREPARATION PROGRAM

The preservice teacher education program at USC is small, preparing fewer than 75 elementary teacher candidates each year. In the Fall of 1987 the program was transformed from the traditional apprenticeship model to a research-focused collegial one. The program pairs student teachers for their student teaching experience. Collegial preparation provides candidates with opportunity for: (1) reflection, (2) learning to work collaboratively with a partner, (3) studying the student teaching experience, (4) deriving meaning from personal experience, and (5) helping to structure the clinical experience. The program was designed to create a bond between partner student teachers to enhance their ability to become professionals and teacher leaders.

The preservice teachers at USC participate concurrently in a general methods course and in student teaching for an entire school year. Faculty for the program include the director of student teaching, the methods professor, and university-employed coordinators. All involved faculty members have extensive elementary teaching experience. A team approach is utilized, with faculty members meeting biweekly to discuss progress in the methods course and matching expectations in clinical experience. University coordinators serve as the liaison between the university program and the clinical school site, meeting with supervising classroom teachers weekly to observe and discuss student progress.

FORMATION OF THE PROFESSIONAL PRACTICE SCHOOL

The PPS began operating in July, 1990. The original grant was the result of collaborative efforts by the Director of Student Teaching at USC, representatives from the Los Angeles Unified School District, and the Vice President of the United Teachers of Los Angeles. Norwood was selected from an applicant pool of ten schools.

The participants in the PPS from Norwood were nine teachers, a media resource teacher, and the principal. Though the teachers were on different calendar schedules, they considered themselves a school-within-a-school. The major participants from the university included the Director of Student Teaching who is a professor of education specializing in teacher education and instructional leadership, and a clinical professor of education specializing in language arts and technology who serves as a university student teacher coordinator. The general methods professor contributed on occasion and a doctoral student served as participant-observer for the project.

Governance for the project was the responsibility of one of the teachers and the principal, who were named codirectors. Funds for the project were administrated by the university with the professor of education named as principal investigator of the grant.

IN THE BEGINNING

How do a school and a university begin the transformation from separate institutions to a collaborative endeavor to promote teacher professionalism? The university participants focused initial efforts on the building of collegiality among project participants. The issue of roles and responsibilities quickly surfaced. Traditional norms were anticipated by some school site members, and as the project began, preconceptions were sometimes fulfilled. For example, the university members assumed the role of participant researchers tracking the progress of the project. The school site personnel focused on maintaining the norm of individual autonomy for classroom decision making.

Suspicion of goals and motives surfaced. One school participant commented:

> I'm not sure how the USC professors see the term restructuring. I see a lot of power play from both ends—the University and AFT—and we are caught in the middle. I'm not clear how USC is planning to incorporate this [project].

The need for the development of colleagueship, openness, and trust was immediately apparent to the teacher codirector and the professor of education. Initiated by the university participants, individual interviews were conducted with school site and university project members by the doctoral student serving as participant-observer. Participants were asked to describe personal and curriculum goals for the project. A cumulative list was generated and recirculated to school-site participants, who were asked to prioritize the list. The two university members did not take part in the prioritization of the goals. During an all-day meeting of all participants, results of the prioritization of goals were shared; common goals for the project were identified and substantive conversation about those goals took place. Using a form of backward mapping (Elmore, 1980), discussion focused on what the curriculum and instructional program in a model school environment might look like. Together, university and school-based participants began to discover that common goals existed. As trust began to build, openness increased. Conversation focused on issues related to the study of teaching. The development of collegiality had begun. By common consent the focus of the restructuring effort became the curriculum and instructional program. This served as the foundation of the Professional Practice School and the glue that would hold the project together.

VARIED PERSPECTIVES

Creating professional practice schools requires a new kind of collaboration between school site and university participants. Both are expected to change organizational structure, alter the pattern of relationships that characterized past associations, and rethink what the education for new teachers should be. In the words of Neufeld (1990)

> The formation of professional practice schools will not be a straightforward organizational or conceptual task. For the parties involved, it will be an adventure that requires a good bit of risk-taking, a tolerance for not "getting it right" the first time, and a firm commitment to the long-term goals" (p. 142).

It is logical that as collaborative activity is engaged in at the PPS, the school-based and university participants will bring to that activity not only multiple perspectives reflective of their disciplines of knowledge and varied beliefs, but also their prior experiences. These will all affect interaction. It is equally logical to assume that having collaborated in different ways in the past concerning a variety of topics, participants' perspectives regarding that collaboration will differ. Analysis of perspectives is critical to understanding the development of any Professional Practice School. In reporting on this PPS, we therefore, find it most useful to offer a discussion of the issues thus far encountered from the sometimes diverse perspectives of the university and the school-based participants. To do this, we address three major emphases of restructuring efforts of the 1990s: the study of teaching, teacher decision making, and teacher professionalism. For in-depth discussion of current reform efforts, see Cuban (1990), Holmes Group (1990), and Shulman (1990). As author-participants representing both the university and the school site, we offer varied perspectives concerning each issue under separate heading (University Perspective and Teacher Perspective), and in the active voice. The intent is to provide the reader an opportunity to respond to a very personal account of involvement by the authors. When appropriate, we have included statements made by other participants as additional reference to help clarify perspective on an issue (see endnote 1 for documentation references).

THE STUDY OF TEACHING

From the beginning of the project, participants' efforts have been focused on the study of teaching as a means of school improvement. Investigation of teaching and learning processes, the language of teaching, beliefs about teaching, and how student teachers should engage in the study of teaching have dominated conversations. However, while participant discussions centered on common interests, different perspectives and values were apparent. Examination of various issues illustrates the authors' attempts to share varied perspectives and draw from them a plan for what the PPS should be.

TEACHING AND LEARNING PROCESSES

University Perception.   When the project began, we at the university recognized that some school-based participants questioned university motivation for participation in the project. While aware that the instructional program needed to be the creation of the teachers who would be teaching it, we wanted a teaching center for student teachers where the cooperating teachers would engage in reflective supervision and where the program reflected current research about teaching and learning and would reinforce recent trends in curriculum and pedagogy (Zeichner & Liston, 1985). During the past several years, the USC Teacher Education Program has been emphasizing models of teaching and collegial professional development in order to help new teachers assume responsibility for leadership and decision making. We were concerned that our students have an internship in a rich environment conducive to the study of teaching. However, as project participants, we were hesitant to express our opinions.

As the PPS teachers discussed their instructional goals at the initial goal setting session, we were reassured that both school and university shared many of the same beliefs. Through much discussion, the planned and evolving instructional program centered on the development of a thinking curriculum organized around thematic units that would integrate disciplines and use a variety of instructional strategies. Project teachers began to work in partner teams to plan thematic units after first requesting help from the university participants on how to develop teaching units. However, realization of this "idealized" program has moved slowly. It is frustrating for university-based teachers to be observers rather than participants in the curriculum development process.

An exciting part of the instructional program planned during the project's 1st year was the development of a club program, the purpose of which was to empower the children by giving them curriculum choices through an elective program. As initially planned, teachers and student teachers were to lead clubs, in special areas of their own personal expertise, comprised of cross-age groups of children who would choose to engage in the study of something unusual and of great personal interest. These "learning modules" would be repeated throughout the school year so that children would have the opportunity to study several different areas of interest.

Organizational problems resulting from the different calendar schedules of the teachers and school-day time issues delayed the realization of the club program. Finally, during the Spring semester this goal was partially accomplished by using student teachers and two PPS teachers to teach the clubs. What had begun as a concept to meet goals for student learning was reduced to a means to resolve time-related issues, an example of how organizational problems encroach upon philosophically based goals as a site attempts to restructure while daily business continues. (See Elmore and Associates, 1990, for a discussion of how routinized organizational practices inhibit new ideas and change.)

Teacher Perception. Time together as a PPS has helped the teachers determine our instructional aims in the context of thematic units that relate to a specific curriculum orientation. Various curriculum conceptions have been explored in order to identify and validate individuals' preferred conception. For the most part, we tend to favor an orientation linked with our school mission, that is, the cognitive processes development approach. It has been very challenging and sometimes frustrating to consistently teach to that approach. The tendency is to backslide and teach as before, or as one was taught. But meeting to develop thematic units has helped us reflect on our practices, expand our thinking, and actually reach some of our goals.

THE LANGUAGE OF TEACHING

Like all professions, teaching has a unique language; like all languages, it evolves. At the Professional Practice School, we have found that the language of teaching affects the study of teaching.

University Perception.   Prior to the creation of the PPS, Norwood was a site for USC student teaching and several of the current PPS teachers were supervising teachers. Student teachers brought with them to the Norwood classrooms, a language of teaching that differs from older or more traditional descriptions. Probably the best example of this was the student teachers' use and talk about Joyce, Weil, and Showers' models of teaching (1992). On an informal and individual basis, discussion between the university coordinator and the supervising teachers about current language descriptions and teaching models preceded the PPS grant. Once the project was underway, several project teachers requested that university members allot time to explain and demonstrate particular models of teaching. This led to several project teachers' experimentation with the models in their own classrooms. Most importantly, it has been interesting to hear the discussion between student teachers and project teachers become enriched and consonant as they share mutual language symbols and descriptions.

Teacher Perception.   The university participants have shared with PPS teachers various models of teaching consonant with our school mission. Thus far these models have included Group Investigation, Concept Attainment, Advance Organizer, and Synectics. The teachers feel it is our task to be well versed in these models, not only for demonstration purposes, but also for the sake of ensuring that instructional aims match pedagogical strategies. As another teacher observed:

> It is comforting to know that student teachers are learning alternatives to the seven step lesson plan. They greatly benefit from observing and interacting with a master teacher who has mastered and regularly practices appropriate models of teaching and who regularly reflects on his/her practices.

EFFECTS ON TEACHER EDUCATION

Bringing together university faculty and school-based practitioners to reflect on the study of curriculum and teaching practices has implications both for children and for preservice education. The following perceptions describe how our partnership has influenced practices.

University Perception.   The PPS has influenced the USC teacher preparation program in several ways. Though university coordinators interact with all of the USC students' supervising teachers, conversations at other training sites are, by necessity, brief and related to the specific teaching partners. With PPS teachers, conversations about teaching and preparation for teaching are intense and sustained. There is a focus on how individuals learn to teach; is there a developmental pattern? Project teachers are able to give important feedback about what USC students know and understand about teaching and what they do not know or misunderstand. This insight helps USC make immediate adjustments in the student teachers' curriculum and methods class. (In addition, see the discussion below about problem-solving clinics.)

Another area of impact has occurred through discussions about the Hispanic population at Norwood, concerning bilingualism and second-language learning. Special needs of the Hispanic child, cultural values, and corresponding school activities have been explored. While the student teachers learn several language acquisition models and sheltered English strategies, they also are in need of specific cultural information, and of historical and linguistic knowledge to help them appreciate the Spanish language, Hispanic culture, and life experiences. PPS teachers will be helping with content ideas and may be providing some Spanish language teaching to help student teachers use Spanish in the content fields. In addition, bilingual project teachers are serving on USC entrance screening committees to evaluate prospective student teachers' use of Spanish. We are seeking more bilingual teacher candidates, and project teachers are contributing ideas for recruitment.

Another area of impact on the teacher education program has been the collaborative development of Problem-solving Clinics for student teachers at Norwood, and other school sites. A series of clinics were created as a result of increased reflection with project teachers about current shortcomings or misconceptions student teachers should address and correct. Content for the clinics has been developed by a team of university and school-based participants, and it is sometimes taught by project teachers at the school site.

Teacher Perception.   Involvement with teacher education and the study of how student teachers learn to teach has made a significant impact on the teachers' own professional practice at Norwood. We have reviewed models of teaching and have seen how to implement them. Teachers have become aware of the value of peer coaching and the need to foster collegial relationships.

The Problem-solving Clinics have become a major component of the student teaching experience at the PPS. Here, students come together to explore areas of concern, share experiences, and put into practice the suggestions offered each other. The clinics have had a definite impact on PPS teachers, as some have helped write cases and lead seminars. This puts a fair amount of pressure on in-service professionals to keep current on educational issues and help identify causes of, and remedies for, poor student achievement and other classroom concerns.

Recently, for example, a team of project colleagues was asked to lead a seminar on developing thematic units. Student teachers suggested various themes or big ideas, and then voted for their preference. They chose the theme of relationships, and the two PPS teachers went to work in front of the student teachers, debating the possible generalizations and correspondent learning activities to integrate subject fields. In the teachers' planning discussion, they referred many times to their need to develop their own materials and to consult outside sources for the materials and knowledge they were lacking. Thus, student teachers witnessed a practical example of collegial interaction focused on planning for active, integrated, and interdisciplinary learning experiences. Since not all of the student teachers teach at the PPS, their task was to return to their respective schools and attempt the same type of planning with their collegial partners.

DECISION MAKING

In discussions of school improvement, three major issues have affected PPS participant interactions during all-day meetings: (1) student evaluation, (2) time and scheduling, and (3) project teacher recruitment and membership. The latter two issues have been particularly tension producing for both the university and school-based participants. (See Elmore and Associates, 1990, for a discussion of the internal tensions of school restructuring.)

ASSESSMENT

University Perception.   Initial hesitance by project teachers to consider different means to evaluate students, surprised the university participants. After agreeing so enthusiastically concerning the focus of project efforts on improving the curriculum and instructional practices, we were unprepared for the teachers' willingness to rely on district use of standardized testing for assessment and evaluation of student learning (See

Perrone, 1991). It was hoped that as the study of teaching processes progressed, interest in alternative assessment would be generated, and PPS teachers would feel comfortable with abandoning school norms. As the project progressed individual members assumed leadership to discuss the integration of assessment with teaching and learning.

At a recent all-day meeting, PPS teachers led the session focused on authentic assessment. They prepared exhibits and engaged PPS members in discussion of ways to have children demonstrate what they are learning. This served as an example of teachers taking charge of staff development time, making key decisions about what they want to study. However, actual implementation of plans has been slow.

Teacher Perception. Built into project planning is the issue of authentic assessment. Evaluation of student achievement is beginning to be based on student performance and products. Such evaluation is congruent with learning activities involving exploration, discussion, research, and projects. Perhaps the greatest gain is the more recent realization, for the most part, that the learning process itself is more valuable than the end result; that the planned and unplanned learning experiences empower the student as a problem-solver and inventor/creator in his own right.

A sterling example of authentic assessment is the student portfolio—a collection of the student's written projects, self-evaluations, and personal reflections on his own education. The portfolio provides concrete evidence of growth over time. It is an instrument utilized at Norwood to affirm the learner as independent and self-fulfilled, one that assists students in determining with their teacher what they have accomplished and what they have yet to achieve. It empowers students to "teach" their parents about learning experiences at parent conferences, for it is the student (not the teacher!) who makes the evaluative presentation via the portfolio.

TIME

The PPS validates that time is a critical component of schooling and of restructuring (Barr & Dreeben, 1981; Cohen, 1990; Denham & Lieberman, 1980). The consequence of the school site teachers' different calendar schedules is that some decisions need to be reconsidered since all teachers are never in attendance at the same staff development sessions. Another consequence of the year round calendar track system is that not all tracks synchronize with the university calendar.

Teacher Perception. Since becoming the PPS, various models of teaching have been explored, and teachers have seen how and when they are most appropriately implemented; units for thematic, interdisciplinary learning have been developed and teachers have attempted to link units with authentic assessment; teachers have become increasingly aware of the role of room environment in the learning process and have made efforts to enrich and relate it to the theme under study. Also, teachers have addressed the value of peer coaching and collegial relationships and attended planning sessions for the purpose of exploring and implementing the above practices. They've taken on student teachers and have attempted to role model these practices, and have developed some of the content for the problem-based clinics attended by student teachers.

Norwood students and their parents continue to need individualized "quality time" with teachers before and after school. PPS teachers need to maintain and increase collegial relationships with non-PPS faculty requiring input and assistance in other school related matters. Though the PPS is a "school-within-a-school," it has not ceased to be an active and necessary part of the rest of the school, especially now that the PPS has received much staff development and the PPS teachers have much to offer to others.

Where is the time for all of this? Assuming that the goal is not merely to "cover the bases," how can the teachers accomplish all the goals they have set for themselves with the high degree of quality that the PPS seeks to develop? Teachers are constantly experimenting with ways to "generate" time. One way is that recently student teachers began conducting classroom activity clubs so children could pursue a hobby of their choice. The student teachers have enriched their own experience and that of the children in new and different ways; the project teachers have enjoyed hosting the activities and sharing in the students' delight. The greatest gain from the clubs is the hour a week free from teaching responsibilities. It has helped ease the planning crunch, but obviously it is not enough. The PPS teachers have looked at ways to "bank" time, by beginning school 15 minutes earlier, 5 days per week, in order to dismiss the students 75 minutes early 1 day per week. This plan would free the project teachers from their lunch period on, to deal with project goals, such as coplanning thematic units, peer coaching, and assisting in problem-based clinics. Banking time is currently one of the issues Norwood School is addressing in its school-based management program. However, to date, the school district has not consented to the plan, though we are hopeful that it eventually will.

University Perception. Time is certainly at the mercy of the organizational structure; the project confirms the "nested layer" concept of Barr and Dreeban (1981). At the school site, the issue of "banked" time affects a variety of other programs, school services, and class schedules. For example, university participants have been present when discussions focused on such questions as: will beginning school earlier in the morning affect the free breakfast program? If time were banked in the afternoon, would it affect siblings who need to walk home with project children? How will other teachers react to a special time schedule for project teachers?

Time and time alternatives are also at the mercy of individuals' commitment and independent-dependent-interdependent relationships. One PPS teacher has been heard to comment that project participation has been an intrusion into personal (independent) development. Another PPS teacher seems to resent the need to facilitate others' development. For a discussion of autonomy and its effect on collegiality see Lemlech & Hertzog-Foliart, 1992; and Little, 1990. Some project members have teamed to begin the development of thematic units and to practice models of teaching; for others, priorities differ. Agreed upon lunch meetings and after school planning meetings are subject to perceived need (level of commitment); as a result committee meetings are sporadic.

RECRUITMENT

Several teachers who initially were PPS participants withdrew. The time commitment was one factor that influenced withdrawal; another was the perceived effect on relationships with other nonmember faculty. Because some project teachers' work schedules do not correspond to the USC calendar, there is a shortage of qualified supervising teachers for student teaching. Recruiting new members has been a frequent topic of discussion.

Teacher Perception.   The PPS seeks to recruit new members to expand its positive influence on the practice of teaching at Norwood. At present a goal is to have 12 committed teachers who will participate actively and consistently in the project. We now have a little more than half that number. Some teachers have left the project because of the pressing time requirements. Many experienced teachers have expressed interest, but very few are willing to commit their time and energies. Those teachers who wish to join will be required to submit a professional portfolio to current members for discussion and evaluation. It is hoped that as the project group expands, the school as a whole will become enriched and distinguish itself as a proud institution of high expectations and high achievement—for students, student teachers, teachers, and administrators alike.

University Perception.   The underlying purpose of a PPS is to provide an environment where really good practices are modeled. In particular these really good practices relate to the teaching and the content of the curriculum. Other assumptions integral to the PPS concept have to do with the relationship of preservice and inservice education, the relationship between university and school practitioners, and ongoing inquiry into best practices. None of these purposes can be accomplished without individuals with vision (Barth, 1990).

We, as university teacher educators, are as concerned about our students (the student teachers) as school practitioners are about theirs, and consider it important to place student teachers with "master" teachers. Therefore, the university wants to recruit the very best teachers in the school district, with a free market in which teachers apply for membership. The university believes there is a need to search beyond Norwood when teacher vacancies exist to find expert teachers who will share the PPS vision. Though teacher members of the PPS understand our perspective, their concern with faculty relations inhibits recruitment beyond the immediate school.

PROFESSIONALISM

Once project ownership was established, PPS participants needed to concentrate on intra-group relationships. Collegiality within the group would affect the improvement process (Barth, 1990; Darling-Hammond & Sclan, 1992; Fullan & Hargreaves, 1991; Schlechty, 1990; Sykes, 1990). Interview data and records of group meetings indicated that group commitment, decision making, and expressions of empowerment seemed to be heightened or diminished by concerns about relationships with other faculty members, personal feelings of esteem, authority, and efficacy.

RELATIONS WITH OTHER FACULTY MEMBERS

University Perception.   From initial concerns about elitism to later concerns about recruitment, school-based participants have been greatly affected by and concerned about their relationships with other school faculty members. Sometimes these concerns preceded the study of teaching and affected working and collegial relationships.

Teacher Perception.   As the faculty (as a whole) at Norwood attempts to establish school-based management with an eye toward total school restructuring, the project teachers feel they are now able to give much valuable input in terms of curriculum design and implementation. PPS teachers share what we have learned about the development of thematic units and authentic assessment, notably portfolio assessment. We endeavor to make our own classrooms models for the rest of the school by creating a room environment that reflects active learning.

During discussion about relations with other faculty members, PPS teachers made the following comments: "I become concerned about other faculty members' perceptions of me. Do they see me as a peer apart from them?" "I find myself taking on leadership positions with confidence and authority. I feel more accepted by the rest of the faculty." "I am more aggressive about my beliefs and sharing what I have learned. I want them to `buy into' the thinking curriculum." "I am both discouraged and encouraged. PPS has been helpful in helping to direct less experienced teachers to look beyond their own classroom." "Seems some are resentful of PPS; think it's a big joke!"

COLLEGIALITY

As supervising teachers and potential supervising teachers, PPS teachers were very interested in the functioning of the USC Collegial Teacher Preparation Program. Those PPS teachers who had supervised partner student teachers recognized that novice teachers gained insight into teaching processes by observing each other. This occurs because responsibility to observe *what* is happening in the classroom leads to reflection about why it is happening. The experienced supervising teachers recognized that the neophytes were forced to focus on the "other" instead of just on the "self." The content and context of novice teachers' discussions have changed from the visceral to substantive, reflective conversations.

University Perception. Studies of collegiality among student teachers conducted by USC prior to involvement in the PPS project have provided insight about what might make a difference in staff development programs with experienced teachers. A beginning study of partner student teachers identified helping and reflective interactive behaviors (Lemlech & Kaplan, 1990). An ongoing study of student teachers' collegial interactions has identified how professional relationships progress through six stages of development, including peer interaction, partnering, competition, focus on the study of teaching, integration of skills, and culminating in reflective and professional behaviors that constitute collegiality (Lemlech & Kaplan, 1991). As participants in the PPS project, we wondered whether an understanding of the collegial process among student teachers would inform the development of collegiality in a professional practice school.

It was recognized that project teachers had cordial and helping relationships with each other, but our experience validated that proximity and helping behaviors do not make individuals colleagues. (See: Fullan & Hargreaves, 1991; Lemlech & Hertzog-Foliart, 1992; Lemlech & Kaplan, 1990; Little, 1990; Zahorik, 1987.)

The goal for all-day staff development sessions was to facilitate the development of collegial relationships. To accomplish this, we attempted to cultivate an hospitable environment for significant talk about teaching. Perspectives of time, of relationships among PPS members, of beliefs about teaching, and of professionalism have changed as a result.

Teacher Perception. In the opinion of this teacher, no PPS teacher feels exactly the same about teaching as before the project began. Ever since Norwood came into partnership with USC, there has come to exist a renewed sense of professionalism, of true pride in one's work, that makes our campus an exciting place. Teachers have begun to view students as problem solvers who are more likely to learn if they are allowed to have input into their units of study. We see ourselves as colleagues with the administration in formulating and assessing educational opportunities, and with the university in determining the student teacher's course of study.

A number of PPS teachers have made the following statements: "I have become closer with all of the members and developed a level of trust in working with them and voicing my opinions." "I communicate freely; I do not hide anything—emotions, ideas, etc." "A very comfortable rapport has developed between PPS teachers." "There is open and candid communications which did not exist before. There is trust."

When asked, how their beliefs changed about teaching, teachers have commented: "I see myself as facilitator and coach instead of disseminator of knowledge—feel more committed to and proud of my profession than ever!" "I'm working on finding a balance between process and content— but at least I know I'm not alone." "I believe different strategies need to be used to bring about the achievement/product I desire. I value using the different models of instruction in various need settings."

When asked for comments concerning professionalism they said: "I have a keener sense as to what my role is as a professional person." "I was unsure of my status in this area; felt that sufficient experiences were lacking in my career to honestly call myself a prideful professional." "I have a renewed, heightened sense of myself and my peers as well-educated, informed professionals." "I have become more professional because I have more knowledge." "I'm more intellectually challenged." "I can make decisions on what my professional development needs are and how to meet them, thanks to the project."

TEACHER ASSESSMENT

The issue of teacher assessment is tied to the question of recruiting additional teachers to the PPS. When the issue was discussed, project members recognized that there needed to be criteria to determine who should be a teacher in the PPS and how readiness should be determined.

University Perception.   The major concern for the university project members was finding additional competent teachers for supervising student teachers. The group agreed to examine criteria used to select teachers for participation. In addition, the PPS teachers expressed the belief that if Norwood students were to be assessed through portfolio accomplishments, perhaps teachers could also.

Teacher Perception.   If student portfolios are desirable as proof of reflection and accomplishment, teacher portfolios should have equal merit. The PPS teachers have therefore decided that each project teacher will develop a professional portfolio featuring a statement of teaching ideology, sample unit and lesson plans, self-evaluations and statement of future professional goals, peer recommendations, letters from students and parents, photographs of student exhibitions, videotapes of special presentations, and evidence of participation in professional development activities, such as: planning thematic units, peer coaching, assisting in problem-based clinics or any other item that teachers feel is representative of their professional practice. Teachers will examine, revise, and update their portfolios as a means of demonstrating competency in the on-going task of self-assessment.

CONCLUSIONS AND IMPLICATIONS

Effective teaching research of the late 1960s through the 1970s influenced policy makers, school districts, teachers in schools, and preservice teacher education programs to focus almost exclusively on basic skill instruction and specific teaching functions (Rosenshine, 1983). As a consequence, teachers (and principals) failed to extend their thinking about significant teaching goals and willingly limited their involvement in key decision making activities that affected students, the school milieu, and their own professional growth. For this reason restructuring efforts have had to convince teachers of their efficacy and responsibility for decision making (Sykes, 1990). This was the case in this project. This chapter began with some basic questions that focused our inquiry. These questions will be repeated to allow comment on some developing patterns.

  • *How likely is it that teachers and teacher educators, jointly, will assume responsibility for restructuring a school-within-a-school to model professional practice?* Teachers and teacher educators can work together to accomplish common goals, but parameters need to be clearly defined. The "regularities of schooling" influence the teacher members. For school-based personnel, the maintenance of the day-to-day operation of schooling must take precedence, and this takes considerable energy. Needed changes affect school staff much more than they do university personnel.

Roles, functions, and relationships for group meetings and for implementation decisions need time to develop. Initially, university members found themselves organizing the all-day meetings and planning the agenda, but as the project progressed, school-based members assumed some responsibility. Patience is a virtue since perceptions, experiences, and beliefs of all involved differ, and time is needed to create common group understandings.

• *Can norms of colleagueship, openness and trust be developed between campus-based educators and inner city teachers to accomplish the aims of restructuring?* Appreciation of what individuals can contribute to each other's education (and professionalism) is an important aspect of a joint relationship. But appreciation doesn't happen until there is openness and trust. Not until you can recognize each other's strengths and weaknesses are you able to contribute to each other's effectiveness and establish a basis for professional collaboration and colleagueship. Open, professional dialogue focused on the study of teaching helps to build these norms. Through discussion, project members were able to meld the competence of experienced teachers with teacher educators' knowledge of current research on teaching to develop a collaborative relationship. Participants in a project such as this need to consciously work to keep communication as open as possible.

• *Will teachers assume responsibility for making decisions related to teaching and learning processes, school environments, use and management of resources, and assessment of teacher and student performance?* Unequivocally, yes. But the assumption of new roles for decision making needs to evolve from an understanding of how decisions affect the instructional program and student learning. New roles and responsibilities need support and encouragement both internally and externally. University members of restructuring teams need to remember that to some extent they are on the outside, looking in; they can encourage, collaborate, serve as consultants, and exert a modicum of pressure. Internally, principals and district personnel need to facilitate the process by providing time for teachers to take on new and additional responsibilities.

• *How will project faculty relate to the school's faculty as a whole?* Not until project members had established group cohesiveness and varying degrees of collegiality were they able to cope with their sense of ostracism by the rest of the faculty stemming from project identification and exclusiveness. Group cohesiveness and collegiality fostered confidence, self-esteem, and professionalism. This was ultimately communicated to the rest of the faculty, and project members began to realize the potential to enhance knowledge and professionalism of other faculty through their contributions to school-wide faculty meetings, participation in school leadership committees, and through mentoring relationships with inexperienced faculty members.

• *How can student teachers contribute to restructuring efforts?* Student teachers assumed responsibility to contribute to the school curriculum by enriching children's experiences through the club program. This served to release project teachers for planning responsibilities. Student teachers can also provide a critical link between university professors and school-based educators. The student teachers in this project demonstrated how collegiality develops, how teachers can serve as peer teachers for each other, and how peers can be comfortable and open with each other. In addition, by citing problems encountered by student teachers, project participants have an impersonal, value-free focus for initial discussions of teaching processes and how individuals learn to teach.

• *Will there be reciprocal effects on the practices of project teachers and of university teacher educators?* Collegial relationships helped project participants:

> Make the consideration of curriculum and instruction the focus for restructuring efforts thus opening up the study of what needs to happen in classrooms to improve student performance;
> "Make public" what is happening in classrooms by sharing prideful lessons and gaining comfort recognizing that it is "ok" not to be expert in everything. Campus-based educators can make similar declarations;
> Provide a direct (and reciprocal) link from what preservice teachers study to what is reinforced in practice;
> Illuminate the developmental nature of learning to teach, thereby bolstering efficacy of experienced teachers through greater awareness of what needs to be modeled for the neophyte;
> Identify and expand the decision-making potential of classroom teachers prompting self-esteem and feelings of professionalism.

• *Will fundamental beliefs about teaching be altered as a consequence of the collaboration?* Shared readings, professional dialogue, presentations, and focused reflection helped project members consider and reassess their beliefs about teaching. Nowhere is the domino theory so evident as in the decision-making realm of curriculum and instruction. Once project members came to terms with their idealized curriculum, there was no turning back. Each aim required new insights, new teaching methodologies, new environments and ultimately new assessments, and each new insight and methodology contributed to changing fundamental beliefs affecting classroom practices.

NOTE

[1]The authors have served as participants in the project since it's inception. Lemlech and Hertzog-Foliart are faculty at the university; Hackl is a classroom teacher at the school site. Documentation of this case study was achieved through personal observation field notes kept by the authors, participant interviews, questionnaires, reflective responses to focused questions, and audio tapes of group meetings.

Acknowledgment.   This paper was prepared for and presented at the 1992 Annual Meeting of the American Education Research Association, San Francisco, California.

REFERENCES

Barr, R., & Dreeben, R. (1981). *School policy, production, and productivity.* Chicago: University of Chicago.

Barth, R. S. (1990). *Improving schools from within.* San Francisco: Jossey-Bass.

Cohen, M. (1990). Key issues confronting state policymakers. In R. F. Elmore and Associates *Restructuring schools: The next generation of educational reform (251–288).* San Francisco: Jossey-Bass.

Cuban, L. (1990). Cycles of history: Equity versus excellence. In S. B. Bacharach (Ed.) *Education reform making sense of it all.* Boston: Allyn and Bacon.

Darling-Hammond, L., & Sclan, E. (1992). Policy and supervision. In C. D. Glickman (Ed.). *Supervision in transition.* Alexandria, VA: ASCD.

Denham, C., & Lieberman, A. (Eds.) (1980). *Time to learn.* Sacramento, CA: California Commission for Teacher Preparation and Licensing.

Elmore, R. F. (1980). Backward mapping: Implementation research and policy decisions. *Political Science Quarterly.* 94(4), 601–616.

Elmore, R. F., & Associates. (1990). *Restructuring schools: The next generation of educational reform.* San Francisco: Jossey-Bass.

Fullan, M., & Hargreaves, A. (1991). *What's worth fighting for?* Ontario, Canada: Ontario Teachers' Federation.

Holmes Group. (1988). *Tomorrow's teachers: A report of the Holmes group.* East Lansing, MI: Author.

Holmes Group. (1990). *Tomorrow's schools. Principles for the design of professional development schools.* East Lansing, MI: Author.

Joyce, B. R., Weil, M., & Showers, B. (1992). *Models of teaching.* Fourth Ed. Boston: Allyn and Bacon.

Lemlech, J. K., & Kaplan, S. N. (1990). Learning to talk about teaching: Collegiality in clinical teacher education. *Action in Teacher Education, 12*(1), 13–19.

Lemlech, J., K., & Kaplan, S. N. (November, 1991). Collegial teacher preparation, reflective practice, and social studies teaching. Paper presented to College, University Faculty Association of the National Council for the Social Studies, Annual Meeting, Washington, DC.

Lemlech, J. K., & Hertzog-Foliart, H. (April, 1992). Restructuring to become a professional practice school: Stages of collegiality and the development of professionalism. Paper presented at the annual meeting of the American Educational Research Association, San Francisco.

Levine, M. (1988). *Professional practice schools: Building a model. Monograph 1.* Washington, DC: American Federation of Teachers.

Little, J. W. (1990). The persistence of privacy: Autonomy and initiative in teachers' professional relations. *Teachers College Record, 91*(4), 509–536.

Neufeld, B. (1990). Professional practice schools in context: New mixtures of institutional authority. In M. Levine (Ed) *Professional practice schools: Building a model. Volume II.* Washington, DC: American Federation of Teachers.

Perrone, V. (1991). *Expanding student assessment.* Alexandria, VA: Association for Supervision and Curriculum Development.

Rosenshine, B. (1983). Teaching functions in instructional programs. *The Elementary School Journal. 83*(4), 335–352.

Schlechty, P. C. (1990). *Schools for the 21st century.* San Francisco: Jossey-Bass.

Shulman, L. S. (1990). *Aristotle had it right: On knowledge and pedagogy.* East Lansing, MI: Holmes Group.

Sykes, G. (1990). Fostering teacher professionalism in schools. In R. F. Elmore and Associates *Restructuring schools: The next generation of educational reform* (p. 59–96). San Francisco: Jossey-Bass.

Zahorik, J. A. (1987). Teachers' collegial interaction: An exploratory study. *The Elementary School Journal, 87,* 385–396.

Zeichner, K. M., & Liston, D. P. (April, 1985). *Theory and practice in the evolution of an inquiry-oriented student teaching program.* Paper presented at the meeting of the American Educational Research Association. Washington, DC.

Chapter 8

CREATING PROFESSIONAL DEVELOPMENT SCHOOLS: POLICY AND PRACTICE IN SOUTH CAROLINA'S PDS INITIATIVES

Barnett Berry and Sally Catoe

The purpose of this case study is to build a better understanding of the enabling as well as constraining conditions of reforming teacher education—especially those conditions related to the establishment of professional development schools (PDSs). The focal point of the case is the University of South Carolina College of Education (COE) and its 3-year effort to create PDSs. The university is a somewhat typical state flagship university, with its emphasis on research grants to financially support its comprehensive mission. However, under its new president, a teaching focus is beginning to be realized. The COE—a charter member of the Holmes Group—is working with eleven local area public schools (nine elementary and two middle schools) as PDS planning sites. The college's efforts have been enhanced through its participation as a partner institution in the state's Goodlad Collaborative—a consortium of five universities coordinated by the Center for School Leadership. The Center is a state-funded agency established to connect public schools and higher education in education reform (e.g., school restructuring) initiatives.

In this study, we sought to capture the perspective of the university and the school site within a broader policy context. Because of the varying degrees of implementation between the COE and its 11 PDS planning sites, we focused on a school that has been identified by university and K–12 practitioners as the most advanced. This site—Pontiac Elementary—opened 2 years ago, and at that time, the district superintendent encouraged the school to initiate site-based management. Drawing on the expertise of a successful principal who had a track record of empowering teachers, Pontiac has used the PDS effort as an "umbrella" for curriculum and technology reform and as a vehicle for securing necessary grant monies to fuel innovation. Over 30% of Pontiac's 600 students are on free or reduced-priced lunch—which is noteworthy, given that this sprawling suburban district generally serves more economically advantaged students. Pontiac's restructuring efforts are centered on the school administration's respect for teachers, their time, and the power they have in working together. At Pontiac, teachers are learning to use math manipulatives (congruent with National Council of Teachers of Mathematics standards), using on-line technology, and emphasizing process learning by integrating literature and writing. In so doing, Pontiac Elementary is becoming an exemplary site for the education of educators.

With a focus on the COE and Pontiac, we set out in our study to answer the following four questions:

1. How are PDS efforts differentiated—in both theory and practice—from more traditional school-university partnerships?
2. How are preservice and inservice educators being educated in PDSs and how are the processes different from traditional approaches?
3. How are PDS efforts leveraging the learning culture of both the university and the K–12 school?
4. What are the barriers to institutionalizing PDS efforts into the mainstream of university and school practice at the school level, district level, university level, and state policy level?

To answer these questions, from the spring to fall of 1992, we conducted a series of surveys and interviews of key participants (professors, teachers, administrators, and others) and stakeholders (legislative staffers and other state-level policy players), reviewed pertinent documents, and observed important meetings.[1] In this chapter, we describe: the process of and progress in creating PDSs; school and COE efforts to transform partnerships, education, and culture; prevailing barriers across the system; and initial outcomes and emergent themes. Thus, our study examines the content and processes of creating PDSs within the COE and one "advanced" K–12 planning site. The chapter also examines respective barriers that both the COE and the school face. We promise no authoritative road map; yet what follows, we hope, are clear, explicit images of both promises and pitfalls of simultaneously renewing K–12 schools and teacher education—the sine qua non of PDSs.

PROCESS AND PROGRESS IN CREATING PDSs

Despite much work over the last 3 years, creating PDSs has been, as one teacher educator noted, a series of "starts and stops." To some degree, the COE's efforts may be described as what Fullan (1991) would classify as the "ready, fire, aim" approach to change. The COE has initiated a great deal of activity and conversation. However, as our interviews and survey data revealed, there is a decided lack of agreement among the faculty over a definition of a PDS model or models. In fact, specific questions asked of faculty in both the COE and the schools about the PDS model(s), more often than not, extracted the answer, "I don't know." While some progress has been made, tangible evidence is sometimes difficult to ascertain.

Initially, the COE's efforts were fueled by the rhetoric of the Holmes Group and the leadership of the COE's new dean, Richard Ishler. Under him, a core group of teacher education faculty began speaking about their "unhappiness" with student teacher placements, partly because of the "little control" over where they were placed, with whom, and what kind of experiences they might have. In the spring of 1990, the COE invited practitioners to a meeting to explore how PDSs might be based on the Holmes Group (1986, 1990) principles. Very little happened until the Fall of 1990 when a second meeting was held and 11 schools were identified as planning sites for developing models for the simultaneous restructuring of K–12 schooling and teacher education. Each site was assigned a teacher education faculty member. Of the eleven faculty members, only three are tenured. At this time, there are no nonteacher education (e.g., educational administration) or arts and science faculty directly involved in creating PDSs across the 11 planning sites. COE faculty act as individual partners with their respective schools, and if a faculty member were to cease working with the school, then progress would probably come to grinding halt.

By 1991, some formal discussions inside the COE began to examine Goodlad's (1990) 19 postulates and task forces were created to begin to define PDSs. Preliminary guidelines "that sounded good" were established by a small group of teacher education professors and area teachers and administrators, but by the Summer of 1991, the faculty, as one professor noted, "were not sure exactly what they wanted . . . and nobody was completely satisfied." A later meeting, attended by representatives from the Holmes Group and interested local schools, encouraged the college to establish a PDS Institute.

The institute offered 3 hours graduate credit for K–12 participants who were charged with developing PDS proposals for their planning sites for COE consideration. The proposals were to set out each site's respective vision for becoming a PDS and its relevance for their school change plans. While the institute provided a new forum for university-school discussions, to some degree its structure reified the status quo. As one teacher noted, the university faculty, who led the institute, were not visible in the schools and were positioned as "the instructors," while the K–12 practitioners were treated as "students." In fact, as another teacher noted, the school proposals were viewed by both K–12 and university faculty as "assignments to be turned in." In addition, several teachers lamented that a "sense of competition" was created among the participants when they perceived that in the near future only a few schools would be chosen to be PDSs. As one teacher noted, the proposals were "varied and creative and covered virtually everything the school had to offer—including the cafeteria sink . . . but many were not specific doable plans for university and school collaboration." Although the proposals were turned in during May 1992 and disseminated to the 11 PDS planning sites in June, some schools have yet to receive any feedback (except individual grades for student work in the institute). Follow-up meetings have been difficult to arrange due to overloaded work schedules and the lack of time. As one teacher mourned about the lack of site-level progress, "We have just not been able to find the time for a group of teachers, the university faculty member, and the principal to meet."

By fall 1992, the COE informed its PDS planning sites that a set of criteria for PDSs needed to be developed, a clear description of PDSs needed to be articulated, the roles and responsibilities of the school and university needed to be defined, and funding issues needed to be resolved. Most recently, a "PDS Council" has been proposed to govern and manage the development of the planning sites, and there is now general agreement that each school needs to establish a site-level governing council. Each school council will be comprised of the principal, representative group of teachers, the COE faculty member assigned to the school, and parent representatives. Currently, each PDS planning site is working to establish: (1) the role of student teachers and interns, (2) the selection and role of mentor (or cooperating) teachers, and (3) a framework for defining best practice. At the end of its 3rd year of creating PDSs the COE hopes to finally define what a PDS is—especially in light of its work with the state's Goodlad Collaborative.

Also, during this time period, the COE dean announced his intent to form a task force that will represent the COE, the college of arts and sciences, the college of social work, and the PDS planning sites. However, while the task force is charged with creating a "blueprint" for the creation of a School of Pedagogy (as envisioned in Goodlad's postulates), another funding crisis has beset the university, requiring cuts in all programs. In addition, university administrators have delayed the formation of the task force; and the dean reports that as he attempts to bring more coherence to the teacher education reform movement, some of the other deans across campus have questioned his efforts "as nothing more than a power play to create a new governance structure." Perhaps, this anxiety among the deans should be anticipated given the current university mandate to cut budgets 12% and the new administration's rhetoric regarding the consolidation of programs and departments.

Notwithstanding the intermittent efforts to create PDSs and university-wide uncertainties, progress is being made. By the end of the 1991–92 academic year, the 11 PDS planning sites had become schools where K–12 practitioners can assist with better coordinated practica and student teaching experiences. During the course of the 1991–92 academic year, 88 of the college's 300 undergraduate and master's level interns were placed in these 11 sites for their student teaching and internships. This number represents 29% of last year's COE placements. However, many of these placements (especially for undergraduate student teaching), as one teacher educator noted, "were just by accident" and "did not have much to do with the PDS efforts." More importantly, 45 of the college's 100 master's level interns had experiences in these 11 PDS planning sites, and over half of these placements emerged from the newly created Master of Arts (MAT) program in Early Childhood and Elementary Education. This program—one of 68 in the COE—has surfaced with a promising approach that may lead to a defined model (or set of models). The reasons are three-fold:

1. A critical mass of quality, mature, post baccalaureate students who have a unique commitment to teaching
2. A critical mass of faculty who are committed to teaching and learning consistent with the ethos of PDSs
3. Coursework and internship experiences that facilitate team learning

In June of 1991, a cohort of 27 full-time COE students entered the MAT program in Early Childhood and Elementary Education. It was a year's course consisting of summer coursework, and blocked classes in the fall and spring, with practica and internship experiences infused throughout the K–12 school calendar, and additional summer coursework leading to a MAT degree. Three themes shape the program. First, there is a constructivist approach whereby interns have choice in field-based projects and the amount and kind of peer assistance they receive as well as extensive opportunities to reflect on and evaluate their practice. Second, interns are prepared as teachers-researchers, with opportunities to inquire into effects of instruction on different groups of students. Third, a cadre of interns is exposed to an integrated curriculum in chosen schools whereby "connections can be made" across subject matter and age levels.

Of the 11 PDS planning sites, Pontiac has been a leader in drawing on the potential and the power of COE student teachers and interns. In fact, in 1991–92, Pontiac had 11 placements (8 MAT and 3 undergraduate)—more than any other PDS planning site. How these efforts can begin to leverage more significant change throughout the COE, across the university campus, out to the K–12 schools, and through the policy system is one question addressed in this chapter.

SCHOOL EFFORTS TO TRANSFORM
PARTNERSHIPS, EDUCATION, AND CULTURE

Pontiac has been successful, at least based on the following evidence. Test scores are rising. The school has received over $200,000 in grants that have forged curriculum integration (math and science) and introduced new technologies. Novice teachers has enhanced the capacity of the school. On-site visits reveal that the school is a whirlwind of activity and everywhere one looks children are busy, having fun, and learning. The administrators and most teachers are "constantly on the go" to create a better education for their students. But, at the root of Pontiac's efforts to transform partnerships, education, and culture is teacher empowerment—a concept driven by the principal, Richard Inabinet, and an assistant principal, Beth Elliott, who have, according to one teacher, "never lost [their] teacher perspective." As another teacher noted: "I think professionalism really comes into play here. The one reason I wanted to come to Pontiac is because I heard teachers had so much power and so much input. . . . You can go to Richard with your ideas because he knows you have thought them out."

Transforming Partnerships

In many ways the PDS effort between Pontiac and the COE is atypical of traditional school-university partnerships. Indeed, 100% of the Pontiac faculty responding to our survey agreed that their "PDS effort is distinctively different" from other school-university relationships. Interview data revealed that some teacher educators and teachers have become equal partners in structuring the experiences of the student teachers and interns, and many of these experiences are beginning to connect to the school's efforts to revise its curriculum. Although primarily assigned to one classroom, the interns work with a variety of teachers at different grade levels. The inclusion of 11 student teachers and interns in the everyday workings of the school have made a difference not only in services to children, but also by freeing up mentor teachers for school change activities.

Initially, with the impetus from the district superintendent and the COE dean, a number of university faculty members were involved with Pontiac. At the outset, a COE administrator was instrumental in delivering a site based management course at the school that spawned Pontiac's new governance system. In addition, a university science professor (one of the few actively involved with K–12 schools) and a teacher education professor delivered a math-science course. A special education professor worked with the Pontiac faculty in shaping the school's first grade readiness programming. However, the partnership has been defined by one teacher educator, Chris Ebert, and her work with Inabinet, Elliott, and a cadre of teachers (who account for about one third of the faculty). It has been this critical mass of people that has been instrumental in shaping a collaborative spirit at Pontiac. The teachers claim that Ebert—who is at the school 2–3 times a week—is responsible for creating a voice for teacher as researcher, assisting teachers in mentoring novices, and articulating a new vision regarding elementary science and language arts teaching. While the administrators, teachers, the interns, and Ebert might not always agree, they do listen to each other. Other university players, while important, have entered and exited. Ebert has become "one of the teachers" and when she is not at the school, "she is missed." As one teacher noted: "Chris has been our inspiration. . . . She does not just come into our classes and say 'do this'. . . . She will say 'What do you think about this?'"

While Ebert noted that she became involved with Pontiac "by accident," she has since become a troubleshooter who generates ideas and covers classes. Indeed, Ebert's involvement at Pontiac is somewhat extraordinary (much like several other COE faculty at other PDS planning sites), given the limitations on her time. She is also a member of the school's newly formed site council. As part of the PDS Institute, Pontiac developed its own proposal. Written by teachers, administrators, Ebert, MAT interns, and student teachers, the proposal called for change in the areas of governance, curriculum and instruction, technology, professional growth, and research. However, as Ebert noted, voicing concern regarding the ambitions of Pontiac faculty and the capacity of the COE to respond: "The school has gone beyond what university has asked for. . . they have constructed very specific objectives—objectives that virtually demand that the university respond. I don't think the university can or will."

TRANSFORMING EDUCATION

Teachers and administrators at Pontiac believe that the new approach to educating preservice teachers is making a difference. Teachers voice strong agreement regarding the "powerful and useful" student intern experiences, their responsibility for the interns, and a belief that interns should receive sufficient support in learning how to teach. While the teachers voiced considerable agreement regarding the support they receive in learning how to mentor, they noted a relative lack of resources and time allocated to actually do the job (See Table 8.1). Nevertheless, teachers are beginning to see the interns as coteachers who are able to make decisions. With the impetus from a wide range of sources, teachers are more involved in curriculum planning, mentoring, inservices, and graduate classes than they were prior to becoming a PDS planning site. Even teachers who are *less involved* in the school's PDS and/or restructuring efforts claim to be "well informed" regarding the work of the interns.

To be sure, some teachers are benefitting from district-sponsored mathematics professional development (e.g., "Math Their Way") and conferences. However, at the same time, teachers reported that they still "suffer" at the hands of college faculty from traditional inservices who "talk at

Table 8.1. Where We Are in Building and Creating PDSs

Pontiac School Faculty (n = 18)

Survey Item	Percentage Disagree (Responding 1, 2, 3)	Percentage Agree (Responding 4, 5, 6)
In my school, student teacher (or intern) experiences are more powerful and useful than the traditional student teaching (or intern) experiences.	28	72
As a result of our PDS efforts, teacher inservice has been more powerful and useful than traditional inservice.	53	47
In my school, student interns receive sufficient support in learning how to teach.	06	94
My school's teachers have more responsibility in mentoring prospective teachers than teachers in other schools.	19	81
In my school, teachers receive sufficient support in learning how to mentor student interns.	39	61
My school's teachers have sufficient resources and time for their mentoring responsibilities.	59	41

Note: For the above survey items, respondents were asked to rate their level of agreement (or disagreement) with the statements by circling the appropriate number along the continuum: 1 = strongly disagree; 2 = disagree; 3 = tend to disagree; 4 = tend to agree; 5 = agree; 6 = strongly agree.

them." Indeed, our survey revealed that the teachers were less sanguine about their inservice education, when compared to the new approaches to preservice education (see Table 8.1). One of the more powerful inservice experiences has been the AIMS workshop (on integrating math and science). But this inservice workshop has been disconnected with the COE preservice curriculum. What has been most striking is that the COE and the district have not been communicating with regard to pre- and in-service plans. Ebert's communication with the district regarding in-service has been, according to her, on an "ad hoc basis," emerging only from her "good reputation" and not from a systematic attempt to connect both pre- and inservice. School administrators have been very concerned about teacher time and the need for "highly focused" professional development. However, as another indicator of disconnected pre- and inservice efforts, we found that Pontiac educators are in six different USC masters or doctoral programs—each with different objectives, sequences, content, and philosophical approaches.

TRANSFORMING CULTURE

Pontiac's PDS efforts are indeed leveraging a learning culture, for teachers, administrators, and interns. As a result of their PDS and restructuring efforts, over 70% of the teachers reported that they changed the way they reflect on practice while 61% reported they changed their conception of collegial work. Similarly, over one-half (55%) of the teachers reported that they have changed the way they teach and their conception of what needs to be known in order to teach (see Table 8.2). (These perceptions are in stark contrast with those of the teacher education faculty, of whom only 21% reported that as a result of PDSs they had changed the way they teach [refer to Table 8.5 below].)

However, just because Pontiac is bordering on cultural transformation, it does not mean there has been a wholesale change in curriculum and conceptions of teaching and learning. The majority of teachers believe that the PDS efforts have forged changes regarding reflective practice (71%) and collegial work (61%). But far fewer believe that the PDS efforts have changed curriculum (41%) and conceptions of teaching (40%). While Pontiac is probably far more innovative than most South Carolina schools, Inabinet's curricular leadership has focused, in his words, on "a blend of tradition and innovation." However, if there is a lack of curricular change, it is not because of dogmatism. Without question, Pontiac's educators are pressured by the state- and district-mandated high-stakes basic skills, standardized achievement testing. When test scores were not as high as expected, the school turned to a more structured phonics based approach to reading, that in some respects runs counter to the constructivist philos-

Table 8.2. Where We Are in Changing Teaching and Learning in PDSs

Pontiac School Faculty (n = 18)

As a result of PDS and/or restructuring efforts, teachers at your school have changed:	Percentage Disagree (Responding 1, 2, 3)	Percentage Agree (Responding 4, 5, 6)
the content of the curriculum.	59	41
their conception of teaching.	60	40
the way they teach.	45	55
their conception of collegial work.	39	61
their conception of learning.	51	49
the way they interact and work with students.	51	49
their conception of what needs to be known in order to teach.	45	55
their commitment to teaching and/or to the work of the PDS.	65	35
their reflections upon their own practices.	29	71

Note: For the above survey items, respondents were asked to rate their level of agreement (or disagreement) with the statements by circling the appropriate number along the continuum: 1 = strongly disagree; 2 = disagree; 3 = tend to disagree; 4 = tend to agree; 5 = agree; 6 = strongly agree.

ophy of the teacher education curriculum. Many of Pontiac's classes are indeed structured, and one can find students in different classes at the same grade level on the same page and worksheet at the same time. While a potential rift exists between the whole language focus of the teacher education program and the structured phonics approach of the school, there is constructive dialogue. Ebert, the teachers, and the interns discuss how whole language approaches can be applied to the highly structured basal readers series. Concomitantly, interns learn how to accommodate and mesh the different methods together, but not without strain and some consternation. In the case of creating PDSs, the well documented tensions that exist between curriculum change and high-stakes testing again arise (see Darling-Hammond & Wise, 1985).

The PDS efforts have illuminated the commitment and intense efforts of many teachers, and in doing so, in the words of one teacher, have "forced many others to become involved." The administration is very serious about teacher professionalism and allowing time for teachers to reflect upon best practice. Inabinet has used grant money for retreats, modest stipends for summer curriculum work, and every so often, the kind of "working lunch that one would have at an uptown law office." Teachers meet often, many times informally, and their camaraderie filters down to the interns. As one intern told us: "There is no competition among us." This is somewhat remarkable given the tight elementary school job market.

There is strong understanding that successful team work requires both new effort and practices. The teachers respect their new involvement in teacher education, and to a slightly lesser extent, their involvement in research and inservice with university professors (see Table 8.3).

Ebert has worked closely with the administration and teachers to design teacher-researcher and mentoring courses. Unlike most college courses, teachers will earn graduate credit without having to sit in a college classroom. Instead, both courses are designed to work with individual and small groups and are designed to address the needs teachers have regarding the investigation of curricular approaches and their effects (the teacher-researcher course) and the supervision of student teachers and interns (the mentoring course). Teachers are committed to the work and

Table 8.3. Where We Are in Building and Creating PDSs

Pontiac School Faculty (n = 18)

Survey Item	Percentage Disagree (Responding 1, 2, 3)	Percentage Agree (Responding 4, 5, 6)
As part of our PDS efforts, teachers have taken on new roles and responsibilities in teacher education.	06	94
As part of our PDS efforts, teachers have taken on research opportunities in partnership with university faculty.	35	65
My school's teachers are active in teaching college level courses.	100	00
University professors are taking on more responsibility in teaching public school classes .	82	18
My school's teachers and university professors work together to plan and conduct school inservice programs.	32	68

Note: For the above survey items, respondents were asked to rate their level of agreement (or disagreement) with the statements by circling the appropriate number along the continuum: 1 = strongly disagree; 2 = disagree; 3 = tend to disagree; 4 = tend to agree; 5 = agree; 6 = strongly agree.

have voiced proud ownership of the content and process. We suspect that even more cultural changes will occur once Ebert teaches at the school more ("I'm just getting started") and more teachers assist with the teaching of COE methods courses. What is most profound about the transformed learning culture is the teachers' own growing interest in teacher professionalism and the self-discovery of becoming more responsible for the education of future educators. Few PDS planning sites view teacher education as their responsibility with the intensity that is found at Pontiac. But those Pontiac teachers who are most involved are distinctly different. These teachers are learning to recognize that they need to help enforce standards of practice. As one teacher asserted: "We want to be involved in teacher education, that's what the bottom line is. . . . I feel like it is so important to us to send out good teachers, not just teachers, but good teachers. . . . We have seen weak teachers. . . . If we are going to get the respect that is due our profession, we have got to take charge and build our profession up." Not only are more Pontiac teachers interested in finding time to see others teach, they are more interested in having someone—including Ebert—see them teach. And this openness can indeed transform a learning culture and change a school.

COE EFFORTS TO TRANSFORM
PARTNERSHIPS, EDUCATION, AND CULTURE

Since becoming dean of the COE 3 years ago, Richard Ishler has placed the establishment of PDSs high on his agenda. He has provided exemplary leadership for the college's recent national accreditation. Faculty report that Ishler has "truly plugged away" at creating PDSs, despite a rigid departmental structure and the resistance of some COE faculty who, as reported by several informants, "entered the professoriate in order to escape the public schools." Given the status-cloaked ethos of research it is not surprising to see few COE faculty actively involved with PDSs. Indeed, the COE garnered $2 million in research grants this past year, creating less time for PDS involvement. Faculty are literally all over the place teaching courses, conducting research, working in centers, consulting, and writing. One faculty member noted that the COE has a "better reputation across campus than many departments of education," but still aspires to higher status and accomplishment.

TRANSFORMING PARTNERSHIPS

Over the years, the COE has had its fair share of work with and in the public schools. However, for the most part, many faculty consider the current

PDS effort as "tentative" given the poor reputation the COE has with the field. Relatively few COE faculty members, only about 25% of the 93 faculty surveyed, responded to our survey concerning the creation of PDSs and of the ones who responded, 60% are from the teacher education faculty. Yet, despite this apparent cynicism, those who were involved with the 11 PDS planning sites are enthusiastic about their work. Those most involved in PDSs (virtually all from teacher education) claimed that their efforts were resulting in far more complex and sophisticated conversations about clinical experiences, more time in schools, freer contact with practitioners, and a decreasing perception of university faculty as visitors at a school. In addition, 82% and 76% respectively of the teacher education faculty reported that PDS teachers and college faculty are taking on new roles and responsibilities. Another finding was that 80% reported that PDS and college faculty are working together to plan inservices and experiences for student teachers and interns (see Table 8.4).

However, despite the positive responses of some teacher education faculty, a number of other faculty considered the PDS efforts no different than previous attempts at collaboration. In fact, many faculty who responded to the survey had little upon which to comment or critique. Open-ended responses to questions about the nature of the PDS model, how interns are being educated, necessary incentives for fuller implementation, and so forth included a great number of "don't know," "minimal knowledge," or no answer at all. Importantly, though, those that did answer let us know that too many faculty had been left out of the process, there was too little understanding of the (PDS) definition, and PDSs were viewed only as an teacher education project.

In spite of the COE starts and stops, several of the PDS planning sites have progressed—with herculean efforts on the part of individual entrepreneurial faculty and administrators (both K–12 and higher education). Unfortunately, although some faculty have had enduring collaborative relationships with nearby schools, their work has not been identified and recognized as PDS labor. For some, this adds to their confusion; for those who are not being identified and recognized, this adds to their cynicism and despair.

TRANSFORMING EDUCATION

If one considers all 68 programs, the COE's current approach to educating preservice and inservice is rather traditional. To be sure, some programs and particular coursework are more closely aligned with the field. Yet, faculty have yet to discuss integrating the education of both preservice teachers and administrators, and few faculty outside teacher education have been involved with the PDS planning sites. Within teacher education, secondary faculty have been absent from the PDS dialogue as well as the

Table 8.4. Where We Are in Building and Creating PDSs

Teacher Education Faculty (n = 15)

Survey Item	Percentage Disagree (Responding 1, 2, 3)	Percentage Agree (Responding 4, 5, 6)
As part of our PDS efforts, teachers have taken on new roles and responsibilities in teacher education.	18	82
As part of our PDS efforts, college faculty have taken on new roles and responsibilities in teacher education.	24	76
As part of our PDS efforts, teachers have taken on research opportunities in partnership with university faculty.	27	73
PDS teachers and college faculty work together to plan and conduct school inservice programs.	20	80
PDS teachers and college faculty work together to plan and conduct school inservice programs.	20	80

Note: For the above survey items, respondents were asked to rate their level of agreement (or disagreement) with the statements by circling the appropriate number along the continuum: 1 = strongly disagree; 2 = disagree; 3 = tend to disagree; 4 = tend to agree; 5 = agree; 6 = strongly agree.

action. Connections to the arts and sciences faculty is even more fragile. Although the COE works closely with a group of arts and sciences faculty (e.g., on the unit's planning committee), each department rules rather rigidly over its disciplinary content. Coursework in each discipline is geared only to the majors—who may represent as few as 5–6 % of the students who take the classes. Few attempts have been made to "convince the rest of the university to package its courses differently."

Despite these pervailing problems, the COE's MAT program—while representing only about one-fourth of the college's early childhood and elementary graduates—is making some headway in transforming preparatory experiences. These teacher education students speak to their curriculum which does indeed reflect the importance of both subject matter and pedagogy. One former MAT student claimed the progam was "fantastic" as she learned a great deal about classroom management, positive reinforcement and nonverbal communication, and detecting patterns in children's behavior so that you can begin to predict what is going to happen with some degree of accuracy. In addition, with the program's constructivist philosophy, the MAT students learned a great deal about whole language instruction. As one former intern, who is now in her 1st year of teaching, noted: "The university training has been the strongest influence on my teaching . . . because the holistic approach makes sense to me . . . it fits my view of learning as communal. . . . The university offered proof that it works." Faculty readily speak to the fact that all except two students (one was weaned from the program) from the first cohort of 27 found jobs in the tight elementary teaching market.

TRANSFORMING CULTURE

Much like any campus of a research university, many faculty avoid collective action. The COE departments are quite different from one another—each with differing politics, personalities, budgets, and rewards. Teacher education professors earn $8,000 less than their educational administration counterparts. A lack of trust is readily apparent as the departments fight over student enrollment and program control. These cultural roadblocks are not surprising, given the beliefs of some longstanding faculty and the norms they hold. As one seasoned faculty member spoke of his initiation to COE norms by another some 15 years ago:

> When I first got here, a senior faculty came up to me and said, "When the dean comes to you he will put his arm around you and will say, "I want you to be on my team." He warned me, "Don't say anything to him and remember *there are no teams around here.*"

When examining the survey responses of the teacher education faculty, some patterns are relatively clear. First, a seemingly significant percentage of faculty (over 40%) noted that because of PDS efforts, they have changed the content of their courses and their concept of collegial work with K–12 teachers and they have noticed a change in the way their colleagues reflect upon their own practice. Second, COE faculty see more evidence of cultural changes (at least related to beliefs about teaching and learning) amongt PDS teachers than among their own university colleagues (see Table 8.5).

PREVAILING BARRIERS ACROSS THE SYSTEM

Identifying system-wide barriers to creating PDSs was, at times, quite simple. Many barriers were obvious as most respondents quickly pointed

Table 8.5. Where We Are in Changing Teaching and Learning in PDSs

Teacher Education Faculty (n = 15)

As a result of PDS and/or restructuring efforts, teachers at your school have:	Percentage Disagree (Responding 1, 2, 3)	Percentage Agree (Responding 4, 5, 6)
changed the content of my course(s).	54	46
changed the way I teach.	69	21
changed my concept of collegial work with K–12 teachers.	54	46
noticed a change in my colleagues' concepts of learning.	69	21
noticed a change in the way PDS teachers interact and work with students.	30	70
noticed a change in the way PDS teachers work with the university.	08	92
noticed a change in the way my colleagues reflect upon their own practices.	54	46

Note: For the above survey items, respondents were asked to rate their level of agreement (or disagreement) with the statements by circling the appropriate number along the continuum: 1 = strongly disagree; 2 = disagree; 3 = tend to disagree; 4 = tend to agree; 5 = agree; 6 = strongly agree.

out numerous roadblocks to establishing PDSs. One clear example related to statewide funding of teacher education. The state's higher education funding formula devalues teacher education relative to other fields of study. For example, in 1993–94, the formula generated for engineering will be equal to $59,697 per faculty, a 20:1 student/faculty ratio, with 59% earmarked for instructional support. The formula generated for teacher education will be equal to $43,633 per faculty, a 22:1 student/faculty ratio, with 33% earmarked for instructional support. For practice teaching, the formula generated will be equal to $38,359 per faculty. Recent analyses indicate that while statewide college faculty salaries are higher than the southeastern average, statewide teacher education salaries are lower. To make matters more dire, this year the legislature only funded higher education at 74% of the formula, and an institutional allocation does not necessarily translate directly into what a particular unit on campus—such as teacher education—receives.

However, as we pruned and grafted the survey, interview, and observational data, we found the identification of barriers to PDSs to be a bit more complex. We grouped the barriers into six general, yet interrelated categories: (1) miscommunications and a lack of education; (2) the limits of time and rewards; (3) territorial imperatives; (4) overstuffed agenda and curricular disconnections (5) policy disconnections; and (6) the press for equality amongst K–12 schools.

MISCOMMUNICATIONS AND A LACK OF EDUCATION

Our surveys and interviews revealed resounding cries regarding barriers to creating the eleven PDSs: "no clear vision," "no distinct definition," and "an evolving definition that creates a feeling that progress is not being made." To some extent this lack of clarity is due to miscommunications and inadequate mechanisms for PDS (and non-PDS) participants to communicate. While miscommunication is readily apparent across the system, it is most pronounced within the COE. Teacher education faculty have learned about PDSs by reading journal articles, Holmes Group reports, attending sessions at professional meetings, and working with colleagues at other institutions. However, we found a significant lack of conversation within the COE and across the departments. At the core of the problem is meaningful communication and understanding and shared values. Despite all the COE has done to leverage change, developing this consensus sometimes appears to be unimaginable. For example, during the course of our interviews, one arts and sciences faculty—who had attended several PDS meetings (including some PDS Institute meetings)—had difficulty describing to us what a PDS is or what it could be. He claimed: "I have attended the meetings, but I'm still sort of confused. . . . I am trying to recall—they have all these buzzwords. Can you explain to me which of these programs I have been working with?" Analysts willingly speak to the criticalness of teachers' professional development as the linchpin of K–12 school reform. But where is the message about the professional development of university faculty? Despite the 3-year effort to create PDSs, too many key players still do not understand and embrace the basic concepts. Without professional development can university faculty—both within COE and across campus—play the role it needs to play in creating PDSs?

THE LIMITS OF TIME AND REWARDS

Again, like any other study of school change (e.g., see Fullan, 1991), time is viewed as the major barrier. Virtually every Pontiac teacher reported concerns about the scarcity of time for conferencing with interns and organizing and implementing new curricular approaches. Yet, Pontiac teachers have more time than most elementary teachers (with approximately 50 minutes per day of team planning time, plus a 30-minute unencumbered lunch period). But the exigencies of school life prevent most teams from planning together, except once a week. Teachers have learned that the more they learn and plan together, the more they need to learn and plan together. Given the current work structure, there is very little time for Pontiac teachers to play a more powerful role in teacher education. Similarly, those COE faculty who are active in PDS have no more time to give. To accomplish what they are doing, these university faculty need to be on site 2–3 times per week. For several faculty, their traditional academic writing has suffered and college committee work has been somewhat neglected. Ebert claimed to be "spread too thin," noting that she "could easily be at Pontiac 5 days a week." If she did not already have tenure, Ebert's school site efforts would not be so forthcoming.

University faculty expected specific rewards for this new PDS work, while the school faculty did not. Ebert expressed grave concerns about how much the K–12 PDS teachers were doing without adequate reward. On the one hand, the reward for PDS teachers was to have the opportunity to shape the next generation of teachers and teachers have long been socialized not to believe they should be compensated for extraordinary contributions. On the other hand, university faculty tend to look at time and rewards much like a business person. As one administrator noted:

> Would you tell the faculty, "Well, we're not giving you any raises this year, but you all have an extra assignment: you all have to go out and work in the schools also." I mean, people get paid to work at the university. I guess the issue is: "What could we drop that we are doing now?"

Most COE faculty highlighted the university reward system (and the "publish or perish" imperative) as a major barrier to investing the time and effort inside K–12 schools. One university administrator agreed:

> Publications are a barrier . . . we reward folks for research, and people perceive it as a barrier. . . . There's some justification for it—in other words, a truly outstanding researcher WILL get rewarded—truly outstanding teachers MAY get rewarded, but not as readily because there's nothing that catches the eye. Other universities don't come and try to steal our teachers very often; they try to steal our researchers 365 days a year.

However, one university administrator—who has worked closely with the tenure and promotion system—claimed that university faculty have not been willing to change to a reward system that could indeed support PDSs. The administrator noted:

> The educational psychology faculty just submitted their revised criteria and procedures. They're very traditional. There's a group that I thought really

could have done something innovative and unique, and they came in with something extremely traditional. I think the faculty could be pushing a lot more change, and they're not.

TERRITORIAL IMPERATIVES

Numerous miscues and misperceptions have arisen because of "territorial imperatives"—primarily from the interrelated issues of a divisive public education funding structure, institutional mistrust, and partisan politics. With regard to funding, one informant told us that: "Here is where government structure gets in the way with the separate funding for higher education and K–12. And, to make matters worse joint projects that are funded are hard to keep because they come under 10 times more scrutiny." Fundamental to the issue of lack of coherent leadership is the state's education funding structure that pits K–12 against higher education and members of the fragmented education community against each other. As one keen observer of the state's education policy system noted:

> The funding issue is critical. Competitiveness is a big issue here because it's difficult to get money for collaboration. Who's going to give it up? You're trying to get new money when the state is trying to cut back on the core operations. You would have to have support from the college presidents and either the local superintendents, the teachers' association, or the school board association. . . . Some key people in those groups are going to have to understand what a PDS is.

To make matters more convoluted, current teacher education reform efforts led by the State Department of Education (e.g., as initiator of new program approval and teacher licensure standards) and the Center for School Leadership (e.g., as initiator of the Goodlad Collaborative) are seemingly at odds with each other due to the political association represented by their respective leaders and boards. While both the SDE and CSL reform efforts focus on higher standards and collaborative arrangements, many would be key players have been excluded from important state-level conversations. Creating PDSs requires complex connections and multiple points of leadership and influence. Currently, the PDS concept is ill-defined and complex concept. With such territorial imperatives, PDSs may be even more difficult to define, support, create, and maintain.

OVERSTUFFED AGENDAS AND CURRICULAR DISCONNECTIONS

Both Pontiac and the COE have overstuffed agendas. Teachers lament the number of initiatives on the table, and COE faculty are incredulous over the college's multiple, multifarious education reform agenda (re: centers, initiatives, grants, and so forth). The core, committed "PDS-type" faculty are "spread too thin" and do not have time to make the necessary connections within the college, much less across the university campus, and into the K–12 schools.

In addition, despite the significant brokering of services and information by the Center for School Leadership, to this point, the Goodlad Collaborative seems to be essentially a set of five alliances, each including the Center and one of the institutions. The Center—which has its own overloaded agenda—has worked with the teacher education departments in these sites to establish PDSs and scrutinize their teacher education programs in relation to Goodlad's 19 postulates. However, most colleges report that they are still in the initial stages of creating PDSs, with each taking different approaches to engaging K–12 and higher education faculty. Most have not substantively involved arts and sciences or non-teacher education faculty (Scannell, 1992). Some Goodlad Collaborative participants have lamented that when information sessions are conducted those who "need to know" do not attend and those who are "in the know" are "too busy to attend."

The COE is connected to the Goodlad Collaborative and its work—but this work does not necessarily filter to Pontiac. At this time, the Center is not necessarily informing the PDS work at Pontiac, and the work at Pontiac is not necessarily informing the PDS work of the Center. As one Pontiac teacher noted, "The Center is only connected to Pontiac by accident." Very few teachers, COE faculty, and district administrators regularly communicate enough. Those at the school level have difficulty seeing (or have time to see) the "big picture" while those at the district and university level have difficulty seeing (or no time to see) the "small picture."

POLICY DISCONNECTIONS

Without stronger ties among COE-Pontiac preservice efforts, Pontiac-District inservice efforts, and the statewide Goodlad efforts, fragmentation, and dilution of labor will continue and foster curricular and policy disconnections. The issue here is not just hard working educators doing too much, but also competing policy initiatives that do not share a common view of teaching. Without a consistent view of teaching, PDSs will be nothing more than one more reform initiative that makes sense to neither policymakers nor practitioners. Presently, teacher education and evaluation standards as well as student testing are being reviewed. However, rhetoric regarding revisions far surpasses action, and many roadblocks to creating both a common view of teaching and, ultimately, PDSs remain.

The current system of teacher education program approval is an "i-dotting and t-crossing" exercise and distracts teacher educators from forward-looking reforms. Similarly, the state-mandated beginning teacher evaluation system (with its requirement of demonstrating 51 discreet, teaching behaviors in a 50-minute or less class period) is an aggravation and, to some extent, an anathema to the kinds of teaching and learning exemplified in the MAT elementary program. Again, time and effort are diverted as COE faculty drill interns to pass the beginning teacher evaluation assessment and hope that they are not taught to teach without any inventiveness. As one intern observed, "I do not want to be an APT [the beginning teacher evaluation assessment system] teacher—it takes all the creativity out of teaching." Finally, student testing (and its accompanying school incentive programs) places a premium on scoring high on decontextualized, multiple choice basic skills assessments. These assessments and reward systems drive schools (and PDSs) to choose prepackaged reading curricula that increase the likelihood of students "scoring high," but do not necessarily encourage a curriculum that prepares educators to "teach for understanding" (Holmes Group, 1986). Even with its high test scores and now deregulated status, Pontiac still cannot afford to be too different, moving away from the curriculum implied by the basic skills assessments. The school's emphasis on teaching isolated skills emerges from the beliefs (and evidence) that students do indeed learn the skills that are tested. However, its direct impact has been an overcrowded curriculum. As other studies have found, what is tested is emphasized while other subjects and models of performance are deemphasized (Darling-Hammond & Wise, 1985). At the first grade, science and social studies are covered in only 50 minutes a day while language arts and reading are covered over a 2 hour and 20 minute period. As one faculty member noted: "Very little social studies and science are taught. . . . What is being taught is called social sciences. . . . Very little science is being taught. . . . The curriculum is being squeezed."

Perhaps these disconnected policies reflect a lack of trust in teacher education. As one state-level observer noted, the state education department has "a long history of brow beating teacher educators" and demonstrated a "lack of faith in teacher education." By the same token, teacher educators have a long history of distrusting the state. This distrust has led to, as one state-level observer noted, "some resistance to linking preservice and inservice education which is the heart of PDSs." Unfortunately, this "lack of faith" in teacher education may be justified to some extent, at least on the basis of the perception that teacher educators do not appear to want to change.

THE PRESS FOR EQUALITY AMONG K–12 SCHOOLS

The tension between a university that seeks to create a resource-enriched PDS and a school district that seeks to maintain equality among its schools emerges as an important barrier. On the one hand, the university seeks to create unique, exemplary, innovative schools that are abundant with staff, ideas, and learning opportunities. On the other hand, administrators and school board members may lose political capital when resource-enriched PDSs, as one district administratored noted, "get too far out ahead of others." We heard from some district administrators that "what is done for one school needs to be done for others." For some, the problem is nothing more than, as one district administrator noted, "petty jealousy" in an organization where resources are scarce. For others, including one district administrator, "equality is essential," as there must be a careful distribution of resources across diverse school districts with longstanding political and racial divisiveness. It is this latter variable that is most confounding and perplexing as we think about how to create PDSs. As one astute COE faculty member told us:

> Over the last 20 years of desegregation efforts we have been trying to make schools equal. [Unequal schools] have almost become a phobia now. Districts are very fearful of giving any one school an obvious magnet—because then they have to face the general public that says, "You're not being fair; my youngster is going to a school that does not have the same opportunities that you're providing for this school." School boards have been very reluctant to allow uniqueness, because uniqueness means inequality and inequality used to be associated with poor education—second class citizenship—continuation of the differentiation of races.

If PDSs are to be created and maintained, tensions must be resolved. On the one hand, these concerns may lead to the creation of PDSs only in less advantaged schools—where insufficient resources may mitigate against best practice. On the other hand, these concerns may lead to the political inability to create PDSs anywhere at all.

INITIAL OUTCOMES AND EMERGENT THEMES

This case study reveals that in South Carolina many notable measures are being undertaken in order to begin creating PDSs. Indeed, progress has been made; but the simultaneous renewal of student learning and the education of prospective and practicing educators has been uneven at best. Yet, both the COE and especially, Pontiac have made considerable headway. The case reveals that attempts to change the public schools are rudimentary compared with attempts to change higher education. Just consider the distinction of the level of PDS understanding between those "less involved" faculty at Pontiac and the "less involved" faculty at the COE.

The distinction could not be more conspicuous—with the former proudly claiming their role and influence in school-wide decision making while the latter are lamenting that they "just do not know what is going on." To be sure, insufficient rewards for higher education faculty are a critical barrier for their involvement. But insufficient rewards are not nearly as critical as insufficient and loosely coupled concepts, policies, and communications, as well as the longstanding university culture that mitigates against collective action. As Teitel (1992) reminds us, the "same relatively decentralized environment that fosters (or tolerates) PDS development contributes to the challenge of integrating and institutionalizing it" (p. 84). Prevailing barriers across the system—discussed previously—do not bode well for future of PDSs. Problematic higher education policies, particularly funding formulae influencing lower investments in teacher education, remain as issues to be addressed. If these organizational, political, and cultural exigencies are not to totally halt progress, then new leadership must emerge. Based on these initial outcomes of our study, we argue that this new leadership must focus on three, interrelated themes that frame the future of creating PDSs.

PRESSING FOR THE "P" IN PDS

For PDSs to unfold, much more authority and discretion must be afforded to teachers and those who support and work with them. There must be more discretion (and thus more time) devoted to defining "what a PDS is" and communicating this knowledge to an increasingly complex web of teacher groups, university faculty, administrators, and policymakers. The demand for defining the "P" (or professional) in PDSs is escalating. We have found that the many variables that inhibit the creation of PDSs are based on a lack of common understanding and acceptance of teacher professionalism. Sykes (1990) has noted that the professionalization of teaching requires more regard, resources, and knowledge for teachers. However, the lack of time and rewards reflect disrespect for the intensive intellectual activity of public school teaching. The current teacher evaluation and education standards do not reflect the intellectual work of teaching. The lack of PDS (and teacher) involvement in reframing the state's program approval process counterindicates teacher-generated knowledge. Territorial imperatives build political walls that prevent the dissemination of best practice generated through PDS and related efforts.

While Pontiac's powerful voice of teacher professionalism is heard at the school, not enough teachers, administrators, university faculty, and state policymakers are listening. Unlike most schools, Pontiac's learning culture is predicated on the teachers' growing interest in teacher professionalism and their self-discovery of becoming more responsible for the education of future educators. Indeed, they are learning how teacher education reform can work within the organizational context of an evolving school-university partnership. But, who are learning from them?

SERIOUS REWARDS FOR SERIOUS COLLABORATION

There must be more time, better structures, and serious rewards for cross-institutional and cross-system collaboration. By this, we mean that those within the public schools and higher education systems must be encouraged to work together across their institutions as well as across their systems. Currently, the COE is a hub for the 11 PDS planning sites. But the sites—as spokes emanating from the hub—have yet to significantly connect to and learn from each other. Similarly, the Center for School Leadership, a statewide network that was established to build interorganizational bridges, has important knowledge and has learned to share it with a small set of colleges, but the colleges themselves have yet to learn how to learn from each other.

Those who are creating the PDS knowledge base—like the school- and university-based faculty at Pontiac—must work with those creating new standards for teaching and teacher education. However, those who are doing the real work of teacher education reform are busy enough with their everyday duties to keep up with an explosion of information, ideas, and initiatives reflected in statewide and national PDS (as well as other educational reform) efforts. Although the PDS creation requires interorganizational learning, the policy system places a premium on competitiveness between schools and universities. There has been little rancor on anyone's part resulting in any of the disconnections reported in this case study but, when there must be a premium placed on connectedness, there seem to be many variables that (across many layers of organizational bureaucracy) limit the linking, sharing, and understanding of the knowledge base.

Inferring from our case study evidence, we would recommend that leadership match rhetoric with reality, that incentives be established to create interagency collaborative projects (along with requisite joint governance and budgeting structures), that comprehensive management information systems be founded to facilitate communication, that joint faculty appointments be considered, and that specific graduate training programs be created that prepare and legitimize professionals to work across colleges of education, the arts and sciences, and the public schools. With such efforts, "territorial imperatives" are more likely to be overcome and the innumerable teacher education reform initiatives can be networked.

NETWORKING THE NETWORKS

For some time theorists have been focusing on systems that forge the interaction between organizational conditions and processes that produce behavior (Katz & Kahn, 1966; March & Simon, 1958) and networks that get the job done (Laumann and Pappi, 1976). Recently, reports have emerged that speak to the power of teacher networks (Lieberman and McLaughlin, 1992). Laumann and Pappi's (1976) analysis of "networks for collective action" revealed the need for "reachability" of those who know ("elites") and those who need to know as well as how and when to "activate" elites.

In the case of creating PDSs, we have found (at the very least) a wide variety of networks represented by the State Department of Education, the Commission on Higher Education, the Center for School Leadership, the COE and its PDSs, and the COE and its other reform initiatives. Several other important teacher/teaching reform initiatives—of which we are aware—are not yet part of the PDS dialogue and effort. We have found that the "elites" who need to network are "too busy" to network, and when they do, they are not very good at it. At this point, we found individual college faculty and teachers developing critical knowledge for creating PDSs. Advanced PDS planning sites exude a collaborative spirit, but are underutilized in defining what a PDS is and can be. Sites must be illuminated and the faculty within them must be drawn upon to advance and connect the PDS agenda. Only when the time and efforts of these K–12 and higher education faculty are valued both within their own institutions (through visible rewards) and across the system will significant change be leveraged. For this to work will require more effort, but also a better definition of what networks there are, which networks are better suited to more directly connect to each other, and how and when the networks need to communicate to each other.

Over the last several years, South Carolina has embarked on a variety of important and provocative K–12 school change efforts, but discussion, plans, and resources for incorporating these supposed exemplar sites of K–12 renewal with the renewal of teacher education through PDSs seem lacking. To make these connections, there must be, as Teitel (1992) has asserted, a whole new set of interorganizational relations advanced by boundary spanners—that is individuals who are accepted in all institutions and able to sell ideas and mediate actions. So much of the success of creating PDSs in South Carolina (and we suspect elsewhere) will depend on these boundary spanners. We wonder who these people are? How do you develop a cadre of them? Where will they find time for new networking responsibilities? Will they be allowed to span politically sensitive boundaries? We do not know. But, what we do know is that they are needed in networking the networks that support and create PDSs.

NOTE

[1]Observations were recorded at key meetings (e.g., COE faculty meetings, the monthly PDS Institute, etc.). Surveys and interview protocols were developed based on the NCREST case study outline. Surveys were administered to teacher education faculty and administrators as well as teachers and administrators in one purposefully selected PDS planning site. Of the 93 COE faculty only 25 responded. Of these, 15 (or 60%) were from the Department of Instruction and Teacher Education (ITE), 6 were from Educational Leadership and Policies (ELP), and 4 were from Educational Psychology (EP). We administered a similar survey to the faculty of the PDS planning site. Of the 33 faculty members, 18 responded.

Also, 44 in-depth interviews were conducted with administrators, teachers, college faculty, and student interns directly involved with the PDS, arts and sciences and COE faculty, university administrators, and key individuals associated with state teacher education policy. In addition, interviews were conducted with key district administrators (two school districts) and state and university officials.

The process of data collection and analysis was recursive and dynamic. In many respects, our approach to the study cannot be separated from our own roles. One of us is a COE faculty member who has experience assessing school reform and is a former senior advisor to the current State Superintendent of Education. The other is an experienced classroom teacher and a graduate student in the COE—who has been active in the PDS planning efforts over the last three years. Our different perspectives and roles allowed for considerable debate and checks on our own biases and understandings.

REFERENCES

Darling-Hammond, L., & Wise, A. (1985). "Beyond standardization: state standards and school improvement." *Elementary School Journal, 85,* 315–336.

Fullan, M. (1991). *The new meaning of educational change.* New York: Teachers College Press.

Goodlad, J. (1990). *Teachers for our nation's schools.* San Francisco: Jossey-Bass, Inc.

Holmes Group. (1986). *Tomorrow's teachers: A report of the Holmes group.* East Lansing, MI: Author.

Holmes Group (1990). *Tomorrow's schools: Principles for the design of professional development schools.* East Lansing, MI:Author.

Katz, D., & Kahn, R. (1966). *The social psychology of organizations,* 2nd ed. New York: Wiley.

Laumann, E., & Pappi, F. (1976). *Networks of collective action: A perspective on community influence systems.* New York: Academic Press.

Lieberman, A., & McLaughlin, M. (1992). "Networks for educational change: Powerful and problematic." *Kappan 73* (May), 673–677.

March, J., & Simon, H. (1958). *Organizations.* New York: Wiley.

National Center for Restructuring Education, Schools, and Teaching (1992). *Mission Statement.* New York: Teachers College—Columbia University.

Scannell, D. (1992). A review of the 1991–92 accomplishments for members of the South Carolina Goodlad collaborative. Report prepared for the Center for School Leadership. Rock Hill, SC.

Sykes, G. (1990). Fostering teacher professionalism in schools. In R. Elmore and Associates. *Restructuring schools: The next generation of reform.* San Francisco: Jossey-Bass.

Teitel, L. (1992). "The impact of professional development school partnerships on the preparation of teachers." *Teaching Education 4* (Spring), 77–85.

Chapter 9

CHANGE FOR COLLABORATION AND COLLABORATION FOR CHANGE: TRANSFORMING TEACHING THROUGH SCHOOL–UNIVERSITY PARTNERSHIPS

Sharon P. Robinson and Linda Darling-Hammond

Collaboration: (1) To labor together; to work jointly with others or together, esp. in an intellectual endeavor; (2) to cooperate with or willingly assist an enemy of one's country and esp. an occupying force; (3) to cooperate with an agency or instrumentality with which one is not immediately connected.

Webster's Ninth New Collegiate Dictionary

But to produce innovation, more complexity is essential; more relationships, more sources of information, more angles on the problem, more ways to pull in human and material resources, more freedom to walk around and across the organization.

Rosabeth Moss Kanter, *The Change Masters*, p. 148

Professional development schools (PDSs) are organizations that cannot be created by either public schools or universities acting alone. They grow out of and depend upon collaboration for their very existence. Each partner brings a critical element to the relationship. Public schools provide venues for the authentic clinical development of teachers now generally accepted as essential for new teacher development and for professional development of veteran teachers (Darling-Hammond, Gendler, & Wise, 1990; Goodlad, 1990; Holmes Group, 1986). Universities provide access to theory and knowledge production. As Webster's definition of collaboration suggests, joint work between these two kinds of organizations can produce cooperation, but it requires each to stretch to meet the other different, if not antagonistic, party.

In PDSs, public school and university faculty interact in a conscious effort to merge theory and practice, knowledge and skill development. Practitioners in both organizations must change the way they relate to each other in order to support the development of teaching professionals—and of a teaching profession—grounded in a synergy of theory and practice as the basis for reflection and action. The unifying goal of a PDS is developing and transmitting knowledge in ways that lead to practice that is both *responsible*, i.e., based on profession-wide knowledge, and *responsive*, i.e., sensitive to the needs and concerns of individual students. Merging these two bases for professional practice requires the perspectives and wisdom of both partners.

As the preceding chapters suggest, the joining of school and university forces in PDSs can create a whole that is greater than the sum of its parts, qualitatively transforming the possibilities for developing teacher knowledge and knowledge about teaching. These examples affirm Hawley's (1990) observation that the unrelenting criticism of traditional, university-based teacher education can be met by more innovative solutions than are typically offered by universities alone. He suggests that rather than rearranging courses and extending field experiences, there should be a fundamental reconsideration of the roles and functions provided by all organizations that have an interest in and responsibility for teacher development. Hawley joins others who assert that schools and universities should begin a collaboration to improve teacher education by redistributing responsibility for teacher development based on asking: "Who should contribute what to teacher learning, and at what stage of teachers' cognitive and professional development can these contributions be made most efficiently and effectively?" (p. 9).

The PDS models described in this volume provide an array of possible answers to these questions. They also illustrate that, just as collaboration between universities and schools is required to create changes in support of teacher learning, organizational changes in both institutions must also be pursued in order to enable this kind of collaboration to occur. Those involved in PDS efforts find they must change the curriculum and the organizational structures of both teacher education programs and schools in order to collaborate effectively.

Organizational changes are also required to sustain teachers' learning opportunities and to enable applications of new knowledge. As more is known and understood, practice evolves; if this new learning is to be put to use, organizations must themselves evolve to accommodate new practices. Just as collaboration spurs this organizational learning, so do the resulting organizational changes enhance the collaboration by enabling each partner to bring more to their shared enterprise. Personal and organizational development join theory development as the province of practitioners in the schools and in the academy.

At their best, PDSs exemplify what Peter Senge (1990) calls "learning organizations." The case studies illustrate how, as they mature and put down roots, PDSs draw upon the five disciplines of organizational change Senge describes in *The Fifth Discipline:*

- Individual knowledge and expertise supporting the personal mastery of all parties
- Mental models or paradigms that govern learning
- Shared vision that inspires further learning and effort
- Team learning among organizational members that generates new understandings and new questions
- Systems thinking, the integration of all knowledge and expertise to form a comprehensive understanding of practice throughout the organization.

Senge's disciplines of organizational development are more than esoteric theory. They describe the process of collaboration for change that undergirds the challenge of designing and implementing new forms of organization. As we describe below, collaborations between public schools and universities involved in creating PDSs rely heavily on these disciplines.

THE CHALLENGES OF COLLABORATION

Efforts among public schools and universities to create PDSs involve collaboration between distinctly different institutions that share the common goal of developing and supporting professional teaching practice. Such endeavors are so inherently difficult that in 1984 Seymour Sarason wrote, "I had come to see these collaborations as instances of 'two cultures' interacting—that is, two cultures misunderstanding and clashing with each other" (p. 19). This dire observation was inspired by Sarason's experiences with numerous collaborative efforts involving public schools and universities that had produced disappointing results, and by the fact that so few successful experiences had been well documented.

Among the factors that distinguish the cultures of public schools and universities are the uses of time, differences in norms and work styles, and traditions regarding status. Public school educators are captive to, and often frustrated by, the clock and the calendar. University personnel may not appreciate that bus duty and close student supervision leave little patience for lengthy discussions of underlying theories of a new instructional method or organizational arrangement. School faculty may find it hard to understand that teaching courses, supervising student teachers, conducting research, and participating in college committees can produce an equally intense but differently structured schedule. With their very different work schedules, educators in both organizations quickly learn how difficult it can be to schedule meetings. Public school personnel begin the day early, with bus duty and homeroom. University personnel often have late afternoon or evening classes. School personnel may think a meeting beginning at 7:30 in the morning is quite reasonable, while university personnel may want to meet at 3:00 in the afternoon. Either arrangement will require a significant sacrifice for one party or the other. The issues of time for collaboration have surfaced in every PDS studied.

Participants in public schools and universities also often have different attitudes toward problem-solving, characterized by Whitford as the contrast between the "ready, fire, aim" culture of schools and the "ready, ready, ready" culture of universities. School-based practitioners have been socialized to embrace a pragmatic approach to problem-solving: implement the new curriculum or regulation as quickly and with as little additional disruption as possible. University-based practitioners are socialized to embrace a more theoretical approach to new situations and problems, with more deliberation by committees prior to taking—or even considering—action. For school personnel, new demands and problems require immediate resolution in whatever manner can be accommodated in each individual classroom; collective consideration of underlying theoretical issues may seem an unaffordable luxury.

However, as the relationship evolves, the cases also provide evidence of how school faculty find time to collectively deliberate, reflect, and plan from a more studied and philosophical stance while university faculty are moved to take action, and in the acting, to develop new understandings of what is possible for their programs and students as well as for their partnership school.

Another source of challenge is the usual initial lack of parity in school and university relationships. By tradition, career advancement in public schools is based on graduate study in higher education. As such, a student-to-teacher rather than collegial relationship may define the interactions between the participating school and university faculty. Meanwhile, there are undertones of inequality in how the knowledge bases of practitioners and academicians are frequently viewed. The "wisdom of practice" (Shulman, 1987) is generally not initially accorded the weight of academics' research- and theory-based knowledge by either party. However, as several of the case studies demonstrate, parity in the relationship evolves as evidence of mutual learning and genuinely shared decision making emerges.

These factors illustrate how the cultures of schools and universities conspire to make collaboration a source of risk, consternation, and frequent failure. Because the creation of PDSs involves decisions regarding substantive issues such as curriculum, pedagogy, and administration, these fundamental issues and areas of difference cannot be avoided. Educators from two very different organizational cultures must find ways to address these issues using collaborative processes.

As is true of all change efforts, the processes of change and collaboration are as important as the content of the enterprise: change agents must pay attention to both or they will accomplish neither the goal of changed relationships nor the goal of changed education (Lieberman, Darling-Hammond, & Zuckerman, 1991). Learning to collaborate while overcoming the cultural barriers described above is as essential to creating successful PDSs as is the intellectual integrity of the substantive issues that must also be addressed.

Below we describe how these processes for collaboration and change have unfolded in a number of school-university partnerships in addition to the PDSs described earlier in this volume.

EXAMPLES OF SUCCESSFUL COLLABORATION

Contemporary efforts to create PDSs can escape Sarason's prediction of failure; they can be successful if care is taken to document the experience of collaboration for reflection and learning. Fortunately, in recent years both experience and research regarding collaboration between public schools and higher education has grown. The *National Directory of School-College Partnerships* (Wilbur, Lambert, & Young, 1987) demonstrates the extent of collaborative efforts ranging from projects focusing on "at-risk" students, to writing instruction, to jointly conducted research. Gaudiani and Burnett (1986) have documented the experience of the Academic Alliance, a movement to create local communities of academic scholars and public school teachers that meet monthly to share knowledge and take responsibility for their own professional growth. This collaboration results in improved practice in both university and public school classrooms.

Gordon Van de Water's (1989) research on the Educational Equality Project focuses on various approaches to improve the academic success of students likely to experience inadequate access to educational opportunities. This report identifies 10 characteristics of successful school-college collaborations (p. 4). These characteristics of successful collaborations and their significance for PDSs are discussed in the next section.

Among the supportive change-agents for school-university collaborations is the NEA National Center for Innovation, which facilitates the creation of PDSs and other partnerships. Through the Center, more than 200 schools in over 60 communities are linked in a network of learning designed to improve student achievement. At its core, the Center is a strategy for professional development for all who participate—teachers, teacher educators, administrators, policy makers, and parents. Specific projects involve schools, school districts, and universities in various approaches to restructuring public schools and teacher education. Learning is the result of addressing the complexity of school change from the perspectives of all stakeholders, and candid consideration of alternative approaches to problems of mutual interest.

During the winter of 1992 the Center conducted a survey of project sites to determine the nature of school-university collaboration. This survey revealed extensive collaborative activity, including the implementation of PDSs such as the Wells, Maine program reported in chapter 2. Other activities include action research projects, the design of teaching materials, and support for professional development. The survey results suggest that these activities are mutually beneficial, contributing to improved teaching, learning, and curriculum, and more collegial cultures in the schools and higher education institutions involved. The Center's work has also enhanced appreciation for just how messy and necessary the process of collaboration can be and how ambitious the creation of a new collaborative organization such as a PDS really is.

Two of the PDS projects that have participated in the NCI network are particularly noteworthy. One project involves San Diego State University and the Chula Vista City Schools. The PDS, which opened in the fall of 1991, is housed in a new elementary school that was designed to support the physical and technological requirements of modern teaching practice and professional development for teachers. The entire school has been designed to support fiber-optic and satellite communication, and the professional development wing has the wiring and cooling systems necessary to support additional technological applications. The building contains conference rooms and a research center where computers will support word processing, desk-top publishing, and access to databases such as Educational Resources and Information Clearinghouse (ERIC).

The entire school is designed as a "pod," with six buildings of four classrooms each plus common teacher workspace. The classrooms in the professional development wing have one-way observation glass. This project was guided by specific goals for student instruction, preservice teacher learning, and inservice professional development. Implementation plans to meet these goals were designed over the course of 2 years of collaboration, planning, and study (San Diego State University & Chula Vista City Schools, 1992).

The other project involves Kansas State University (KSU) and the Manhattan/Ogden School District in Manhattan, Kansas. This project was inspired by findings of a study regarding the quality of elementary preservice preparation in mathematics, science, and technology instruction. A survey completed by student teachers and their cooperating teachers indicated that all respondents viewed the preparation in elementary mathematics and science as inadequate to meet the demands of initial professional practice. The collaboration, launched in 1990 with a 5-year grant from the National Science Foundation, involves KSU faculty in the colleges of education and arts and sciences, and teachers and administrators of the Manhattan/Ogden School district.

The project includes establishment of PDSs, collaboration in the design and implementation of new mathematics and science content courses, new teaching methods courses, shared faculty for instruction at both KSU and in the PDSs, shared professional development of all project participants, and an action research agenda to support continuous enhancement of the project. In the fall of 1991, three clinical instructors from each of the three elementary schools selected to become PDSs began to split their work, half on the project and half on classroom teaching. The duties of the clinical instructors include coteaching the 1st year curriculum with university faculty. While the PDS model has not yet been fully implemented, the project participants have achieved a consensus regarding the major premises to guide this effort, such as involving content specialists, education specialists, and school-based practitioners in the collaboration, integrating theoretical professional studies with clinical skill development, and extending knowledge about teaching and learning through an organized, shared agenda of experimentation and research (Parker, Shroyer, Thompson, Wright, & Zollman, 1990).

These two PDS initiatives, along with those described throughout this volume, exhibit many of the characteristics of learning organizations and of successful collaborations described in the literature on organizational development.

CHARACTERISTICS OF SUCCESSFUL COLLABORATION

The ten characteristics of successful collaborations identified in Van de Water's (1989) research have a great deal in common with the characteristics of learning organizations described by Senge (1990) and with the emerging features of successful PDSs. This section explores these characteristics.

MUTUAL SELF-INTEREST AND COMMON GOALS

Just as members of learning organizations must have a sense of shared vision to guide their collective actions, participants in successful collaborative activities must have a clear sense of enlightened self- and mutual-interest. Classroom and university-based educators must recognize that perceptions—and realities—of teacher quality reflect upon both communities. As such, there is mutual interest that can be exploited to benefit the status of both classroom teachers and teacher education faculty, as well as the well-being of students. PDSs offer a new "playing field" on which both communities can win when they act as a team. Teamwork requires a shared set of ideals and strategies for their pursuit as well as a sense of common concern.

Snyder's case study of two New York City PDSs (chapter 5) provides a graphic example of how difficult it is to launch such efforts in the absence of a clear sense of mutual interests and goals, and how crucial it is to develop such shared vision for any progress to occur. It was difficult, but necessary, for each party to give up representing the traditional interests of their own group in order to find "one common, new voice, that of the PDS." Eventually, being a PDS member became a new and distinct role, one with its own set of mutual interests, enabling a different way of thinking to emerge.

Snyder notes that because mutual interests had not been well-established initially, "the project had become trapped in a specific strategy rather than liberated by a common vision." Once a sense of mutual interests was discovered, progress toward the common goal of significant mentoring for beginning teachers could occur, with strategies becoming flexible and negotiable means, rather than ends in themselves.

In contrast, the Kansas State University and the Manhattan/Ogden School District collaboration began with a keen sense of mutual self-interest. The collaboration involved creating three PDSs to address the mutually identified problem of poor preparation in math, science and technology. This was considered to be a problem of arts and sciences faculty, teacher education faculty, and school district personnel. Those involved in the project recognize that improved instruction in these subjects will enhance the professional integrity and efficacy of school and university personnel alike. Their sense of mutual self-interest guides them toward a common, widely shared goal.

MUTUAL TRUST AND RESPECT

In a successful collaboration, all parties must recognize and utilize the talents and perspectives of each participant. Further, they must be honest in assessing skills to be developed within the group. All parties must feel safe so that learning can occur. As participants in the Los Angeles PPS noted (chapter 7), "Appreciation of what individuals can contribute to each other's education (and professionalism) is an important aspect of a joint relationship. But appreciation doesn't happen until there is openness and trust." Open dialogue about issues of practice allows colleagues to recognize each other's strengths and needs so that professional collaboration can occur and supportive norms can be established.

Shared study, like the team learning Senge (1990) describes, is an important means for creating the common language and respect needed for collaboration. Similarly, in the Kansas State University/Manhattan School District project, the parties acknowledged that university instruction in mathematics and science did not model instruction appropriate for future elementary teachers. To address this and other professional development needs, during the 2nd year all participants were invited to a series of shared learning experiences on topics such as action research, active learning strategies, and alternative assessment of student achievement.

Mutual respect for the unique knowledge, perspectives, and roles of all parties is a recurring theme. An important basis for this trust and respect is familiarity. The Wells school district and University of Southern Maine's "evolution of relationships" supported the PDS there. Miller and Silvernail (chapter 2) argue that the previous 3-year relationship between the school and university in Wells, Maine "is a matter of considerable importance . . . in developing a PDS," just as the tangled web of previous projects between the University of Louisville and Fairdale High enabled serious collaboration in that case (chapter 4). Mehaffy (1992) also argues that prior experience with other collaborations was especially important in the early success of the San Diego State University/Chula Vista Elementary School District PDS project.

Reports from the Kansas State University project also indicate extensive collaborative experience, such as a mentor-teacher program and the Leadership Cadre, prior to the PDS project. In other cases where such prior relationships were absent, a rocky start was experienced. This suggests that, ideally, PDSs should proceed based on a foundation of previous collaborative experiences. In all cases, a climate of trust and respect including collective learning activities, should be created.

SHARED DECISION MAKING

Decisions ranging from goal-setting to operations must be shared so that needs and perspectives of all parties can be taken into consideration. Successful shared decision making will often require that participants develop skills regarding how to reach and measure the strength of a consensus, how to communicate across organizational and cultural barriers, and how to resolve conflicts. These skills are not common to contemporary teacher education programs or schools, but those involved in creating PDSs will find them essential.

All of the PDS initiatives involve numerous committees, task forces, and councils that engage stakeholders in the decision-making process. In all cases significant learning has occurred as groups slowly began to look for and discover ways to support honest conversation, structure decision making, and find consensus. As Lemlech, Hertzog-Foliart, and Hackl note in chapter 7, "Patience is a significant virtue since perceptions, experiences, beliefs of all involved differ, and time is needed to create common group understandings."

These common understandings born of opportunities to communicate and share in direction-setting both solidify the mutual trust and respect that are essential for collaborations and contribute to the team learning and shared vision that motivate continued work together.

Clear Focus

Many issues arise and must be resolved during the process of creating PDSs. The entire effort must be guided by a strong consensus regarding the outcome, a vision of the new organization to be created, and the mission of that organization. Achieving this mutual understanding and focus is time consuming; it is a topic that those involved in the collaboration should revisit and refine over time. This is an important step that reinforces the mutual trust necessary for success.

The Kansas State University participants have articulated six major premises as the defining objectives for their PDSs. These are to

1. Establish collaborative relationships among content specialists, education specialists, and practitioners
2. Strengthen practical field experiences and integrate theory from professional studies with practice in clinical settings
3. Extend the knowledge base in teacher education
4. Encourage experimentation and risk taking
5. Create a long-term, continuous commitment to learning
6. Professionalize teaching practice through new roles and differentiated responsibilities

These defining standards also provide the means of accountability for individuals and the group.

In similar fashion, PDS faculties at Wells, Fairdale, and Lark Creek worked through statements of guiding beliefs. These give shape to the growing efforts and create momentum for continued initiatives to reduce the creative tension between the real and the ideal, a critical guiding force in learning organizations (Senge, 1990). The generative quality of such work is suggested by the efforts of the founding members of the PDS network convened by the National Center for Restructuring Education, Schools, and Teaching, who decided to create a vision statement to guide their collective work across widely diverse PDSs (see Darling-Hammond, Adams, Berry, & Snyder, in press). This statement of shared goals, commitments, and practices has been used in the various sites, as well as by other professional organizations, as a tool to encourage reflection on goals and progress, further articulation of beliefs and direction, and to stimulate continual growth and improvement.

MANAGEABLE AGENDA

Organizing the PDS collaboration requires mapping the activities so that all are aware of how their efforts, and the efforts of others, contribute to the outcome. While no one party should be expected to do it all, everyone should have a clear understanding of the entirety, and the enormity, of the venture. This kind of "systems thinking" contributes to the capacity of learning organizations to continually invent and adapt, with a sense of the whole giving shape and coherence to efforts even while they are flexibly, and usually nonhierarchically, managed.

In the Kansas State project, for example, the complex change agenda was organized through planning teams—including school and university practitioners, content specialists, and students—that were responsible for determining program requirements, preservice courses, and clinical field experiences. This work provides the sense of the whole that will influence the design of the PDSs.

In addition to a view of the journey's destination and a map for its pursuit, it is important to celebrate achievements and benchmarks along the way as the work goes forward. As in other change efforts, a big vision with small building blocks can create consensus and progress (Lieberman, Darling-Hammond, & Zuckerman, 1991):

> The vision pulls people together so they know what is at stake, while goals and projects provide a concrete focus for what otherwise might be grand, but empty, words. These smaller building blocks help focus energy and help affirm that real changes are taking place. (p. 37)

The interdisciplinary January Experience at I.S. 44 is a good example of a discrete project that mobilized collaboration over a limited span of time in a PDS that was having difficulty moving toward its goals. This concrete affirmation of the productive power of collaborative work enabled the establishment of greater trust, respect, and a sense of shared accomplishment that in turn enhanced future collaboration on a broader agenda.

COMMITMENT FROM TOP LEADERSHIP

Collaborations are hard, time consuming ventures that may not look like the appropriate work of the organization. As Berry and Catoe point out in chapter 8, there are very few sources of legitimation and support for cross-institutional collaboration. Institutional leaders can assist the effort by giving legitimacy to this work and providing support in acquiring necessary resources, especially the resource of time away from the traditional work of the organization while the future work is being invented.

Mehaffy (1992) reports that involvement of key personnel from both the school district and the university is essential to the success of the San Diego project. Institutional leaders provide validation for the work and encourage the involvement of other stakeholders, such as curriculum coordinators and academic department heads. Additionally, involvement of institutional leaders will facilitate the "official" sanctions required from governance bodies for policy waivers and resource requests.

The same kinds of leadership supports have been notable in facilitating the work of the Louisville and Wells projects. Without superintendents willing to commit energy and attention to reform initiatives and university leadership willing to support internal change, such bold restructuring efforts could not have been launched or sustained. By contrast, the lack of leadership commitment from key university and district officials in the New York City cases clearly slowed progress toward developing and institutionalizing the PDS concept.

FISCAL SUPPORT

PDSs are institutions designed to improve the clinical preparation of educators. These schools will add to the cost of teacher development as they add to the integrity of teacher education and the later effectiveness of beginning teachers. The collaboration has operational expenses. Participants should not be expected to take on the task without adequate operational support. Otherwise, it will not be taken as a serious commitment of the sponsoring institutions, and individual participants will measure their energy accordingly.

Those involved in the collaboration must be intellectually honest and politically savvy regarding this matter. As Berry and Catoe note in chapter 8, key constituents whose support will determine long-range funding options must be educated about the concept and benefits of PDSs if the schools are to receive continued support.

All of the PDSs described in this volume had received at least small external grants to get started. The cases demonstrate how crucial these funds were for staff development and planning activities. Equally important, the receipt of outside funding legitimized the projects and enabled participants to take risks and break from the status quo. The best funded of these efforts is the Kansas State project, which is supported by a 5 year, $1,700,000 grant from the National Science Foundation. This scale of funding enables a much more comprehensive and ambitious set of initiatives than other PDSs have been able to undertake. At the same time, it poses the challenge to local institutions to pick up costs and maintain the effort when these funds run out.

Both the benefits of funding and the demoralization resulting from loss of additional funds are well-documented in the Fairdale High School case in chapter 4. In the long run, a persuasive case for core funding by states, as well as universities and local districts, will be needed to sustain the gains that have been so hard won.

LONG-TERM COMMITMENT

All parties should be clear about the extent and significance of the change required to create PDSs. This venture will result in changes for the public schools and the universities involved. Both institutions are steeped in traditions and have biases regarding the other that will need to be addressed and reconciled. Change may seem very slow, but as mentioned above, those involved in the collaboration should celebrate accomplishment along the way so that evidence of progress is widely known.

Miller and Silvernail's view in of the Wells PDS as a set of evolving relationships (chapter 2) seems apt to the long-term nature of the required commitment for such a collaboration. In the initially troubled New York City projects described in chapters 5 and 6, the importance of "maintaining a commitment to the collaboration," even when other aspects of the PDS were uncertain, was critical to the eventual successes of the projects. Given the magnitude and uncertainties of the task, and the degree of continued problem-solving and invention required, a PDS cannot expect to succeed as a "quick fix" approach to the dilemmas of teaching and teacher education.

DYNAMIC NATURE

PDS work is highly developmental. Members of the collaboration must have the opportunity to revisit plans, incorporate new understandings and ideas, and change priorities as experiences dictate. Even when consensus is the result of long and intense debate, subsequent evidence should be brought to the consideration of the group. In fact, carefully developed plans should be expected to change from time to time.

One of the realities of PDS development is that participants must spend as much of their time seeking to transform their home institutions as they do trying to establish a new relationship and set of joint practices. The effort to transform existing institutional constraints in ways that remove obstacles and create new possibilities demands continual dynamic planning and action. As Snyder notes in chapter 5, in changing the behavioral and programmatic regularities in more than one institution, the PDS must overcome "the inertia of the status quo that inhibits any movement in directions away from 'what is.'" In order to do this, the PDS must pick up substantial momentum of its own, so that it has the energy and clear direction needed to create new ways of doing business and new forms of organization. At each inevitable collision with existing norms and traditions, dynamic planning and rethinking are needed so that the PDS does not become trapped by the very existing regularities of schooling it is seeking to change.

For these reasons, "systematic ad-hocism" is probably one of the more useful metaphors for the development of PDSs. As Miller and Silvernail explain it in chapter 2:

> Systematic ad hocism is characterized by having a map rather than an itinerary, being long-range, being adaptive, and being value-based. This approach to planning has . . . enabled experimentation and risk-taking and encouraged authentic partnership. Most importantly, it has encouraged constant assessment and invention—which may be essential ingredients in the transformation of teacher education.

INFORMATION SHARING AND COMMUNICATION

Establishing efficient means for members of the collaboration to communicate within and across institutional boundaries is essential to success. Members must develop conscientious habits of sharing information which is of interest to professional colleagues in another organization. In a complex change process such as this, what may seem insignificant to one member could be very helpful to another. Information should be treated as a cherished commodity and shared widely. It is an essential ingredient in the learning process.

This principle is variously illustrated in all of the PDS cases. Many teachers noted that the efforts of the initial planning and decision making groups to share information widely and to insure that all communications were open were the key factors in establishing trust and willingness to participate. Evidence from Kansas State and San Diego State illustrates the challenge of effective communication and information sharing. A Kansas State participant hints at the urgency, frustration, and hope associated with effective communication:

Another difficulty has been communication and coordination among planning teams. We have conducted several meetings of the codirectors who represent all planning teams in an effort to enlarge the sphere of communication. We have distributed team notes and agendas to each school and central office administrators to enhance communications. We now realize that this problem will always be with us because of the size of the project team. The most natural solution is to accept the progress we are making and to realize that this project is not going to move as quickly as we had once anticipated. (Parker, Shroyer, Thompson, Wright, & Zollman, 1990)

Though communication takes time, investment in communication and information-sharing eventually pays off. A principal at one of the New York City PDSs observed that the PDS helped the school restructure itself in part by virtue of the open channels of communication the PDS established with the staff in the school and the willingness of the committee members to meet and to honor staff concerns and questions. A teacher confirmed this, noting that meetings were conducted to explore issues very carefully, ensuring that everyone feels they have a voice. "The university, the UFT, teachers, administrators—we've got all of us working together toward one common goal."

As a consequence of this kind of communication, the initial barriers to collaboration—cultural differences, mistrust, and distinct agendas—can be overcome, and the benefits of cooperative work can be realized.

CONCLUSIONS

The 10 characteristics of successful collaboration discussed above are recurring themes and helpful guideposts for current and future PDS projects. Elaborating on the same concepts, Fullan and Steigelbauer (1991) assert in *The New Meaning of Educational Change*, that the future of education must engage all professionals in the process of instigating and managing collaborative change. Their goal should be moving from transient innovations to more lasting institutional development, constantly challenging one another with "what if I" or "what if we" proposals (p. 346).

Viewed in this light, PDSs are much more than a fashionable new idea. They are an imperative of professional responsibility in education. They are the means for joining practitioners in public schools and universities in preparing and admitting future members to their profession who are willing and able to engage in the kinds of personal and organizational development demanded by learning organizations. They are both the exemplars and the birthing places of tomorrow's schools "where people are continually discovering how they create their reality. And how they change it" (Senge, 1990, p. 13).

REFERENCES

Darling-Hammond, L., Adams, C., Berry, B., & Snyder, J. (in press). *The evolution of professional development schools.* NY: National Center for Restructuring Education, Schools, and Teaching, Teachers College, Columbia University.

Darling-Hammond, L., Gendler, T., & Wise, A. E. (1990). *The teaching internship: Practical preparation for a licensed profession.* Santa Monica, CA: The RAND Corporation.

Fullan, M. G., & Steigelbauer, S. (1991). *The new meaning of educational change.* New York: Teachers College Press.

Gaudiani, C. L., & Burnett, D. G. (1986). *Academic alliances: a new approach to school/college collaboration.* Washington, DC: The American Association for Higher Education.

Goodlad, J. I. (1990). *Teachers for our nation's schools.* San Francisco, CA: Jossey-Bass Publishers.

Hawley, W. D. (1990, March). *New goals and changed roles: A realignment strategy for improving the education of teachers.* Paper presented at the 1991 NEA Standards Clinic, Washington, DC.

Holmes Group (1986). *Tomorrow's teachers: A report of the Holmes Group.* East Lansing, MI: Author.

Kanter, R. M. (1984). *The change masters.* New York: Simon & Schuster.

Lieberman, A., Darling-Hammond, L., & Zuckerman, D. (1991). *Early lessons in restructuring schools.* New York: National Center for Restructuring Education, Schools, and Teaching, Teachers College, Columbia University.

Mehaffy, G. L. (1992, February). *Issues in the creation and implementation of a professional development school.* Paper presented at the Annual Meeting of the American Association of Colleges of Teacher Education, San Antonio, TX.

Parker, B., Shroyer, G., Thompson, N., Wright, E., & Zollman, D. (1990). *Development of an innovative model for the preservice preparation of elementary teachers for enhanced science, mathematics, and technology teaching.* Unpublished paper.

San Diego State University & Chula Vista City Schools. (1992, February). *The Chula Vista professional development school: An educational partnership.* Paper presented at Annual Meeting of American Association of Colleges of Teacher Education, San Antonio, TX.

Sarason, S. (1984). Two cultures meet: The Queens College-Louis Armstrong Middle School collaboration. In S. Trubowitz, J. Duncan, W. Fibkins, P. Longo, S. Sarason, *When a College Works with a Public School.* Boston: Institute for Responsive Education.

Senge, P. M. (1990). *The fifth discipline: The art and practice of the learning organization.* New York: Doubleday.

Shulman, L. S. (1987). Knowledge and teaching: Foundations of the new reform, in *Harvard Educational Review, 57*(1), 1–22.

Van de Water, G. B. (1989). *The governance of school-college collaborations: Lessons learned from the eq models program*. New York: The College Entrance Examination Board.

Webster's Ninth New Collegiate Dictionary. (1987). Springfield, MA: Merriam-Webster.

Wilbur, F. P., Lambert, L. M. & Young, M. J. (1987). *National directory of school-college partnerships: Current models and practices*. Washington, DC: American Association for Higher Education.

About the Contributors

Barnett Berry is an assistant Professor of Educational Leadership and Policy at the University of South Carolina. He earned his Ph.D (1984) in educational administration and policy studies from the University of North Carolina-Chapel Hill. Dr. Berry has worked as a social studies teacher in an inner-city high school, a social scientist for the RAND Corporation, a consultant to a wide range of foundations, research centers, and professional associations, and associate director of the South Carolina Educational Policy Center. Most recently, he served as a Senior Executive Assistant for Policy at the South Carolina State Department of Education.

Sally Catoe is a seventh grade social studies teacher at Summit Parkway Middle School in Richland School District Two, Columbia, South Carolina. She earned a Master's Degree from the University of South Carolina and is working on completing her doctoral degree in general curriculum. Ms. Catoe's experience is elementary, middle school and state-level curriculum design.

Linda Darling-Hammond is Professor of Education and Co-Director of the National Center for Restructuring Education, Schools, and Teaching (NCREST) at Teachers College, Columbia University. She has worked as a public school teacher and curriculum developer, a senior social scientist and Education Program Director at the RAND Corporation, and member of numerous education boards and commissions at the national, state, and local levels. She is currently editor of the *Review of Research in Education* and coeditor of the *New Handbook of Teacher Evaluation*. Her research has focused on issues of teaching quality and educational equity.

Arlene Hackl is an experienced bilingual teacher in Los Angeles. She has taught gifted classes at Norwood Elementary School for 12 years.

Hillary Hertzog-Foliart is clinical professor of education at the University of Southern California. She specializes in language arts, the integration of technology in the curriculum, and teacher education.

Pamela L. Grossman is an associate professor in Curriculum and Instruction at the University of Washington. In her first year at the university, she served as assistant director to the Puget Sound Professional Development Center and subsequently directed and taught in the pilot teacher education program developed through the PSPDC. Her research interests are in the areas of teacher knowledge and teacher learning.

Johanna K. Lemlech is the Stephen H. Crocker Professor of Education at the University of Southern California. She specializes in curriculum, instructional leadership and teacher education. She has authored three textbooks on teacher education.

Jean Lythcott is associate professor of Science Education at Teachers College Columbia University. She was involved with the Professional Development School from the beginning and maintains work with The January Experience as a key area of program and research.

Lynne Miller is a Professor of Educational Leadership at the University of Southern Maine and Director of the Southern Maine Partnership, a school-university collaboration entering its ninth year of operation. She writes widely in the areas of professional development, teacher education, and school reform. She is coauthor (with Ann Lieberman) of *Teachers, Their World and Their Work* and *Staff Development for the 90's*, both published by Teachers College Press.

Sharon P. Robinson is currently Assistant Secretary for Educational Research and Improvement in the U.S. Department of Education. She earned her doctorate from the University of Kentucky in educational administration in 1979 and served as Director of the National Education Association's (NEA) Instruction and Professional Development division from 1980 through 1989, providing staff leadership for the NEA reform agenda. She headed the NEA's National Center for Innovation and the Center's Teacher Education Initiative.

Jon Snyder has been a teacher, school administrator, curriculum and staff developer, researcher and teacher educator. He was formerly Associate Director for Research for the National Center for Restructuring Education, Schools, and Teaching at Teachers College, Columbia University and is currently Director of Teacher Education at the University of California at Santa Barbara.

David L. Silvernail is Professor of Educational Research and Evaluation and Director of the Center for Applied Research and Evaluation at the University of Southern Maine. His research has focused on teacher beliefs and issues related to student assessment and accountability. He is currently working on a manuscript on the implications of the British educational reforms on school and classroom practices.

Frank Schwartz is a teacher who helped facilitate the original Professional Development School program at Intermediate School 44 while serving as the school's liaison with Teachers College, Columbia University. He now coordinates the PDS collaboration that includes Teachers College, Columbia University, Manhattan's School District 3, and the UFT.

Betty Lou Whitford is Professor of Secondary Education in the School of Education at the University of Louisville. Her research and writing focus on the relationships among school organization, professional development, and educational change, work that grows out of extensive experience with school-university collaboration. She holds A.B., M.A.T., and Ph.D. degrees from the University of North Carolina at Chapel Hill.

Index